THE CITY AND GUILDS TEXTBOOK

LEVEL 3 DIPLOMA IN

BUSINESS ADMINISTRATION

THE CITY AND GUILDS TEXTBOOK

LEVEL 3 DIPLOMA IN BUSINESS ADMINISTRATION

VIC ASHLEY
SHEILA ASHLEY

About City & Guilds

City & Guilds is the UK's leading provider of vocational qualifications, offering over 500 awards across a wide range of industries, and progressing from entry level to the highest levels of professional achievement. With over 8500 centres in 100 countries, City & Guilds is recognised by employers worldwide for providing qualifications that offer proof of the skills they need to get the job done.

Equal opportunities

City & Guilds fully supports the principle of equal opportunities and we are committed to satisfying this principle in all our activities and published material. A copy of our equal opportunities policy statement is available on the City & Guilds website.

First edition 2015

ISBN 978 0 85193 253 8

Publisher: Charlie Evans

Development Editor: Claire Owen

Production Editor: Fiona Freel

Cover and text design by Design Deluxe

Typeset by Saxon Graphics, Derby

Printed in the UK by Cambrian Printers Ltd

British Library Cataloguing in Publication Data

A catalogue record is available from the British Library.

Publications

For information about or to order City & Guilds support materials, contact 0844 534 0000 or centresupport@cityandguilds.com. You can find more information about the materials we have available at www.cityandguild.com/bookshop.

Every effort has been made to ensure that the information contained in this publication is true and correct at the time of going to press. However, City & Guilds' products and services are subject to continuous development and improvement and the right is reserved to change products and services from time to time. City & Guilds cannot accept liability for loss or damage arising from the use of information in this publication.

City & Guilds
1 Giltspur Street
London EC1A 9DD

0844 543 0033
www.cityandguilds.com
publishingfeedback@cityandguilds.com

CONTENTS

ABOUT THE AUTHORS

Vic and Sheila Ashley are experienced authors in the business and education fields. They have written Business and Administration Student Handbooks at Levels 1, 2 and 3 for the Council for Administration (CfA), online resources for Retail and Business and Administration for the City & Guilds SmartScreen website (www.smartscreen.co.uk), and workbooks supplying the knowledge and understanding for a range of qualifications, available through www.aspect-training.com.

Vic has extensive retail experience, mainly with the Debenhams Group, and has spent 25 years working with awarding organisations including City & Guilds in a number of roles including consultant, lead verifier, regional verifier and external verifier. He is also the chair of examiners for the 14–19 Diploma in Retail Business for AQA–City & Guilds.

Sheila has operated a successful catering business and acted as centre co-ordinator for her own training provider, delivering Assessor and Verifier Awards and Teaching in the Lifelong Learning Sector qualifications.

We would like to thank the following people for their work on this textbook: Charlie Evans, Fiona Freel, Lucy Hyde, Claire Owen, Lynn Preston and Sylvia Sims.

HOW TO USE THIS TEXTBOOK

Welcome to your City & Guilds Level 3 Diploma in Business Administration textbook. It is designed to guide you through your Level 3 qualification and be a useful reference for you throughout your career.

Each chapter covers a unit from the 5528 Level 3 qualification, and covers everything you will need to understand in order to prepare for your assessments.

Throughout this textbook you will see the following features:

Assessment criteria

This section covers assessment criteria 1.1, 1.3, 1.4, 1.6, 1.8, 1.9, 2.1, 2.6 and 2.7

ASSESSMENT CRITERIA – These highlight the assessment criteria coverage through each unit, so you can easily link your learning to what you need to know or do for each Learning outcome.

Motivate

To make somebody feel enthusiastic, interested and committed to something

KEY TERM – Words in bold in the text are explained in the margin to aid your understanding. They also appear in the glossary at the back of the book.

ACTIVITY

Use a dictionary to look up the proper meaning of the commonly confused words shown in the table.

ACTIVITIES – These are suggested activities to help you learn and practise.

HANDY HINT

Avoid producing a presentation with too many slides – you don't want to be seen as presenting 'death by PowerPoint'!

HANDY HINTS – These are particularly useful tips that can assist you in the workplace or help you remember something important.

COMMON MISTAKE

Never assume the audience has previous knowledge of the subject

COMMON MISTAKES – These identify common mistakes to avoid.

CASE STUDIES – Each chapter ends with a case study describing situations you may encounter in your work.

CASE STUDY
INFORMATION SHARING

Following a major fire, Melton Borough Council decided on a £5.6 million project to move to a new town-centre location it will share with its partners, Leicestershire County Council, Leicestershire Partnership NHS Trust, Voluntary Action Melton, and Leicestershire and Rutland Probation Trust.

The new building is designed to improve information sharing and encourage closer co-operation between public sector agencies in order to deliver multi-agency responses that improve outcomes for people and places in the Melton area. Office space in the new building is zoned into cross-agency working neighbourhoods determined by the provision of services directed to mutual customers or places. Teams from different agencies are located together and work collaboratively to provide more efficient and effective services, intervening sooner to tackle emerging social, economic and environmental issues.

Sound management and effective sharing of information and data underpin the success of the co-location project, and the partner agencies recognise that significant effort is required to remove cultural barriers to sharing information. A joint-agency Co-location Information Management Working Group has been established to deliver guidance, standards, governance and protocols to prepare staff for working with information in a co-located, co-production environment.

TEST YOUR KNOWLEDGE QUESTIONS – At the end of every chapter are some questions designed to test your understanding of what you have learnt in that chapter. This can help with identifying further training or revision needed. You will find the suggested answers at the end of the book.

UNIT 318 (B&A 57): TEST YOUR KNOWLEDGE

Learning outcome 1: Understand business communication models, systems and processes

1 Describe two communication needs of internal stakeholders.

2 Explain what is meant by 'internal communication'.

3 Describe the problems that could occur with informal communication.

4 Explain why an organisation uses different methods in its communications plan.

5 Explain why it is important for organisations to evaluate their communications.

MAPPING GRID

		Unit number										
		204 (B&A 16)	227 (B&A 39)	301 (B&A 40)	302 (B&A 41)	308 (B&A 47)	309 (B&A 48)	318 (B&A 57)	319 (B&A 58)	320 (B&A 59)	322 (B&A 61)	345 (M&L 9)
Unit number	204 (B&A 16)					★					★	
	227 (B&A 39)											
	301 (B&A 40)								★			
	302 (B&A 41)								★			
	308 (B&A 47)	★						★	★			
	309 (B&A 48)								★			
	318 (B&A 57)					★			★			
	319 (B&A 58)			★	★	★	★	★		★	★	★
	320 (B&A 59)								★			
	322 (B&A 61)	★							★			
	345 (M&L 9								★			

CROSS-REFERENCING EVIDENCE

The table on the opposite page indicates where it *might* be possible to cross-reference evidence. To use the table, look down the left-hand side, find the unit you have produced evidence for, and then look across to find other units that the evidence *might* cross-refer to, indicated with the ★ symbol.

For example, when you have collected evidence for Unit 308 (B&A 47), some of it might also supply evidence for Unit 318 (B&A 57).

CAREER PLANNING

There are very few jobs for life in the current economy, so it is important that you plan your career. Look regularly at where you are now, where you would like to be in the short- and longer-term, and how you can get there.

A short-term career plan focuses on a period of between one and five years. The most important aspect is to develop realistic goals and objectives. You need to narrow down your choices so that you can focus on the career that you really want and then carry out detailed research into that career. It may be a different career from the one you are currently employed in, or you may want to develop within your existing career.

The research will enable you to identify the qualifications needed to move into a new career or take the next step in your existing career. Compare the qualifications you already have with those identified by your research. If this indicates that you already have the necessary qualifications, you will be ready to look for opportunities to make the move into the position you want. If there is a significant gap, consider whether it is realistic to achieve the necessary qualifications in the short term. Look at obtaining further training, attending college (either on day release or in the evenings) or gaining additional experience, maybe in a voluntary role in your own time.

A long-term career plan focuses on the period beyond five years. As the workplace is rapidly changing, the competences you have now, or plan to gain in the short term, may not be appropriate in the future. There are fundamental skills that will always be in demand and you should concentrate on these for your long-term development. The skills that will always be in demand include verbal and written communication, computing, team leadership and team working, decision making, planning, organising, problem solving, and commitment to life-long learning.

Within the business administration sector, qualifications can lead to career progression. With a level 3 qualification, job opportunities include the following:

- Administration officer – duties might range from helping prepare financial statements to producing monthly management accounts. Other tasks you will be likely to take on include:
  - budgeting
  - raising invoices
  - managing ledgers

  - processing expenses
  - preparing VAT returns.
- Bookkeeper – you will help prepare the profit and loss sheets for the annual accounts. Other tasks you will be likely to take on include:
  - balancing accounts
  - processing sales invoices, receipts and payments
  - VAT returns
  - checking bank statements
  - dealing with financial paperwork and filing.
- Office supervisor – this role is demanding. Your daily tasks may well include:
  - balancing budgets
  - arranging travel, meetings and appointments
  - ordering stationery and equipment
  - supervising and monitoring staff
  - discussing problems
  - reporting to management
  - reviewing and implementing the company's health and safety policy
  - arranging training.
- Personal assistant – you will be helping your manager organise their working life so that they always know where they need to be and what they're doing. Your duties will include tasks such as:
  - typing up minutes
  - organising diaries
  - fielding calls
  - managing junior staff
  - organising travel arrangements
  - researching projects, writing reports or managing budgets (once you have more experience and training).
- Purchase ledger clerk – you may have sole control over payments or work as part of a much bigger purchase ledger team. Purchase ledger clerks are expected to be able to:
  - code and check invoices
  - work out VAT payments
  - pay out money via BACS or by cheque
  - check and reconcile supplier statements
  - file invoices and statements

  - deal with purchase enquiries
  - process staff expenses.
- Sales ledger clerk – your responsibility is to ensure that money owed to a company is accounted and invoiced for. Your main duties will include:
  - setting up new clients
  - producing invoices
  - banking and reconciliation
  - running-off turnover statements
  - chasing up outstanding debts
  - checking VAT has been included on invoices
  - providing creditors with VAT receipts.

The possibilities for progression within the business administration sector really are exciting, with a wide range of careers available including:

- accountant
- advertising account executive
- banker (investment or commercial)
- banking manager
- buyer (industrial or retail)
- commodity broker
- company secretary
- distribution/logistics manager
- human resources manager
- insurance underwriter
- IT consultant
- management consultant
- market research executive
- marketing executive
- public relations account executive
- recruitment consultant
- retail manager
- sales executive
- stockbroker
- systems analyst.

Whatever career path you embark upon, this textbook will help you take the first steps.

ACKNOWLEDGEMENTS

City & Guilds would like to sincerely thank the following:

For invaluable subject knowledge and expertise
Lynn Preston and Sylvia Sims.

For freelance editorial support
Lucy Hyde

Picture credits
Every effort has been made to acknowledge all copyright holders as below and the publishers will, if notified, correct any errors in future editions.

Front cover: © Ant Track / Corbis

Back cover: Shutterstock – © Goodluz, © "LDprod", © Monkey Business Images, © Odua Images, © Pressmaster.

iStock: © gchutka p248; © Neustockimages p107; **Shutterstock:** © 1000 Words p220; © AD Hunter p44; © Adriano Castelli p103; © alice-photo pp 175, 240; © alphaspirit p195; © Andrew Horwitz p103; © Andrey_Popov pp 105, 110; © auremar pp 19, 20; © baranq p214; © BasPhoto p52; © bikeriderlondon pp 100, 237, 238, 240; © Boris Sosnovyy p143; © Brendan Howard p148; © Cameron Whitman p169; © CandyBox Images p115; © Creativa p46; © d_arts p258; © Dean Drobot pp 34, 186, 254; © dotshock p107; © Elena Elisseeva p193; © Elena11 p104; © Ensuper p281; © fiphoto p130; © FooTToo p74; © FrameAngel p73; © gamble19 p60; © Gines Valera Marin p257; © Golden Pixels LLC p188; © Goodluz pp 1, 115, 173, 231; © graphixmania p42; © Hasloo Group Production Studio p99; © Hurst Photo p202; © hxdbzxy p78; © Iakov Filimonov p256; © Iryna Rasko p11; © Jakub Zak p287; © JMiks p282; © Josemaria Toscano p149; © Julia Kopacheva p258; © Kheng Guan Toh p206; © Konstantin Chagin p215; © Kzenon p243; © Laurens Parsons Photography p81; © "LDprod" p91; © Lester Balajadia p228; © leungchopan pp 59, 127; © lightpoet p63; © Lightspring p277; © littleny p105; © Macrovector p259; © marekuliasz p259; © Marie C Fields p275; © Martin Good p132; © mast3r p10; © mhatzapa p258; © michaeljung p120; © Minerva Studio p240; © Monkey Business Images pp 5, 15, 32, 87, 273, 299; © muuraa p258; © Odua Images p234; © Olga Rosi p265; © Orientaly p127; © ostill p117; © Pavel L Photo and Video pp 55, 190; © Pixsooz p48; © Plukhin p103; © pmphoto p259; © pogonici p8; © polat p283; © Pressmaster pp 18, 24, 177, 186, 251; © racorn p109, 246; © Rido p184; © Robert Davies p157; © Robert Kneschke p68; © Robert Mandel p20; © RoboLab p259; © Robyn Mackenzie p85; © Rtimages p293; © Samo Trebizan p295; © Sebastien Burel p133; © Seregam p225; © shooarts p260; © simonox p126; © Sophie James p104; © StockLite p17; © Stuart Jenner p23; © Svetlana Lukienko p267; © Taiga p223; © tazzymoto p148; © Tomasz Bidermann p104; © travellight p217; © trekandshoot p71; © Tutti Frutti p146; © val lawless p57; © Vereshchagin Dmitry p65; © wavebreakmedia pp 3, 43, 111, 168, 196, 285; © Wilm Ihlenfeld p271; © wrangler p161; © YanLev p96; © Yuganov Konstantin p123; © Zurijeta p152.

MANDATORY UNITS

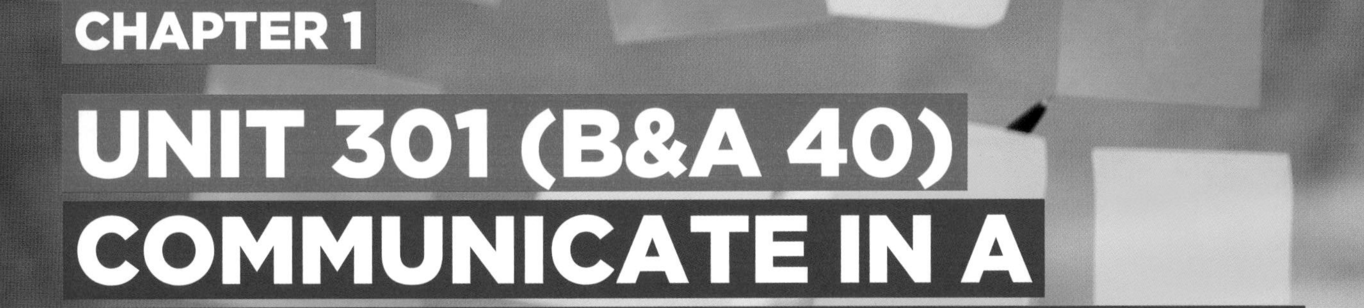

CHAPTER 1

UNIT 301 (B&A 40) COMMUNICATE IN A BUSINESS ENVIRONMENT

Many surveys of recruiters identify communication skills as the single most important factor when selecting managers. Whatever role you have, in whatever organisation, you will need to communicate – with customers, suppliers and colleagues. No one works entirely in isolation.

All communication has a purpose: either to generate action, or to pass on or request information. Effective communication achieves its purpose by prompting the desired effect without the message losing its clarity during the process. If the receiver of the message is unable to understand it, the message will not have the desired effect.

Communication, whether it is written or verbal, has to follow certain conventions if it is to be understood. Conventions refer to the customary way in which things are done. They can be commonly accepted conventions (such as spelling, punctuation and grammar) or company-specific conventions (such as technical phrases or abbreviations).

In this unit you will cover the following learning outcomes:

1 understand business communication models, systems and processes
2 be able to communicate in writing in business
3 be able to communicate verbally in business.

BUSINESS COMMUNICATION

Assessment criteria

This section covers assessment criteria 1.1, 1.3, 1.4, 1.6, 1.8, 1.9, 2.1, 2.6 and 2.7

Stakeholder

A person or group with a direct interest, involvement or investment in something

It is important to understand the communication needs of internal and external stakeholders. Internal **stakeholders** include employees, colleagues, managers and owners or shareholders. External stakeholders include shareholders and others such as governmental bodies, communities, financiers, suppliers and customers.

Internal stakeholders' needs include knowing what business the organisation is in, who the customers are, specific details about products or services, where forms are located and who to see when there is a problem. They also need practical skills required to do their job well, which include communication skills, and interactions that give them a sense of belonging and self-worth, such as being listened to, respected, trusted and valued.

External stakeholders' needs include information to promote sales and publicity, generate sponsorship, announce events, products or services, and to support branding. Marketing professionals use persuasive techniques to influence others in their external communication strategies.

Motivate

To make somebody feel enthusiastic, interested and committed to something

Communicating in a business environment always has a purpose: to send a message to an individual or group of people in order to request action, inform, teach, persuade, **motivate** or inspire. Communication is a process that must be understood if it is to be effective and avoid misunderstanding and confusion. It is successful only when the sender and the receiver understand the same message.

THE COMMUNICATION PROCESS

According to communication theories, the process of communication consists of the following elements:

- The sender – the person sending the communication, who needs to be clear what they want to communicate, who to, how and why.
- The message – the information the sender wants to communicate must be clear and not capable of being misunderstood.
- 'Encoding' – putting the message into a form that can be understood. The sender needs to understand their audience and the level of knowledge of the subject, avoiding mistaken **assumptions** that may arise as a result of missing information or cultural issues.
- The channel – the method of sending the message. Channels may be written (for example letters, emails, memos or reports) or verbal (for example presentations or face-to-face meetings).

Assumption

Presuming something to be the case without knowing for sure

A face-to-face meeting

Think about the channel you will use to communicate.

Think about how your audience will receive the message

- 'Decoding' – reading or hearing the message. The message can be misunderstood through a lack of knowledge, a poorly worded message or not enough time being given to consider its meaning.
- The audience – the individual reading or hearing the message. Even if the message is sent to a group, it is received by individuals, each of whom has to understand the message. Individuals receiving the message may have pre-conceived ideas that will affect their interpretation of the message – the sender needs to take these into consideration when encoding it. If your message is being delivered to a group of people, they each have to understand the message.

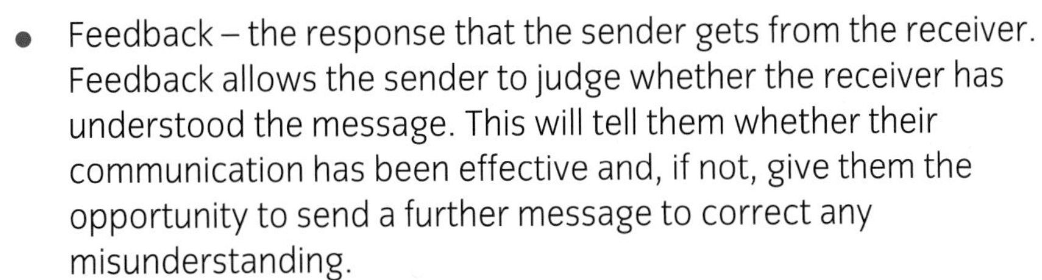

- Feedback – the response that the sender gets from the receiver. Feedback allows the sender to judge whether the receiver has understood the message. This will tell them whether their communication has been effective and, if not, give them the opportunity to send a further message to correct any misunderstanding.
- Context – exterior factors that can affect effective communication of the message. These include factors such as language, culture and organisational culture.
- Intended outcomes – the desired result of the communication.

Consider the following when planning communication:

- Who is the message being sent from?
- What is the purpose of the message?
- When is the message being sent?
- To whom is the message being sent?
- Which model of communication is best in this case?

At each stage of the process, there may be barriers that make effective communication difficult. Barriers may include:

- poor listening skills
- lack of communication skills
- language problems
- technology breakdown
- prejudice and misconception
- conflicting messages
- lack of discussion
- environmental constraints.

It is important that you find ways of breaking down these barriers wherever possible. For instance, if a written message is poorly worded or a verbal message is poorly delivered, it is much more likely to be misunderstood. If too much information is delivered too quickly, the receiver may not have enough time to decode the message.

METHODS OF COMMUNICATION

The following diagram shows different methods of communication.

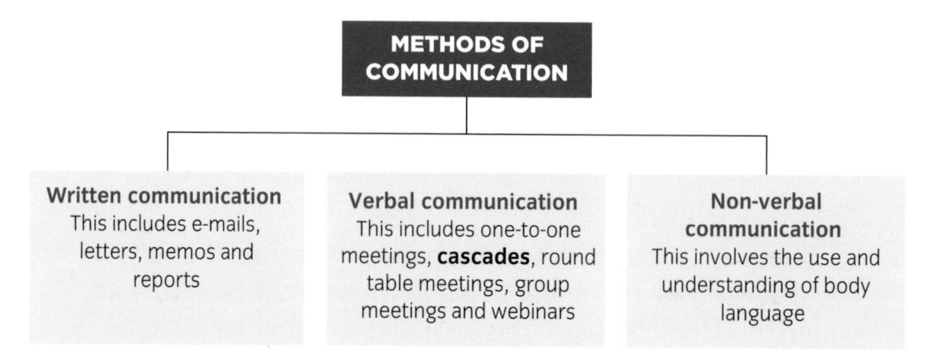

Cascade

A downward flow of information

Each method is best used in different circumstances. More formal communication is likely to need written communication, while verbal communication will often be appropriate to informal situations. Non-verbal communication is, of course, used whenever two or more people are together.

HANDY HINT

Check that messages have been understood, not just received.

Remember that the written word is more 'powerful' than the spoken word, because it can be read again and again while the spoken word is either heard or not.

The common thread with all of the methods of communication is the passing of information from the sender to the receiver in a form that makes the message clearly understood. The method of communication you choose will depend on the urgency and complexity of the information being communicated. You will also need to adapt your communication for different audiences, both internal and external.

PATTERNS OF COMMUNICATION

There are several patterns or networks of communication that represent the direction and flow of communication within an organisation:

- 'The chain' is a hierarchical pattern that characterises strictly formal information flow, 'from the top down', such as in the military and some types of business organisations.
- 'The wheel' is found in a typical autocratic organisation, where one person governs and there is limited employee participation.
- 'The star or all-channel network' allows free flow of communication in a group, encouraging all of its members to become involved in group decision processes.
- 'The Y pattern' is a more complicated arrangement where the group is separated into three and the group members can communicate with the other members of the group through the leader.
- 'The circle' is where the sender can communicate only with group members next to him or her in the circle. Other group members can't receive the sender's message.

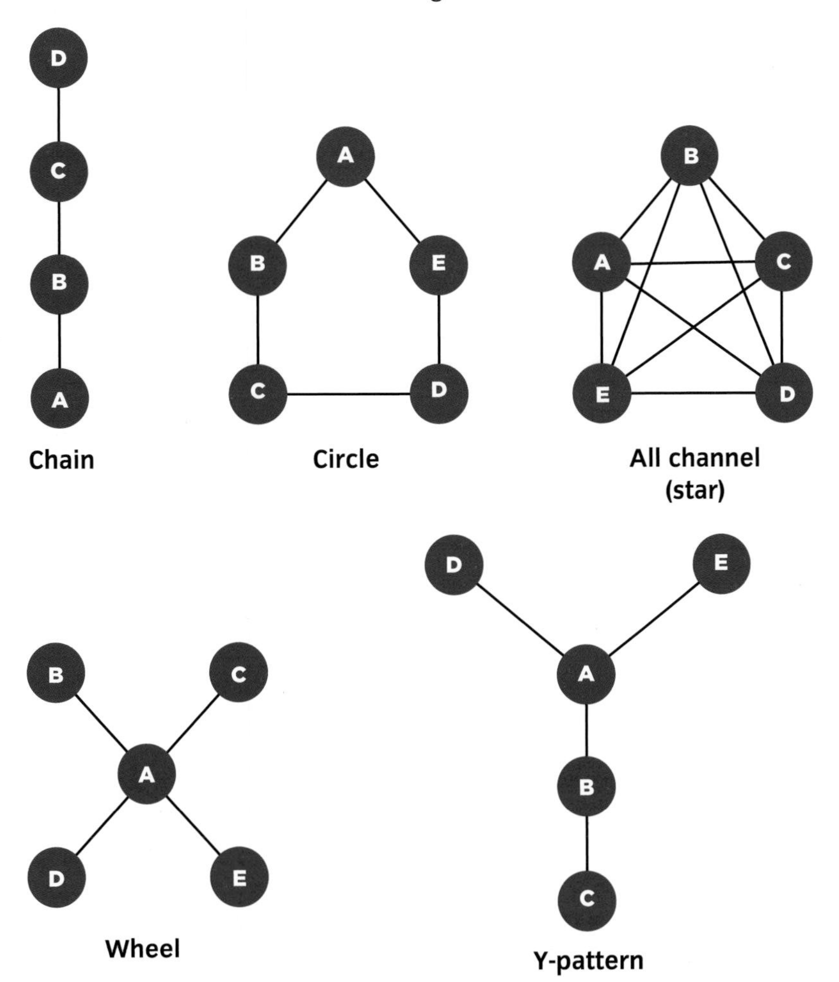

The chosen structure of communication within an organisation will have a significant influence on the accuracy of decisions, the speed with which those decisions are reached and the satisfaction of the people involved. In networks where the responsibility for initiating and passing messages is shared more evenly among the members, better communication will be achieved.

PRACTICAL TIPS

Proofread your written messages before you send them. Read a hard copy of the document rather than reading on-screen, and read the document backwards. This prevents your brain seeing what it knows should be there, rather than what is actually there. Don't rely entirely on the spell check function on your computer, as it doesn't know the difference between 'now' and 'know', for instance – both are correctly spelt but only one will be the correct word in the context.

When communicating on behalf of colleagues or your line manager, it is important to keep them informed of your progress towards meeting any deadlines they have given you. If you are experiencing difficulties, this will alert them to the need to plan for any effect that a delay in the communication going out may cause.

Try to avoid printing out emails

Keep a file copy of your written communications. If you have sent an email, it may be enough to keep a copy in the 'sent items' folder of your emails program, or alternatively your organisational procedure may be to file the emails in folders by subject or by the recipient's name, for example. Try to avoid printing out emails just to file them: this is a waste of resources.

ACTIVITY

Proofread the following excerpt from a sales letter about a new product – some deliberate mistakes have been introduced into it.

Dear Sir or Madam

I'm writing too you about an exiting new oppertunity. We wil soon be launching brand new product which Im sure will be of grate interest to you. Usualy this product wud cost you £100, but as a spesial offer you can know purchase it at the bargin price of £75.

The mane features of this item are:

- its high quality, wich means it will last for years
- it is multi-purpose to meat all your business needs
- it is competatively priced.

Their are many more reasons to by this product, which we would be happy to discus further with you.

If you would like to by this product dont hestitate to contact me today. Otherwise you mite miss out on this amazing deal! Don't except less than the best.

If you have sent a letter, memo or report, your organisational procedure may be to file a hard copy in a filing cabinet but, as the communication will probably have been created electronically, it is more cost effective to keep the record electronically unless there is a real need to print off a copy. Many organisations have shared drives on computers which allow access to files for everyone who needs it. This may raise issues surrounding the security and confidentiality of the content.

HANDY HINT

Read your messages out loud – this will often allow you to hear mistakes that you have not seen.

WRITTEN COMMUNICATION

Assessment criteria

This section covers assessment criteria 1.2, 1.5, 1.6, 2.2, 2.3, 2.4, 2.5 and 2.6

Written communication in a business environment includes emails, letters, memos, agendas and minutes of meetings, notices and reports. Electronic written communication can also include different media such as graphics, sound and video, producing a more engaging communication that is relevant to your particular audience.

While each form of written communication has its own conventions, they all require you to use the three main elements of written communication.

STRUCTURE

The first element is structure, which refers to the way that you lay out the content. To organise the structure of your communication, think about what you want the receiver to understand from your message.

Identify the key points and facts that you are trying to convey and put them into a logical order. Make sure you start with a powerful introduction, as this will create a positive first impression.

Use headings, sub-headings and bullet-points to help the receiver identify the main points of the message. Write in short sentences and paragraphs that are to the point. Each paragraph should start with a main point, followed by supporting information.

Finish the communication with a conclusion or a recommendation, or by re-stating the main point of the message (depending on the purpose of the communication). The last paragraph is the one the receiver will remember longest, so don't use it to waffle on after you have made your main point.

STYLE AND TONE

The second element is style and tone, which refer to the way that you write. All business communication should be to the point, simple, direct and clear. As a rough guide, sentences should contain no more than 30 words, and paragraphs should be no more than 10 lines long.

Written communication in general, and letters and emails especially, should be kept as short as possible while containing all the necessary information. If people receive a lot of letters or emails, they will tend to first look to see who it is from and then read it if it is short. If it looks too long, they will put it aside and read it when they have time. An effective business letter or email should consist of no more than three paragraphs of four or five lines per paragraph.

Business letters follow widely accepted standard layouts and conventions

In any written communication, you need to consider how much information and how much detail should be included, and how formal the message is. This will depend to a great extent on the message's intended audience. If you are writing an article for a broadsheet newspaper, such as *The Times*, you would use a different style from an article about the same subject in a tabloid, such as *The Mirror*.

Write positively: if you have to communicate to your customers about a price increase, point out the excellent value that your product or service still gives, and remind them of the benefits it has over your competitors. The exception might be when you have had to deal with a disciplinary or performance issue involving a team member. After initially discussing the situation verbally you will have to record the outcome formally in writing, and it might be inappropriate to write positively in this situation.

The first sentence of any communication should be interesting in order to help capture the interest of the receiver. The majority of the communication should be relevant to the receiver – people are always more interested in themselves than in you and want to know what the benefit will be to them, so address them directly using 'you' and 'your' as much as possible.

Jargon and abbreviations should be avoided unless they will definitely be understood by the receiver or are explained within the communication. Short, familiar words should be used rather than obscure, complex words. Active words should be used: for example, say 'I think ...' rather than 'It is thought ...'. And use single words rather than phrases that mean the same thing: for example, use a word such as 'now' instead of a phrase such as 'at this point in time'.

Jargon

Language that is used within a group or profession that might not be understood or used by other people

CONTENT

The third element is content, which refers to what you are writing about. The information you need to communicate may have come from a variety of sources, including your own research and information that has been passed to you for the specific purpose of communicating it to a wider audience. You need to think through what your message is, making sure your objective is clear. Check that you have made your essential points clearly and developed your argument logically. Make the content positive and constructive, and don't allow detail to obscure the main issues.

Don't write for the sake of writing: people are busy and don't have time to read unnecessary messages. But do write to congratulate or praise people who deserve it. This may seem unnecessary on the face of it, but it will mean a lot to the recipient. They may have worked very hard to achieve a promotion or a successful sales pitch, and it is worth the time to let them know you appreciate it.

Receiving a letter of congratulations can mean a lot to the recipient

Use plain English. This will allow the receiver to understand exactly what you mean. Plain English is written clearly and is to the point so that the reader can take the required action. Government departments, banks, insurance companies and local councils have moved towards the use of plain English in order to provide clear communication, rather than producing **missives** that aim to impress but often only confuse their clients or customers. The simple rules for writing in plain English are:

- Write in short sentences.
- Use everyday words, not jargon.
- Use personal words such as 'I', 'we' and 'you'.
- Write as directly and to the point as possible.

Customers expect to be treated with respect and using plain English when writing to them is one way to do this. Before you send your message, read it and think how you would feel if you received it. If your reaction is the one you intend, then send it; if not, re-write it.

Missive

A formal letter or other written communication, often a legal communication

HANDY HINT

Consider the writing rules of George Orwell:

- Never use a long word where a short one will do
- If it is possible to cut out a word, cut it out
- Never use the passive voice
- Never use jargon if you can think of an everyday equivalent.

ACTIVITY

Find out which famous quote from former US President Abraham Lincoln could be re-written as: 'Political organisation of the general community, administered directly via the populace, on behalf of each and every one of the citizens.'

SPELLING, PUNCTUATION AND GRAMMAR

Spelling, punctuation and grammar are all vital to effective communication. An incorrectly spelt, badly punctuated and ungrammatical message will give a very poor impression of you to your colleagues if used internally and of the whole organisation if sent to customers, clients or suppliers. Even people whose own standard of written English is poor can recognise when they receive a badly written message!

Poor spelling, punctuation and grammar can also totally alter the meaning of your message, potentially with serious consequences. A misplaced or omitted comma can completely change the meaning of a sentence. Consider the following, which lists the ingredients of a salad:

Tomatoes, onions, goats, cheese

The addition of a comma after the word 'goats' and the omission of the apostrophe from the 'goats' cheese' have made it an entirely different dish!

PUNCTUATION

There are lots of punctuation marks that you need to know how to use correctly if your text is to be completely accurate, but the most important are:

- Full stops – used at the end of sentences or to indicate an abbreviation.
- Commas – used to separate individual words in a list or to indicate where a pause is intended in a sentence.
- Apostrophes – used to indicate a missing letter ('he's' meaning 'he is') or that something belongs to someone (St John's Wood, The King's Head).

SPELLING

Practise spelling words correctly, if you need to. And remember that some word processing programs use American English rather than 'English (UK)' as their basic dictionary: these may indicate that a word is correct when it is actually incorrect, and vice versa, so check this and alter the settings if you can.

As well as improving your spelling, it is important to improve your knowledge of the meaning of words. There are a number of words in the English language which are commonly confused with each other (see the table on this page); learn their correct meaning and you will not misuse them.

Commonly confused words	
accept	except
advice	advise
affect	effect
ambivalent	indifferent
disinterested	indifferent
disinterested	uninterested
eligible	illegible
ensure	insure
farther	further
fewer	less
meddle	medal
personal	personnel
practice	practise
principal	principle
stationary	stationery
than	then
there	their *or* they're
your	you're

ACTIVITY

Use a dictionary to look up the proper meaning of the commonly confused words shown in the table.

GRAMMAR

The third part of language that you need to understand is the correct use of grammar. There are far too many rules of grammar to cover in a book like this, but the key parts of speech to understand are:

- Nouns – these are the names of people, places or things, such as 'laptop', 'medal', 'James' or 'Norwich'.
- Pronouns – these are used to replace nouns to avoid repetition, such as 'he', 'she', 'his' or 'theirs'.
- Verbs – these are used to indicate action or being, such as 'to be', 'to type' or 'to watch'.
- Adverbs – these are used to describe a verb, such as 'to type *accurately*' or 'to watch *closely*'. They usually end in *-ly*.
- Adjectives – these describe a noun, such as 'a *new* laptop', 'a *gold* medal', '*handsome* James' or '*beautiful* Norwich'.

Parts of speech are joined together into sentences, and sentences are joined together into paragraphs. Sentences should express a single thought; paragraphs should contain sentences on a single topic.

NETIQUETTE

If you are communicating over the internet, a form of convention known as 'netiquette' has developed. This requires you to:

- treat your readers with the kind of respect you would expect from them
- not harass or insult people, either your readers or others
- respect copyright restrictions
- not overuse CAPITAL LETTERS
- not send **spam**
- tell the truth
- use correct grammar and punctuation
- not use inappropriate language
- research your facts
- acknowledge your sources.

Spam

An unsolicited, often commercial, message transmitted through the internet as a mass mailing to a large number of recipients

HANDY HINT

KISS: keep it short and simple.

ACTIVITIES

- Research the structure of a formal report.
- Research the layout of a business letter.

ACTIVITY

Correctly punctuate the following paragraph:

> if you fly economy listen up results from the most comprehensive survey ever. into seat sizes has just been revealed and amethyst. Flyaway, and Getaway, airlines have tied at first place we love both. airlines for having top notch customer service in any case and this. news will only sweeten the experience while airlines such as scottish airways have been improving. their food offerings and check in speed it languishes. in 21st place for legroom unsurprisingly frillfreeair is. in 24th place for having a seat width of 16 inches but at least the airline can gloat. at the fact that it has beaten lazyjet in the legroom category which came second, from last frillfreeair had 30 inches; while lazyjet was 29 inches, the worst airline for legroom is Cattleair

ACTIVITY

Correct the following:

> Google survises go offlion in China
>
> Google sez It's serch ingen and uther internet survises have bin cutt of form mutch of China jus as the countrys rewling party pick new leeders.
>
> Data posted on Googles website show it's survises in China becaime largely inaxessable form around 5pm locle tyme inn Beijing.
>
> A Google spookswomen said the companny found no problem in I'ts own compooter or network that wood disrupt It's survises inn China.
>
> That razed the posabilaty that Chinas Commnist Party desided to block Googles survises at a polaticily sensitif tyme
>
> Googles surch ingines, email and other survises have bin perodicly unavalable in China sinse 2010. That were when Google desided to stop censering it's surch ressults to remove websites what Chinas goverment found objecshunnjable

Assessment criteria

This section covers assessment criteria 1.7, 1.8, 3.1, 3.2, 3.3, 3.4, 3.5 and 3.6

VERBAL COMMUNICATION

Verbal communication includes making presentations, using the telephone, speaking to people one-to-one, and holding discussions with two or more people. The principles of effective verbal communication are the same whatever the context.

- Speak clearly – if you are nervous about the situation, you will speak more quickly than if you are relaxed, and this will make it more difficult for people to understand you. Make sure you have prepared (at least mentally) what you want to say, stick to the point, and avoid waffling or unnecessarily repeating yourself. If possible, give examples that your audience will be able to relate to in support of your arguments.

- Speak appropriately – consider the culture, background and level of understanding of your audience and use English correctly. If your levels of grammar and vocabulary come across as below those expected by your audience, you will be seen as lazy, under educated or, at worst, disrespectful if it is perceived that you are 'dumbing down' your delivery. In an increasingly global workplace, it is more important than ever to speak English well if you are to be understood by people who have learnt it as a foreign language.

Consider the culture, background and level of understanding of your audience

- Speak thoughtfully – consider your audience and the effect your message may have on them. Remember to make the conversation about the people you are speaking to, rather than about you, wherever possible. People much prefer talking about themselves – it is everyone's favourite subject. Ask questions and show interest in the answers. Try to remember personal details so that next time you speak to them you can ask how their husband/wife/child/dog is. This will encourage dialogue and give you the opening you need to get your message across. Everybody prefers working with people they like, so make people like you.
- Speak sincerely – if you think someone has made a particularly good effort, tell them so. Show interest in your colleagues by congratulating them, but be careful not to be insincere – people can tell if you are saying 'well done' while thinking 'lucky so-and-so'. Avoid any personal remarks as innocently intended comments on a colleague's physical attributes, for instance, can be misunderstood and lead to a variety of problems.
- Speak confidently – if you don't believe what you are saying then you shouldn't be surprised if no one else does, either. You can demonstrate confidence in what you are saying through the way you speak. Think about the pace, pitch and volume of your voice

– although this doesn't mean you should shout at your audience! Stand upright, make eye contact but don't stare, as that is very disconcerting.

It isn't enough that you understand what you are saying, you must also be sure that the recipient has also correctly understood the message. You can confirm this through:

- Paraphrasing – this means saying what you said in a different way.
- Probing – this means questioning closely.
- Clarifying – this means making a statement clear and free from ambiguity.
- Verifying – this means ascertaining the truth or correctness of a statement.
- Summarising – this means giving a brief recap of previously stated facts or statements.

HANDY HINTS

- When a person is speaking, do not interrupt. Not all conversations are about winning an argument or making a point. Communication is as much about listening as it is about talking
- Speaking to elderly people as if they were children is extremely disrespectful. Remember, they have already been your age, while you have no experience of being theirs.

People hear what you say against a background of their own experiences and opinions, which might completely alter the meaning.

Be clear about what you are saying, but don't over complicate it with too much detail.

Only 10% of what you say is actually received by the listener. Try to avoid using jargon and abbreviations which might not be familiar to them, or long difficult words which you might think will impress them but in fact only obscure the point you are trying to make.

If the purpose of your verbal communication is to resolve a problem, remember that the best way to get answers from people is to ask questions. If you start by stating the problem and ask for opinions or suggestions, you will get a more balanced response than if you start with your solution to the problem and ask if people agree with it.

COMMON MISTAKE

If the message has not been understood, saying it again more loudly will not help.

If you are dealing with poor performance or behaviour, ask for their side of the story before you make a decision on how you are going to handle the situation; you may be surprised to find that the actual problem is completely different from what you imagine it to be.

LISTENING

'Hearing' and 'listening' are not the same thing. We all hear lots of things we don't listen to, such as background noise. Listening is a conscious activity aimed at understanding what you hear. Unfortunately, even when we listen we don't necessarily hear. People speak at up to 175 words per minute, but we are able to listen intelligently at up to 800 words per minute, so there is a lot of spare capacity which we usually fill by thinking about something else.

There are seven levels of listening:

1 Passive listening – you are not really listening at all, simply hearing background noise.
2 Pretend listening – you are giving all the outward signs of listening (nodding, smiling, saying 'of course') but you are really thinking about something else.
3 Selective listening – you have already made up your mind what your response is going to be, so have stopped listening.
4 Misunderstood listening – you are hearing what you want to hear, not what is actually being said.
5 Active listening – you are listening attentively, understanding feelings and gathering facts.
6 Empathic listening – you are understanding feelings and checking facts, with the speaker's purpose in mind.
7 Facilitative listening – you are listening with the speaker's purpose uppermost in your mind.

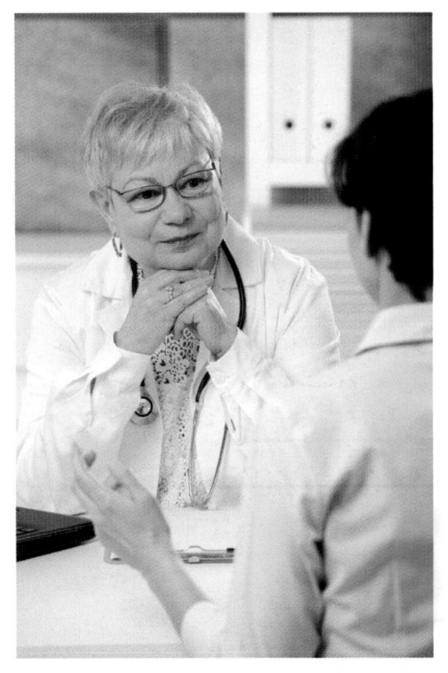

You need to be listening at or above the 'active' level

In a business environment, you need to be listening at or above the 'active' level. In many conversations, nobody is listening and everybody is simply taking turns to speak. Everybody is more interested in giving their own views than in listening to those of other people. At the same time, we all want to be listened to and understood.

Active listening requires you to:

- stop what you are doing
- look at the speaker
- let others speak
- be interested in what is being said
- ask open-ended questions to clarify what you hear
- spend more time listening than talking
- not finish the speaker's sentences
- not interrupt
- avoid answering questions with questions
- plan your response after the speaker has finished, not while they are talking
- only give your own opinions after you have heard the speaker's.

When you have listened actively to what is being said, summarise it in your own words so the speaker can confirm that you have understood it. Even if people are actively listening, there may still be barriers that prevent the message being understood. These can be divided into physical barriers, **experiential** barriers and **psychological** barriers.

Experiential

Relating to experience as opposed to other methods of acquiring knowledge

Psychological

Relating to the mind or mental processes

Physical barriers are things like background noise, the physical environment and stress. The message can be misunderstood if it cannot be clearly heard because of noise from other people speaking or from equipment being operated. Environmental distractions might include bright lights, passing people or traffic, or any other distraction. Stress causes misunderstanding because we do not hear things the same way when we are under stress.

ACTIVITY

Ask a colleague to help with this activity. Ask them to read aloud a short newspaper article. Then ask them to read it aloud again, but to make some changes. Each time a change is read out, you must interrupt them and tell them the change that has been made. This requires you to listen carefully and remember important information and details.

Experiential barriers arise because everyone has a different experience of life which affects the way they understand what they hear. Our culture, background and inbuilt bias all alter our reaction to information we receive. We are also influenced by our perception of the person we are listening to. If we consider them to be an expert on the subject, we automatically give more authority to what they say than we do to someone we think knows less about it than we do.

Psychological barriers include an inability to separate the message from the way we feel about ourselves. This leads to us reacting defensively if we feel the message is intended as a verbal attack, or with feelings of superiority if we feel we know more about the subject than the person delivering it. We may also find ourselves listening to the words rather than the meaning of the message, especially if we feel strongly about particular words being used. For example, if we think calling an actor a 'genius' is overstating the facts, we will focus on the use of the word rather than what is actually being said about her.

NON-VERBAL COMMUNICATION

An important part of verbal communication is, strangely enough, non-verbal communication, in other words what we say without speaking. Body language is an extremely complex subject which even the acknowledged experts disagree about, but there are some simple clues that you give off all the time and which you can learn to read in others.

Smiling is used to indicate friendliness, happiness or non-threatening behaviour

The primary elements of body language are usually listed as:

- The face – the most obvious source of expression, your face can smile, frown, and show anger, disgust or disbelief. Smiling is used to indicate friendliness, happiness or non-threatening behaviour.
- The eyes – perhaps more difficult to control than your facial expression, your eyes can make or avoid contact with other people, and look 'shifty' or express sympathy. Eye contact is usually an indication of interest or concern – but be careful as different cultures interpret eye contact in different ways.
- Posture – the way you hold your head, the way you stand or folding your arms all express your feelings towards other people. Standing erect and leaning forward means that you are approachable.

- Gestures – we all know and understand basic gestures, such as a wave hello or goodbye, but there is a whole language of gestures – and just to confuse the issue further they differ between different nationalities and cultures. Speaking without gestures gives the impression of being uncomfortable with that you are saying.
- Voice – while *what* you say is verbal communication, *how* you say it – tone, volume, pace, pitch, rhythm and **inflection** – is considered non-verbal. Vary these six elements and you will avoid being boring, dull and monotonous.
- Movement – the way you move gives off messages. Moving towards someone may be friendly or threatening, depending on the context and manner, while moving away may be submissive or dismissive. Try not to invade other people's personal space.

Inflection

The way a speaker's voice rises and falls when they speak

There is a whole language of gestures

HANDY HINT

While it is often difficult to be sure that someone is telling the truth simply by listening to their words, if you watch their body language closely you will get vital clues.

You can use combinations of these elements to deliver or interpret non-verbal messages. Make sure your words match your tone and your body language. Look at the person you are speaking to or, if you are speaking to a group, look at each of them in turn unless you are directing a comment or question to one individual.

While you are speaking, look at the audience for signs of confusion and ask the listeners if they are following what you are saying. Give them the chance to comment or ask questions. Remember that verbal communication should always be a two-way process; if you just wanted to get your point across, without comment or discussion, you could have written to them. It is important to confirm that they have understood correctly what you wanted to communicate.

ACTIVITY

Research body language and the meaning of different facial expressions and positive gestures.

ACTIVITY

Ask a colleague to make a note of any negative comments that you make over a period of a week – they should make their notes without you being aware they are doing it, so that it doesn't alter your behaviour. At the end of the week, ask them to share the comments with you. Answer the following questions.

- Are you inclined to use negative statements?
- How frequently do you use them?
- Are they necessary?
- Can you avoid them?
- Is it easy to replace them with positive statements?
- What are you planning to do to eliminate them?

CASE STUDY
BREAKFAST CLUBS

Breakfast clubs give school pupils a good start to the day

Cereal brand Kellogg's has supported breakfast clubs in schools, providing a healthy meal at the start of the day in a safe and friendly environment, for many years. But schools ran into trouble funding their breakfast clubs. Research showed that lack of a breakfast would lead to poorer academic results and worsening behaviour in schools. Kellogg's responded by creating a communications plan to show its commitment. The campaign aimed to get across that:

- breakfast is especially important for young people
- breakfast clubs have a positive impact on behaviour, attendance and ability to concentrate
- by buying Kellogg's Corn Flakes customers were helping to support breakfast clubs.

A government spending review could have resulted in the Kellogg's story being overlooked, and other food companies' support for breakfast clubs could have led to confusion. The campaign's key objectives depended on promoting the right messages to different audiences.

Kellogg's devised a communication plan for both internal and external stakeholders. The internal stakeholders were Kellogg's employees, who were encouraged to get involved through information posted on the company intranet and being invited to attend a breakfast club with two primary schools that was hosted in the Kellogg's building.

Campaign communications involved both formal and informal communications. Formal communications included letters sent to MPs. In contrast, face-to-face interactions at breakfast clubs and briefings to mummy bloggers demonstrated a more informal approach to communication.

An evaluation of the campaign showed that:

- the first six weeks of the campaign reached a potential audience of 9 million people
- over 500 schools received a grant of up to £450
- the money raised provided a million breakfasts.

UNIT 318 (B&A 57): TEST YOUR KNOWLEDGE

Learning outcome 1: Understand business communication models, systems and processes

1. Describe two communication needs of internal stakeholders.
2. Explain what is meant by 'internal communication'.
3. Describe the problems that could occur with informal communication.
4. Explain why an organisation uses different methods in its communications plan.
5. Explain why it is important for organisations to evaluate their communications.

Learning outcome 2: Be able to communicate in writing in business

1. Describe what is meant by 'a barrier to communication'.
2. Describe two types of barriers to communication.
3. Explain structure in written communication.
4. Explain style and tone in written communication.
5. Explain content in written communication.

Learning outcome 3: Be able to communicate verbally in business

1. Explain why appropriate language is important in verbal communication.
2. Describe two positive types of body language.
3. Explain why it is important to check that a recipient understands a verbal message.
4. Explain why it is important to respond to a verbal message in an appropriate way.

CHAPTER 2

UNIT 318 (B&A 57) PRINCIPLES OF BUSINESS COMMUNICATION AND INFORMATION

Improving communication makes all organisations better, with more sharing of ideas and higher morale. Organisations that think of their employees as customers and treat them well create a form of advertising, because employees tell others what happens at work, and it's better to have them saying positive rather than negative things. Organisations need to communicate both with their employees and their customers. An internal newsletter or intranet helps employees know what's going on.

Information systems developed must provide information that is relevant, timely and accurate. Information is only relevant if it can be used to help make a decision. It is only timely if it is readily available when decisions have to be made. And it must be accurate enough to help ensure that the correct decisions are made.

In this unit you will cover the following learning outcomes:

1 understand negotiation in a business environment
2 understand how to develop and deliver presentations
3 understand how to create bespoke business documents
4 understand information systems in a business environment.

Assessment criteria

This section covers assessment criteria 1.1, 1.2 and 1.3

NEGOTIATION IN A BUSINESS ENVIRONMENT

Negotiation is a skill that must be learned. It is used not only when attempting to get the best deal from suppliers or customers, but also on a daily basis when dealing with management, colleagues, trade unions and/or legal advisers. When faced with one or more suppliers who are intent on obtaining your business, or potential customers who are trying to negotiate the best deal for their organisation, you can be sure that they will be skilful and experienced negotiators. If you are to conclude a deal that is beneficial to your organisation, you need to prepare well for the discussions you are going to have. These discussions may be face to face or over the telephone, but you will need preparation in either case.

Before you talk to potential suppliers or customers, you need to be clear in your own mind about what it is you want to achieve. Ideally, of course, from suppliers you want a deal at a great price for a guaranteed quality of product or service, exclusive to your organisation and with penalty clauses for any failure to meet your terms. Your potential customers will be looking for exactly the same from you. In reality you are extremely unlikely to achieve your **optimum** deal, so you must decide before you start:

Optimum

The best or most suitable within a range of possibilities

- what you are going to ask for
- what you are prepared to concede – and what you have the authority to concede
- the point at which you cannot accept any further compromise.

Negotiation in progress

Your starting position will be that you want to receive or deliver certain conditions in terms of quality, quantity, timing, service and price. Some of these will be more important to you than others, so the less important will be those you are prepared to concede. Each will have a minimum level that you are prepared to accept – if the supplier or customer's best offer is below this minimum, you may have to walk away and look elsewhere.

The supplier or customer will recognise that your starting position is just that. The skill lies in not letting them know what your minimum level is, or they will offer this and know you have to accept it. In most cases, you will state your starting position, the other party will state theirs, and you will need to negotiate to narrow the gap between the two. Your goal is to reach agreement as close as possible to your starting position; their goal is to finish as close as possible to theirs.

COMMON MISTAKE

Thinking of negotiations as a process that one party wins and the other party loses is wrong. Both will be looking for the 'win/win' situation.

APPROACHES TO NEGOTIATION

There are a number of tactics used by experienced negotiators to gain an advantage. Negotiations may be concerned with contracting, buying and selling, and staffing or financing. If you learn these tactics you can use them yourself, and you can recognise when they are being used against you and use tactics to counter them.

Tactic	Counter tactic
Two-person negotiating team, one making impossible demands and the other one more reasonable ones, so that the more reasonable demands are accepted	Put up a similar strategy
Offer a low basic price, then charge for extras	Make the specification so detailed that there is no room for extras
Make an offer that seems very attractive, but has a strict deadline for acceptance	Specify at the beginning of the negotiations what your timeframe is for making a decision
Make two offers, one so unacceptable that it makes the other – although also bad – seem reasonable by comparison	Refuse both offers and suggest you will have to look elsewhere
Claim that even their best offer is so unreasonable that there is no way you could accept it	Make your best offer and refuse to be moved

Approaches to negotiation may include:

- Soft negotiation, which involves the negotiation of positions, rather than interests. The negotiator will take a soft approach, treating the other side as friends, seeking agreement at almost any cost and offering concessions easily in the interests of preserving or creating a good relationship with the other side. Soft negotiators will trust the other side and be open and honest about their bottom line.

- Hard negotiation, where the negotiators see the other side as rivals and demand concessions as a condition of the relationship. They distrust the other side and play underhand games to try to gain the negotiating advantage. For example they will refuse to make concessions, mislead their rival about their bottom line and demand one-sided gains as the price of an agreement. They will apply tricks and pressure in an effort to win what they see as a contest of will.
- Principled negotiation, in which the first step is to understand that both you and the other side have a certain set of interests. Although you may have a preferred solution, there are likely to be a number of different outcomes that will work for you and for the other side. Do not go into a negotiation without having a 'plan B': a way to get some of what you need without going through a negotiation. One way to persuade the other side to see the matter your way is to have legitimate standards that you can use to show the other party that you are being reasonable. Know what you need to tell the other side and, equally important, how you need to tell it to them. The adage that people do business with people they like holds true in negotiation. Engaging in reasonable, principled negotiation will help to maintain a good relationship with the other side's negotiator. As that relationship grows in strength, you will be better able to negotiate with this person based on the store of goodwill that has been built. Obviously, a successful negotiation closes with both sides committing to act on the negotiated settlement. However, commitments are important throughout a negotiation and start with the simple commitment to negotiate.
- Distributive negotiation, which is where you look at the property or goal of the negotiation as if it were a fixed amount of something. This is sometimes referred to as a fixed pie negotiation. Each party in this negotiation wants to get as much as they can for their side. For example, if you are buying something, you want to pay the lowest price possible while the seller wants to get the highest price possible. This type of approach is best used if you will only be working with the counter party to the negotiation once or only a few times.
- Integrative approaches to negotiation, which seek to create value between the parties. The idea of integrative negotiation is to work together to find the outcome that best helps both sides. This requires both sides to put more effort than usual into understanding what the other side requires and desires from a deal. It works best when the two sides concentrate primarily on the main point of the deal, rather than coming up with many secondary points which they will then 'trade off' as part of the negotiating process.

ACTIVITY

With a colleague or colleagues, role play negotiations. Both parties should have a starting position and a minimum position that they are prepared to accept, which must be unknown to the other party. After agreement is reached, review what tactics you used, what tactics the other party used and how they were countered.

At the end of the negotiation there will be an agreement. Possibly this may be an agreement to differ, when there is no position that is acceptable to both sides. In most cases, however, an offer will be made that is better than the points at which either side cannot accept, and an agreement will be reached that is acceptable to both parties.

DEVELOPING AND DELIVERING PRESENTATIONS

Assessment criteria

This section covers assessment criteria 2.1, 2.2, 2.3, 2.4 and 2.5

There are many different ways of giving presentations:

- in person
- via audio link
- via video link
- via webinars
- via round-the-table discussion.

The principles for giving an effective presentation remain the same, whatever method of delivery is used. Presenters who know and understand their subject will work from notes that simply state the keywords that they must not forget to mention, and will improvise around these prompts. This usually gives a more free-flowing impression to the audience and encourages interaction. It doesn't work if the presenter is not prepared for questions that need greater depth of knowledge.

If you are preparing keyword notes for yourself or the presenter, make sure they are in a large enough font to be seen at a glance so that the presenter does not have to lift the notes up to refer to them. The notes must appear in the same order as the topics to be covered or the presenter will be in complete confusion trying to gather their thoughts.

The most common sequence used by presenters is:

- tell them what you are going to tell them
- tell them
- tell them what you have told them.

In other words, describe the content of the presentation, give the presentation, then confirm the main points. When preparing the presentation, however, it is better to write the close first, then the opening and finally the main body. This will allow you to clarify in your mind that you understand the purpose of the presentation before trying to produce the individual handouts or slides that will explain the detail.

RESOURCES

Resources required when developing a presentation include information, equipment and people. Providing handouts for the audience allows them to take notes to capture the key points of the presentation and will help them to remember these later. There are different kinds of presentation including formal, informal, promotional, and training presentations and demonstrations.

Reasons for producing handouts include:

- to explain technical terms or concepts for members of the audience who may be unfamiliar with them
- to provide background information that the presenter doesn't have time to give
- to provide statistics that support or explain the presenter's comments
- for use in workshop sessions or brainstorming exercises
- to give a hard copy of a diagram or graph that the audience needs to study in detail
- to give the audience a list of topics to be covered
- to provide the audience with a hard copy of the slides being presented so they can make notes against them.

Handouts must concentrate on the message of the presentation and avoid being an excuse to overload the audience with information.

If you have agreed with the presenter that handouts would be helpful, the handouts must be produced in a way that maximises their effect. Handouts must help the audience remember both the presenter and the message and, more importantly, to understand the message. Within a few days of attending a presentation, studies show that most people will remember only 10% of what they heard, but well-written handouts significantly increase this.

HANDY HINT

Produce handouts only if they contribute to the presentation's objectives.

Well-written handouts will be printed on good-quality paper to give an immediately favourable impression. They should contain graphics whenever possible, as people give more attention to a chart or a diagram. Leave white space around the margins and between paragraphs and pictures, and in general fill no more than two-thirds of the page.

The presenter will probably decide when to give the audience the handouts – before, during or after the presentation. If they are given out during the presentation, they can distract the audience from listening to the presenter. From the point of view of preparing the presentation, you will need to know in advance when the presenter intends to distribute the handouts so that you can make sure they are available.

Some presenters prefer to use a flipchart or whiteboard as the visual aids to support their presentation, but most will want to use a slideshow. These can be presented using transparencies projected through an overhead projector (OHP) or, more commonly nowadays, using presentation software on a computer. A relatively simple laptop computer can project an infinite variety of words and images, including photographs and even videos.

The equipment needed to present a slideshow will include:

- a projector (either an overhead projector or a digital projector)
- a screen to project the slides onto
- spare projector bulbs.

It's often said that 'anything than can go wrong, will go wrong'. This is always particularly true where equipment is concerned, so when preparing a presentation it is always best to have a **contingency plan**. If the presentation is to be given on a remote site, email it to the event organisers in advance, and ask them to load it onto the equipment that will be used and run through it to check that everything works as expected. The presenter can then take a copy of the presentation on their own laptop, or on a disk or pen-drive, as a back-up.

Contingency plan

A plan about how to react to an event that might occur in the future, especially a problem that might arise unexpectedly

PRODUCING THE SLIDES

An important part of preparing for a presentation is to produce slides that are suitable for the content of the presentation and the audience.

The slides must look professional. They should use a consistent format and typeface, as well as colours that will be legible from the back of the room. Avoid the use of too many colours as this can be confusing. Remember that the printed handouts of the slides may well be produced in black and white, so information presented in different colours on the screen may appear the same in the hard copy.

When using a presentation program to prepare the slides, use a master slide to store information about the theme and slide layouts of the presentation, including the background, colours, fonts, effects, placeholder sizes, and positioning. You can then make changes to every slide in your presentation without having to update each slide individually. This is especially useful when you have extremely long presentations with lots of slides.

HANDY HINT

Avoid producing a presentation with too many slides – you don't want to be seen as presenting 'death by PowerPoint'!

Each slide should be numbered and show the logo of the presenter's organisation.

The first slide in the presentation should give the title of the presentation, the event, the date and the name of the presenter. Members of the audience will be able to refer to their handouts of the slides to remind themselves of these details weeks after the event, when otherwise they are likely to have forgotten. The title of the presentation should be memorable in order to catch the attention of the audience, but without being so quirky as to risk detracting from the presentation's professionalism. A question may work well as a title, such as: 'Where next for banking?'

The second slide should set the tone. It might contain the main point of the presentation or a witty quote. If you can make the second slide either controversial or amusing, do.

The third slide should list the objectives of the presentation so that the audience is fully aware of what they can expect.

The fourth slide should list the topics that the presentation will cover. Ideally, there should be three themes. Any fewer and the presentation is likely to be very short; any more and the presenter will likely be rushed to cover all of the information.

Each theme should be covered in a few slides, three to five slides per theme. If a theme can be covered in fewer than three slides, it may not be substantial enough to stand alone; if it needs more than five slides, it may need splitting into two themes.

Each slide should have a heading and around thirty words of text. If you are using an illustration, you should use fewer words on that slide or the audience will find them difficult to read.

Bullet points are a really good way of getting a lot of information onto a slide in relatively few words, but each bullet point must make sense in its own right. For instance, a bullet point relating to the point in the previous paragraph of this book might say:

- Fewer words on slides containing illustrations.

Rather than:

- Fewer words.

or

- If you are using an illustration, you should use fewer words on that slide or the audience will find them difficult to read.

Penultimate

Second to last in a series or sequence

The **penultimate** slide should recap the objectives of the presentation so that the presenter can check that the audience feels they have been met and give them a final opportunity to ask questions or raise issues.

The final slide should give contact details for both the presenter and any other part of their organisation that the audience might wish to contact.

While adding images, movement and video into slide presentations will make them look more impressive, you need to be careful that they do not detract from the message. If the audience is too busy thinking how clever or how attractive the slides are, they will not be able to concentrate fully on the content.

It is a good idea to avoid graphs, charts or tables that cannot be quickly understood. If the audience is going to take more than five seconds to grasp the information, give it to them as a handout and use the slide to make the point that the diagram illustrates. Again, don't put all the words the presenter is going to use on the slide – if you do, there is no point in having a presenter as the audience could simply read the slides for themselves.

You will also need to proofread each slide to ensure the presenter doesn't look bad on the day of the presentation because you have either incorrectly spelt a word or used bad grammar. Remember that they will be the one standing in front of an audience presenting your work, so they need to be happy with it. If it comes down to a choice between what they want and what you think they should have, their view should be accepted.

When you have prepared a presentation for someone else, you will usually receive feedback from the presenter. They will tell you if they were happy with the slides, handouts etc produced or if they want any changes made before repeats of the presentation.

You should ask the presenter to share with you the feedback that they get from the audience. Feedback on the presenter's performance will not be helpful to you, but feedback on the materials that you produced will help you – and the presenter – improve the next presentation.

HANDY HINT

Too many gimmicks like animation or sound effects distract the audience rather than adding to the impact of the presentation. Remember, 'less is more'.

YOUR OWN PRESENTATION

When you are due to make a presentation yourself, remember that the planning and preparation will take longer than the actual presentation, probably two or three times as long, so start planning in plenty of time. Clarify exactly what is required and the facilities that will be needed. Check how much time is available for the presentation and remember that some of that time will be needed for questions, so plan to develop a presentation that will fit comfortably into the time available.

There are different kinds of presentation including formal, informal and group presentations. Most will fall into one of two types:

- an informative presentation, such as a training session, a report on outcomes or a demonstration of a product or service
- a persuasive presentation, such as to promote sales or persuade an audience of the benefits of a plan.

Make sure you know which you are preparing for. The content will vary if the presentation is designed to change the audience's mind or encourage them to make a favourable decision rather than to provide them with information.

You also need to be clear about your audience. The number of people attending will influence the style of the presentation, as will their level of knowledge of the subject. A useful test of the effectiveness of a presentation is the 'last person test'. The last person in an audience is the one with the least knowledge or experience of the subject. If the last person will be able to understand the message that the presentation is trying to deliver, the presentation will have achieved its purpose. If you don't believe this will be the case, you need to re-write the presentation until the last person will understand.

Consider your audience and make sure everyone will understand the presentation

You also need to consider how much audience participation you will encourage or allow. This will affect the timings of the presentation, so remember to allow time for the audience to ask questions, make comments or join in with discussions if this is going to be part of the presentation.

When you start to put the presentation together, you need to be clear what the main point is that you want the audience to understand. It should be possible to present the main point in one sentence which can be explained verbally in no more than twenty or thirty seconds. The main point should be referred to in the opening part of your presentation and confirmed in the closing part. All of the content of the presentation must be consistent with the main point.

You also need to be clear what the objectives of the presentation are. As these will be revealed to the audience at the beginning of the presentation and checked at the end – to ensure the audience agrees with you that they have been met – they must be specific and measurable.

There are two schools of thought on how much of the presentation should be written down before the event. Some presenters work from a script, where every word is decided beforehand. This works if you are experienced enough to be able to memorise the script and confident enough to be able to digress if a question is asked and return to the script after dealing with the interruption. Where it doesn't work is if you simply read the script to the audience. In this case you may as well print off the script and hand it out for the audience to read for themselves.

ACTIVITY

Attend a presentation, making notes on what you think worked well and what you would have done differently. Discuss this with colleagues who also attended the presentation.

PRACTISING YOUR OWN PRESENTATION

When you have finished putting together the presentation, it is absolutely vital that you practise delivering it. If you are inexperienced at making presentations, practice will help you to overcome your natural nervousness. There is nothing worse than waiting to make your first presentation feeling unprepared, knowing you are either going to forget what you wanted to say or finish saying it with half the available time still left and nothing to fill it with. Even if you regularly give presentations, you should practise each new one as you will want to fine-tune the timings.

There are lots of different ways to practise. With experience you will find the method that best suits you. Until then, try all of them. Practise the beginning, the ending, using the equipment, writing on the flipchart and the links from one topic to the next. When you have these perfected, the main presentation will seem easy.

Practise short sections of the presentation separately. This is how actors rehearse. They don't try to learn the whole play at once: they learn a scene at a time until they know the whole of their part.

Practise in front of people. The first time you do this it will feel awkward, but it's better to get over your nerves during a dummy run than on the day. Ask for their advice but beware of the temptation to change everything at the last minute. The idea was to practise: if you re-write the whole presentation or try to make too many changes to your style, you will be back where you started but with less time left to prepare.

Practise in a realistic situation. When you deliver the presentation, there will be distractions. People will move about, ask questions, get up and pop out of the room, so practising in an ideal setting will not prepare you for the real thing.

Practise thinking ahead. If you have memorised your presentation, or at least the keywords that you are using as prompts, you should be able to think a sentence or two ahead of what you are actually saying. This makes the presentation smoother, as each sentence triggers the next.

Practising can help reduce presentation nerves

COMMON MISTAKE

Never assume the audience has previous knowledge of the subject

Practise your body language. You need to be aware of what you are doing with your hands because your audience will be. If your nerves make your hands shake, avoid holding papers in them as this will only emphasise the movement. If you plan to use hand gestures to emphasise points, use them when you are practising. This will help you remember as your brain will link the gesture with the point.

Think about whether you are going to move around. If you are presenting from behind a lectern or a desk, you will be standing still. If you are going to walk while you talk, practise this too – you don't want to be caught out by finishing a point on the far side of the room away from the notes for the next point or the button to press for the next slide.

Practise in front of a mirror, or video your practice presentation. You will see what the audience will see. Ignore the fact that it's you and try to focus on how you look as a presenter. If they (you) look confident, knowledgeable, competent, friendly, approachable, smart and presentable, then that is how you will look to the audience, too.

DELIVERING YOUR OWN PRESENTATION

When the day of the presentation arrives, check that all the necessary resources – whether physical, electronic or web-based – are available and that the equipment is working. Don't worry if you are nervous. Nobody delivers a live performance without feeling anxious. Many famous performers know it is the nerves that make their performance special. If you reach the point where you are completely relaxed before presenting, it is probably time to give it up.

If you have practised well enough, you will have at least the opening completely 'off pat'. Smile, look confident and deliver your opening. Remember that the audience is on your side – they have come to hear what you have to say.

Introduce yourself and tell the audience what you are going to tell them. Remember to emphasise why you are telling them and how long you will take to tell them. Tell them about the breaks you have organised and whether you will welcome questions during your presentation or whether you would rather they kept their questions to the end.

You will now have overcome your initial fear: no one has laughed at you or thrown anything. You will probably be starting to think that this is not such a terrible ordeal after all. You might even find that you are enjoying yourself – just be careful not to relax too much and forget everything you practised for the rest of the presentation!

Avoid starting with a joke. This is a business presentation and jokes are notoriously difficult to deliver, as you will know if you have ever watched a comedian 'die' on stage or TV. Jokes also have the unerring ability to offend someone: whatever the subject of the joke, you can almost guarantee that someone in the audience will be upset or offended by it, and you will have lost their support before you have really begun.

HANDY HINT

Adding humour to a presentation is not achieved by telling jokes. Most of the best comedians make observations that are humorous rather than telling jokes.

If you absolutely must start with an apology, make it as brief as possible and then get on with the positives. The audience will be unaware of or unconcerned by most of the things that you are tempted to apologise for, so don't beat yourself up. Starting with an apology will not gain audience sympathy, but it will start the proceedings with a negative feeling that things will not be as good as they might have been.

It is important to use language that suits the topic and the audience. The wording of a presentation delivered to new starters in an organisation would be completely different from that delivered to senior managers, for instance, even if the subject and content were the same.

Remember that audiences have very short attention spans and the younger the audience the shorter these will be. Each topic in your presentation will only hold the attention for a few minutes, so break them up with pictures or activities wherever possible. Don't expect an audience to sit and listen to you for long periods without giving them some form of diversion. As soon as you see any evidence that they are losing concentration, do something to bring them back. This may involve getting them to move into different groups, asking them to interact by relating their own experiences of the topic, writing their thoughts on sticky labels and attaching them to the walls – anything to get their interest back onto the subject. Be careful to give them a reason for what you ask them to do, or you risk **alienating** them further.

HANDY HINT

The audience remembers the beginning and end of any presentation long after they have forgotten the middle.

Alienating

Causing somebody to change his or her previously friendly or supportive attitude and become unfriendly, unsympathetic or hostile

During the presentation, use the tone, pace and volume of your voice to emphasise key points. Keep watching the audience so that you can gauge their reaction and adapt your presentation accordingly. Summarise your key points throughout the presentation so that you can check the audience has understood them.

Remember that you are the visual aid that the audience is most aware of, far more than the slides or the flipcharts. Use your body language to give an impression of being interested, even enthusiastic, about your topic and the audience will feel the same way.

Sometimes people in the audience will start to talk among themselves. The best way to deal with this is to simply stop talking and look directly at them. They will catch your eye and feel embarrassed at having behaved badly, increasing your authority in the eyes of the rest of the audience.

If you need to, give yourself time to think by asking the audience a question or setting them a task to carry out. If they ask you a question, be careful not to allow it to divert you from the message that you are there to deliver. If the question cannot be answered simply, say you will come back to it later. If you don't know the answer, say so and offer to find out. In either case, remember to give the answer before the audience leaves, if possible, or follow up with the person who asked it so that you can let them have the answer later.

Your presentation will be more effective if you are able to introduce props. If you are introducing a new product, pass samples round so the audience can see and touch them – or, if they are catering samples, even taste them. Each additional sense you can involve will help the audience to understand and remember what you have told them and shown them.

People also remember if they are able to link what you are telling them with something they already know. Using quotes, especially famous ones that they will already be aware of, will help your audience to put what they are hearing into context. Remember to credit the original user, however: attempting to pass off 'we will fight them on the beaches' as an original thought will not gain the respect of an audience who are well aware of where it comes from.

ACTIVITY

Research some famous quotes and make notes of where they might be useful in a presentation that you may have to deliver.

Remember to leave the audience on a high. You won't want to finish the presentation with a song, but remember why stage performers always try to end their act with something rousing or memorable. End by reinforcing the message that you had for them. Go back to the objectives you set for the presentation and let them see that they have been met.

EVALUATING YOUR OWN PRESENTATION

To help identify changes necessary to improve future presentations, it is important to collect feedback on your presentation. While you can reflect on your own performance and the reaction of the audience to identify learning points, you will have been too involved in the presentation to be truly objective about it.

There are a number of different ways to collect feedback on a presentation. One of the most effective ways of collecting qualitative feedback is to ask someone whose opinion you trust to sit in the audience and make notes. Try to avoid asking a family member or a friend to do this, as they will likely tell you what they think you want to hear. You want to know from them:

- what was good about the presentation
- what was not so good about it
- how they would describe your technique
- areas that you could improve on.

Ask them specific questions rather than relying on generalisations and you will get valuable feedback that will help you make a more effective presentation next time.

A second method is to video your presentation so that you can view it later. The first time you watch yourself you will almost certainly be overly critical. Look for one or two areas you can improve rather than describing the whole performance as 'terrible'. You might see that you need to speak more slowly or stop using phrases like 'you know'.

Leave it a while and then watch the video again. This time listen to the reactions of the audience. Note when they reacted the way you expected them to and when they didn't. Look for occasions where you didn't give them enough time for the point to sink in.

Finally, watch the video a third time and listen to what you said. Compare it to what you had planned to say. Did you allow yourself to get distracted and miss an important point? Did you ignore a member of the audience who was trying to ask a question? Once you have looked at the video a number of times you will be able to see yourself objectively and appreciate what you did well and where you can improve.

The traditional way to evaluate a presentation is to ask the audience to complete 'happy sheets' which provide quantitative feedback. These are often badly used, however. People will fill in the answers to questions such as 'Did the presentation meet your expectation?' with a 'yes', but this doesn't actually tell you anything about your presentation. What if they were expecting you to be terrible?

Audience evaluation needs to be specific and measurable if it is to be useful. An evaluation which grades the individual elements of the presentation will enable you to look at the high- and low-scoring areas and, if you give the same presentation more than once, you can compare scores to see if you have maintained your performance in the better elements and improved where you needed to.

ACTIVITY

Use the evaluation grid below to grade two presentations that you are attending as a member of the audience. Use the results to improve your own presentations.

	1	2	3	4	5
Effective beginning					
Good ending					
Appropriate length					
Well prepared					
Appropriate for audience					
Presented in an interesting way					
Open for questions					
Short and simple language					
Contact with audience					
Overall use of visual aids					
Handouts					
Computer use (eg slideshow program)					
Total score (out of 60)					

I specifically liked:

The presenter could improve:

CREATING BESPOKE BUSINESS DOCUMENTS

Assessment criteria

This section covers assessment criteria 3.1, 3.2, 3.3, 3.4 and 3.5

A list of the types of bespoke documents that can be produced would be almost endless. The most common include:

- letters and correspondence
- reports and proposals
- minutes and agendas
- invoices
- compliment slips
- business cards
- catalogues
- newsletters, brochures and leaflets
- posters and notices
- forms – the website www.freebusinessforms.com lists over 700 different business forms.

Bespoke documents are simply documents that have been personalised for use by the organisation, a department within the organisation or an individual. They include stationery (such as compliments slips and business cards), promotional material (such as catalogues, brochures and leaflets) and forms (documents that require information to be filled in).

When designing bespoke documents, remember that documents are visual and make an impression on the reader or user based on the way they look, so you must give a great deal of thought to their format and layout. Poorly designed bespoke forms can affect the efficiency of the organisation and its reputation with customers, clients and the general public. Take the time to produce them well and you can improve the organisation's image, reputation and performance.

When preparing bespoke documents, it is important to:

- Use a consistent layout. There is a huge variety of fonts available and all of them can be used in different sizes and colours, together with italicising, bolding or using capital letters. However, most documents will benefit from using no more than two different fonts. In particular, long documents should retain a similar look and feel throughout as too much variation can confuse the reader.
- Use different sizes of font and bold letters for headings and sub-headings to make the document easier to navigate. For instance, if the main text is in a font size of 12, a subheading could be size 14 and a main heading size 16. Use a combination of serif fonts and sans serif fonts:

   - Serif fonts such as Times New Roman have 'flicks' at the edge of each letter. While they are highly readable over large blocks of text, they can be overpowering in large sizes.
   - Sans serif fonts such as Tahoma can be used for headings and subheadings. They have no 'flicks' at the edge of each letter. They are very readable at large sizes but become unreadable over large blocks of text.
- Only create a design element that has a purpose. The design of your documents should help your content make its point, not overwhelm it. If in doubt, remember that 'less is more'.
- Think about spacing. People find it very difficult to read documents that are crammed full of text. Use white space to separate paragraphs and in the margins.
- Use visual aids such as photographs, diagrams, graphs and charts to break up large blocks of text and make the document page more visually appealing. Remember that 'a picture is worth a thousand words'.
- Use colours. Colours attract the reader's attention and are useful in directing the eye to a particularly important point. Remember to use colour sparingly, however, and not to make your documents look like the product of a small child's art class. There are some colours whose use is traditional – such as red when indicating a negative in financial figures – and these conventions should be followed or the reader may become confused.
- Use bullet points to summarise information and numbered lists to explain sequences of events or activities. Remember to be consistent when creating numbered lists: if you need item numbers, sub-item numbers, sub-sub-item numbers etc then decide on the style to use and stick to it.

ACTIVITY

Look at a letter that you have received that did not impress you. Discuss with your supervisor the impression that it gives of the organisation that sent it.

LETTERS AND CORRESPONDENCE

When producing letters and correspondence, you need to consider:

- the paper colour
- the text colour
- the size and font of the text
- the positioning of the organisation's logo
- the positioning of the organisation's name and address, website, email address, telephone number, fax number, VAT registration number and company registration number.

REPORTS AND PROPOSALS

When producing reports and proposals, remember that a written report should provide information and facts as **succinctly** as possible. A formal report will contain the following:

Succinctly

Expressed with brevity and clarity, with no wasted words

- A title that reflects the subject of the report.
- A table of contents if the report is more than ten pages long.
- An executive summary. This is written last and summarises the essential points of the report, including the conclusions as briefly as possible. It should be able to be read in isolation, allowing the reader to decide whether it is necessary to read the whole report.
- An introduction explaining why the report has been written, giving background information and explaining the method of investigation used.
- Main text where the findings of the report are listed under sections and subsections. Each section will refer to a different topic and describe, analyse, interpret and evaluate the data. Only proven facts should be used, not opinions at this stage.
- Conclusion, which should sum up the main points. Opinions can be expressed if the evidence to support them is given in the main text. This may lead to recommendations.
- Recommendations for improvements or actions based on the conclusions.
- Bibliography listing the publications cited in the report or referred to when putting it together.
- Appendix containing material which is referred to in the report which requires greater detail.

MINUTES AND AGENDA

Producing minutes and agendas is explained in detail in Chapter 3 (Unit 319, B&A 58).

INVOICES

When producing invoices, there are a number of pieces of information which must be included:

- the client's or customer's name and address
- your organisation's name, address, telephone number and email address
- when you expect payment and by what method
- an invoice number.

COMPLIMENTS SLIPS

When producing bespoke compliments slips you need to consider:

- Their size – making them fit a standard DL envelope will avoid the need to fold them.
- The background and text colours – these will often be designed to mirror the organisation's letterheads.
- The positioning of the wording 'With compliments'.
- Positioning of the same information as used on the letterhead (except for the VAT and Company Registration Number, if applicable).

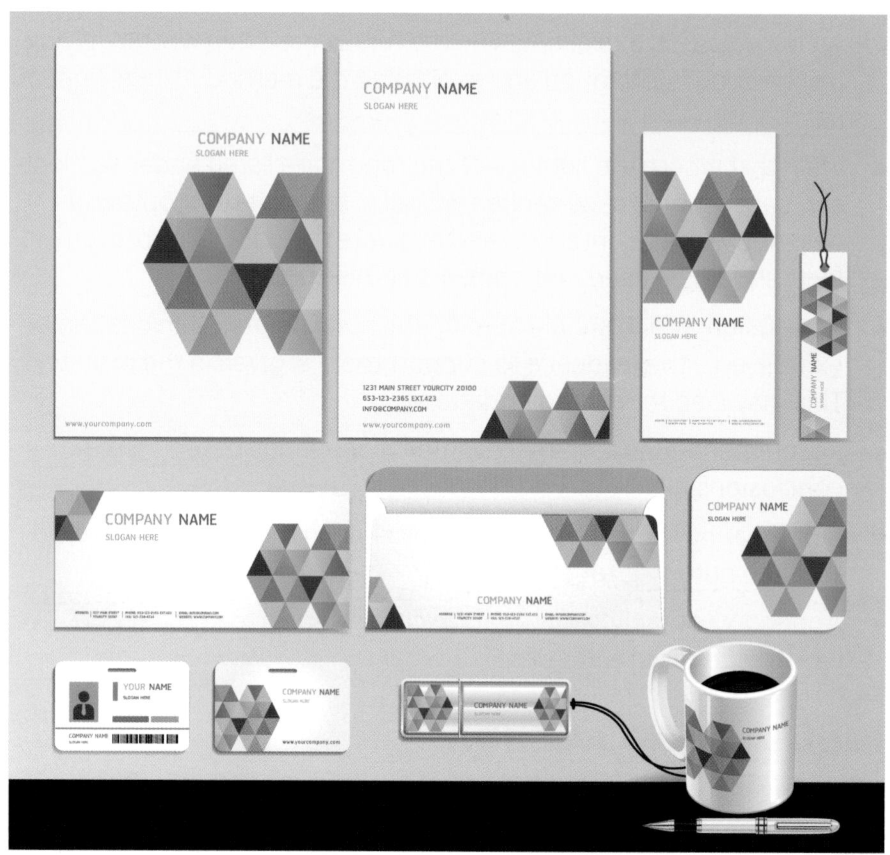

An example of a compliments slip

BUSINESS CARDS

When producing bespoke business cards you need to consider:

- Their size – they need to be small enough to fit conveniently into a wallet but also big enough to contain all the same information as on a compliments slip, plus the name, email address and phone number of the individual carrying them.
- The quality of the material they're printed on – business cards reflect the organisation so print them on good-quality card, not on flimsy card or even paper.

CATALOGUES

When designing bespoke catalogues, you will want to introduce more colour and images to display your products or services more graphically. You need to consider:

- 1 man in 20 and 1 woman in 200 has some degree of colour blindness – the most common form is the confusion of red and green, so be aware of this when choosing colour schemes.
- The colour which is printed is often not exactly the same as the colour on the screen when you are creating the design, so print a test page before committing yourself.
- The size and number of pages – if your product range is extremely wide, can you illustrate every option or should you illustrate only the most popular products and list the others?
- The size of illustrations – pictures, diagrams etc must be large enough to be seen clearly by everybody who is likely to read the catalogue.
- The **demographics** of your audience – the text size and colour, the language and the use of pictures and diagrams will all be affected by the type of person you are trying to communicate with.
- Categorising the content – if your catalogue contains large numbers of products, the order in which you display them and the index you provide will determine how user-friendly it is.

NEWSLETTERS, BROCHURES AND LEAFLETS

When producing bespoke newsletters, brochures or leaflets you will need to consider:

- Their size – they should fit easily into customers' pockets.
- The text and content – leaflets must be interesting and memorable, but above all they must be eye-catching or they will go into the recycling container without even being read.
- The positioning of information – the front page needs to make an impact, while details such as the organisation's contact details can go on the back page.
- The size and positioning of illustrations in relation to the information.

A company's catalogue is an example of a bespoke document

COMMON MISTAKE

Low-resolution web images are not acceptable for print catalogues. They are less than ¼ the resolution and if you use them your products will appear blurred.

Demographics

Groups of people characterised by age, income, sex, education, occupation, socio-economic group etc.

HANDY HINTS

- Readers typically look to the top right of a page first then sweep across the page to the other side. Put your most appealing products on the outside top corners. Make these elements larger than the remaining products on the page spread
- A business-to-business catalogue should be very different from a business-to-consumer catalogue. Catalogues for young people will have a different look from a catalogue for older people. Make the style of your catalogue match the style of your audience.

ACTIVITY

Obtain catalogues form a number of suppliers whose audiences differ in terms of age/sex/income. Create a chart showing how the different designs have been influenced by the demographics of the audience.

An example of a brochure/leaflet

ACTIVITIES

- Source a leaflet or newsletter either from your organisation or another. Discuss with your supervisor whether the presentation could be improved.
- Obtain brochures and leaflets from a number of different sources. Make a list of which would encourage you to read them and which you would discard after a quick glance. Why do they have this effect?
- Design a set of stationery for your organisation, including compliments slips and business cards.

POSTERS AND NOTICES

When producing posters or notices:

- Use all the space available, but remember that white space is an important part of the layout, and good use of it can make a poster elegant and arresting.
- Use colour sparingly. Limited use of a few colours is more striking than a 'rainbow' approach. Think about why you are using colour; it is especially useful for emphasis and differentiation. Avoid colour combinations that clash (eg red on blue) or cause problems for people with colour-blindness (eg red and green next to each other).
- Use white or pastel shades as background.
- The flow of information should be clear from the layout; if you have to use arrows to indicate the flow, the content could probably be arranged better.
- Clearly label diagrams or drawings and provide references to them in the text where necessary.
- The title text should be readable from 6 metres away – at least 48-point text. Remember that if you are creating your poster in A4

format, to be blown up to A1 format later, the final printed font size will be approximately three times the size you are working with.

- The body text should be readable from 2 metres away – at least 24-point text.
- Choose a clear font with large inner space (ie the space inside the loops of letters such as 'o', 'd', 'p'). Good examples are Arial, Verdana, Georgia or Helvetica.
- Keep the word count as low as possible.

FORMS

When producing bespoke forms, you again need to consider the demographics of the people who will be filling them in. If they are for internal use there will be an opportunity for training to be provided, so less information may need to be given on the form itself and some jargon may be acceptable. When designing forms for completion by customers or the general public, it is important to remember they may only ever complete the form once, so they will have no previous experience to fall back on and may find jargon or technical language confusing. In this case, notes explaining how to fill in the form should appear at the beginning. Other design tips when creating forms are:

- use tick boxes wherever possible
- signature boxes need to be a minimum of 60mm × 20mm (2½ inches × ¾ inch)
- address boxes should be at least five lines deep
- boxes for written answers should allow a 6mm (¼ inch) space between lines.

TEMPLATES AND MAIL-MERGE DOCUMENTS

When producing templates, you are usually looking to create a master that can be used, for example, in a mail merge. This allows you to use a word processing document to create personalised letters and pre-addressed envelopes or mailing labels for mass mailings. The mail out will contain fixed text – which will be the same in each output document – and variables – which act as placeholders that are replaced by text from the data source.

The data source is typically a spreadsheet or a database that has a field or column for each variable in the template. When the mail merge is run, the word processing system creates an output document for each row in the database, using the fixed text exactly as it appears in the template but substituting the data variables in the template with the values from the matching columns.

ACTIVITY

Design a set of stationery for your organisation including letterheads, reports, minutes and invoices.

ACTIVITY

Collect samples of forms used in your organisation. Check whether they conform to the standards described in this chapter. If not, make suggestions to the appropriate person to amend them.

COMMON MISTAKE

Forgetting to take a break from your keyboard when you are busy is a common mistake. You will be more productive if you take regular breaks than if you try to work for long periods non-stop.

PRODUCING BESPOKE DOCUMENTS

Before producing bespoke documents, it is important to understand exactly what is required. You need to liaise closely with the user or department that requires the document in order to agree the purpose of the document and the content, style and quality that is required. In some organisations there is a manager or even a department responsible for checking that all documentation meets the organisation's standards and uses the agreed **house style**. In these organisations, new or amended documents must be approved before being put into use.

House style

A set of rules concerning spellings, typography etc to be applied within a company

Text and non-text can be integrated by inserting pictures, graphs and clip art. There are a variety of different features that can be used in word-processing programs. Other applications help with integrating text and non-text into spread sheets and slides. The benefits of agreeing the purpose, content and style for the content of documents are that documents are standardised across the organisation and there are no poorly designed or poorly produced documents giving a bad impression of the organisation to customers or clients.

A variety of different features can be used in word-processing programs

It is also important to agree a deadline for the design and production of the document. A fabulous, award-winning brochure giving details of an event in August is completely worthless if it is not completed until mid-September. It may be necessary to research the information needed to complete the document. The research may be carried out internally, by checking on facts and figures, or externally. External research will mostly be carried out on the internet, using search engines.

Techniques for creating bespoke business documents will include the use of ICT hardware such as printers, software packages, web applications, and print and binding equipment. The hardware involved consists of a processor (which processes the data), a monitor (which allows you to see the data on the screen), a keyboard (which enables you to input data) and a mouse (which enables you to navigate around the screen). In a laptop computer or tablet, all of these are contained in one piece of equipment. Computers are often linked together with other computers to form networks that can share files.

HANDY HINT

Static electricity can destroy computer chips, so when cleaning your computer occasionally touch another metal object with your finger to dispel static build-up.

Software includes desktop publishing (DTP) packages that allow you to create documents using page layout skills on a personal computer. DTP software allows organisations to self-publish a wide range of printed material. They use 'what you see is what you get' (WYSIWYG) screen displays to create documents for either large-scale publishing or small-scale local distribution. DTP provides more control over design, layout and typography than word processing does, although word-processing software has evolved to include some capabilities previously available only with professional printing or DTP software.

The basic purpose of a printer is to produce hard copies of the data from the computer. There are different types of printer which have different features:

- Inkjet printers can produce a wide range of documents including complex colour documents such as photographs.
- Laser printers can print off text documents at high speed but cannot print photographs.

The features of printers vary, including their ability to print in black and white or colour, produce draft- and high-quality copies, the speed at which copies are produced and the ability to switch automatically to energy-saving mode. Many printers incorporate some of the features of scanners, photocopiers and fax machines. Printers can often be networked so that they accept instructions from a number of separate computers.

The basic purpose of a binding machine is to convert loose-leaf documents into bound ones. There are various types of binding machine:

- Channel binding machines, which produce professionally-bound documents in 15 seconds or less by compressing the documents inside a folder – documents can be bound and unbound up to three times, so binding errors or updates can easily be corrected.
- Wire binding machines, which punch holes through the documents and insert wire binders through the holes.
- Plastic comb binding machines, which work in the same way as wire binding machines but insert plastic combs through the holes, enabling thicker documents to be bound.

It is important in order to gain approval for the bespoke document that it is checked for spelling, grammar and punctuation. Remember that spell checking facilities on your computer will only find some errors – it cannot tell whether you meant to say 'its' or 'it's', or spot correct common typing errors such as 'form' for 'from' or 'then' for 'than', for instance. Check that it is set to English (UK) rather than English (US) or it will insist on changing words like 'organisation' to 'organization'.

While proofreading will find spelling mistakes, it will not find errors of fact, so it is important to check issues such as model number, prices etc as errors can lead to confusion and loss of business. Be particularly careful when checking numbers, dates, times and amounts. In the case of promotional material, for instance, it is important that prices and descriptions of products and services are accurate and up to date.

Once a document is complete it should be proofread for errors

Another important aspect to bear in mind when checking documents is confidentiality. Care must be taken not to include any information that is **commercially sensitive** in documentation that will be available to people outside the organisation. Any document must also comply with the principles of the Data Protection Act, the Copyright, Designs and Patents Act and intellectual property rights, which include copyright, trademarks, patents, industrial design rights, **trade dress** and trade secrets.

Commercially sensitive

Information that an organisation would not like to be in the public domain as it may give an advantage to a competitor

Trade dress

A product's physical appearance, including its size, shape, colour, design and texture. In addition to a product's physical appearance, trade dress may also refer to the manner in which a product is packaged, wrapped, labelled, presented, promoted or advertised, including the use of distinctive graphics, configurations and marketing strategies.

The Data Protection Act covers personal data that relates to a living individual who can be identified from the data or from the data and other information in the possession of the **data controller**. There are seven principles of information handling outlined in the act. These say that data must be:

Data controller

The person who decides the purpose for which personal data is to be processed

- fairly and lawfully processed
- processed for limited purposes
- adequate, relevant and not excessive
- accurate and up to date
- not kept for longer than is necessary
- processed in line with the rights of the data subject
- not transferred to other countries without adequate protection.

ACTIVITY

Research the Data Protection Act and the Copyright, Designs and Patents Act and consider how they apply to documents that you produce.

MAKING CHANGES TO BESPOKE BUSINESS DOCUMENTS

When amending forms or documents that already exist, it is important to use a system of document version control, a process by which different drafts and versions of a document or record are managed. Basically, version control is a tool that tracks a series of draft documents which end in a final version. It provides an audit trail for the revision and update of these finalised versions.

Version control clearly identifies the development of the document. It allows you to, for example, retain and identify the:

- first draft that was submitted to someone for comment
- draft that was created as a result of comments
- versions that went back and forth for further comment
- final version that was signed off.

It is also useful when you are working on a document with others. Changes made by different individuals at different times can thus be clearly identified. Having such versions identified and easily accessible allows the development of the document to be easily understood. It also allows the possibility of a return to a previous version to determine when decisions on content were made.

Version control should be used when more than one version of a document exists or when this is likely to be the case in the future, and can be achieved by adding a number at the end of a file title. Each successive draft of a document is numbered sequentially from 0.1, 0.2, 0.3 etc until a finalised version is complete. This would be titled Version 1.0. If version 1.0 is revised, drafts of this would be numbered as 1.1, 1.2 etc until Version 2.0 is complete.

In addition to adding the version number to the end of the file title, it should also be displayed within the document. The version number should appear on any document title page and also in the header or footer of each page. To ensure against accidental loss of final versions of records, a **read-only tag** can also be applied. Should any changes to this document be made, the user will be prompted to save the file with a new title.

Read-only tag

A computer setting that means users are unable to change the content of a file

INFORMATION SYSTEMS IN A BUSINESS ENVIRONMENT

Assessment criteria

This section covers assessment criteria 4.1, 4.2, 4.3 and 4.4

Information systems are used to help the management of an organisation make sensible decisions based on hard data rather than a **hunch**.

Hunch

An intuitive feeling about something

Information systems are developed through a number of stages, from an initial feasibility study through to maintenance of the completed application. Various **methodologies** have been developed to guide the processes involved, including:

Methodologies

The methods and principles used for doing a particular kind of work

- the waterfall model
- rapid application development (RAD)
- joint application development (JAD)
- the fountain model
- the spiral model
- build and fix
- synchronise and stabilise.

ACTIVITY

Research the methodologies listed above to find out what they involve.

Often, several models are combined into a **hybrid** methodology. In general, information system development involves the following steps:

Hybrid

Something made up of a mixture of different aspects or components

- The existing system is evaluated and deficiencies are identified by interviewing users of the system and consulting with support personnel.
- The new system requirements are defined – it is important that the deficiencies in the existing system are addressed with specific proposals for improvement.
- The proposed system is designed – the physical construction, hardware, operating systems, programming, communications and security issues are planned.
- The new system is developed – the new components and programs are obtained and installed, users of the system are trained in its use, and performance is tested. If necessary, adjustments are made.
- The system is put into use – the new system may be phased in and the old system gradually replaced, or it may be more cost-effective to shut down the old system and implement the new system all at once.
- Once the new system is up and running, it is comprehensively evaluated – maintenance must be kept up carefully at all times and users kept up to date concerning the latest modifications and changes in procedures.

TYPES OF INFORMATION SYSTEMS

There are different types of information systems available, including:

- electronic databases
- stock control systems
- management information systems (MIS)
- paper-based filing systems
- commercial systems
- bespoke systems
- systems for different business functions.

Information needs are different at different levels of the organisation, and this will affect which type of information system is best used. Information may be:

- Strategic information, which is the information needed by senior management for decision making. For example, trends in income earned by the organisation are required for setting the policies of the organisation. This information is not required by lower levels of management. Information systems that provide these kinds of information are called decision support systems.
- Managerial information, which is the information used for making short-term decisions and plans, such as sales analysis for the past quarter or yearly production details etc. Management information systems (MIS) provide these information needs of the organisation. They use a set of information processing functions and should be able to handle queries as quickly as they arrive. An important element is the database, which is a collection of **inter-related** data items that can be processed through application programs available to many users.
- Information relating to the daily or short-term information needs of the organisation, such as attendance records of the employees, is provided by the transaction processing systems. Some examples of information provided by such systems are processing of orders, posting of accounting entries, evaluating overdue purchaser orders, payroll processing etc.

The characteristics of the different types of information system are summarised in the table.

Inter-related

In a relationship in which each depends on or is affected by the other or others

ACTIVITY

Research the information systems listed in the table and find examples of where they are used in your organisation.

Type of information system	Characteristics
Decision support system	Provides information to managers who must make judgements about particular situations. Supports decision makers in situations that are not well structured.
Management information system	Provides input to be used in the managerial decision-making process. Deals with supporting well-structured decision situations. Typical information requirements can be anticipated.
Transaction processing system	Substitutes computer-based processing for manual procedures. Deals with well-structured processes. Includes record-keeping applications.

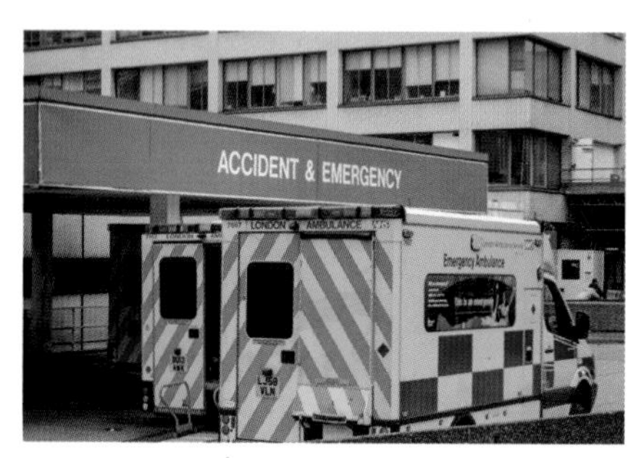

The Freedom of Information Act applies to organisations such as hospitals

LEGAL, SECURITY AND CONFIDENTIALITY REQUIREMENTS

Use of information systems must comply with legal and organisational requirements. Legal issues include compliance with the Freedom of Information Act, which applies to:

- government departments
- local assemblies, authorities and councils
- health trusts
- hospitals
- doctors' surgeries
- schools, colleges and universities
- publicly funded museums
- the police
- non-departmental public bodies, committees and advisory bodies.

The act gives members of the public the right to ask public bodies for all the information they hold on any subject. Unless there is a good reason not to disclose it, the information must be provided within 20 working days.

All organisations must also comply with the Computer Misuse Act 1990, amended by the Police and Justice Act 2006. This was introduced primarily to deal with computer hacking and contains three main offences to do with unauthorised acts relating to computers:

- Section 1 contains the basic 'hacking' offence of gaining unauthorised access to any program or data held in a computer.
- Section 2 makes it an offence to commit a Section 1 offence with a view to commit, or facilitate the commission of, a further offence.

- Section 3 contains the offence of doing any unauthorised act in relation to a computer with intent:
    - to impair the operation of any computer
    - to prevent or hinder access to any program or data held in any computer
    - to impair the operation of any such program or the reliability of such data
    - to enable any of the things to be done knowing that any modification intended to be caused is unauthorised.

Maximum sentences for these offences range from six months imprisonment and/or a £500 fine to 10 years imprisonment and/or an unlimited fine.

Other legislation which applies to information systems includes the Data Protection Act and the Copyright, Designs and Patents Act, which are covered in detail in Chapter 3 (Unit 319, B&A58).

As well as legal requirements, you must consider organisational policies for security and confidentiality. These will cover storage and retrieval of information, the types of information held, and security, storage and rights of access to the information. Organisations that don't establish a strong chain of command for keeping data secure, or that provide inadequate security training for users, create an unstable security system. By taking the time to ensure that data is used carefully and by reputable sources, the risk of a security breach can be significantly reduced.

The four principles that ensure security of information are:

- Confidentiality – information must be secured against unauthorised access.
- Integrity – information must be safeguarded against unauthorised modification.
- Availability – information must be accessible to authorised users.
- Back-up – information must be backed-up so that it can be recovered in the event of a system failure.

MONITORING THE EFFECTIVENESS OF AN INFORMATION SYSTEM

Once the system is in place and operating, it is necessary to monitor its use. This enables you to check that the system is operating efficiently and is not being misused. It also ensures no problems with legislation are encountered, as information being input can be checked for reliability. As in all but very small information systems it is not possible to monitor every task carried out, a form of sampling or auditing must be designed. There are a number of methods of selecting a sample to monitor.

- Random sampling – in this method, each task has the same probability of being selected as part of the sample as any other.
- Systematic sampling – in this method, every *n*th task from a list is selected as the sample, starting with a task randomly selected.
- Cluster sampling – in this method, the list of tasks being sampled is divided into groups called clusters, from which a random sample is then taken from within one or more selected clusters.
- Haphazard sampling – in this method, samples are selected based on convenience but should still be chosen as randomly as possible.
- Judgemental sampling – in this method your knowledge or experience are used to select items that are more likely to have problems or which pose a higher risk.

CASE STUDY
INFORMATION SHARING

Following a major fire, Melton Borough Council decided on a £5.6 million project to move to a new town-centre location it will share with its partners, Leicestershire County Council, Leicestershire Partnership NHS Trust, Voluntary Action Melton, and Leicestershire and Rutland Probation Trust.

The new building is designed to improve information sharing and encourage closer co-operation between public sector agencies in order to deliver multi-agency responses that improve outcomes for people and places in the Melton area. Office space in the new building is zoned into cross-agency working neighbourhoods determined by the provision of services directed to mutual customers or places. Teams from different agencies are located together and work collaboratively to provide more efficient and effective services, intervening sooner to tackle emerging social, economic and environmental issues.

Sound management and effective sharing of information and data underpin the success of the co-location project, and the partner agencies recognise that significant effort is required to remove cultural barriers to sharing information. A joint-agency Co-location Information Management Working Group has been established to deliver guidance, standards, governance and protocols to prepare staff for working with information in a co-located, co-production environment.

UNIT 318 (B&A 57): TEST YOUR KNOWLEDGE

Learning outcome 1: Understand negotiation in a business environment

1 Explain why negotiation is important in a business environment.

2 Explain what is meant by a 'win/win situation'.

3 What counter-tactic can be used when an offer has strict deadlines for acceptance?

Learning outcome 2: Understand how to develop and deliver presentations

1 Name two types of presentation.

2 Name two types of visual aid that might be used in a presentation.

3 How many slides should be used to illustrate each theme?

4 State two reasons not to start a presentation with a joke.

5 What is used to collect feedback after a presentation?

Learning outcome 3: Understand how to create bespoke business documents

1 What are 'bespoke documents'?

2 What is the main difference between serif fonts and sans serif fonts?

3 State two principles of the Data Protection Act.

4 What version number is used for the first finished version of a document?

5 Explain why spell-check must be set to English (UK) rather than English (US).

Learning outcome 4: Understand information systems in a business environment

1 Name two methodologies developed for information systems.

2 Which type of information system helps management make long-term decisions?

3 Name the four principles that ensure security of information.

4 Name two sampling methods that are used to monitor information systems.

CHAPTER 3

UNIT 319 (B&A 58) PRINCIPLES OF ADMINISTRATION

Over 3 million people currently work in business and administration roles in the United Kingdom, and millions more work in positions that require some administration skills. The future success of businesses depends on staff having professional administration skills. Recent developments in business have been towards more horizontal management, with less administrative support available within teams and an expectation that staff at all levels will carry out their own administration. If you do not have access to administrative support and are expected to carry out your own administration, you need to know what you're doing.

In this unit you will cover the following learning outcomes:

1 understand how to manage an office facility
2 understand health and safety in a business environment
3 understand how to take minutes of meetings
4 understand how to chair, lead and manage meetings
5 understand how to supervise an administration team
6 understand how to organise events.

Assessment criteria

This section covers assessment criteria 1.1, 1.2, 1.3, 1.4, 1.5 and 1.6

MANAGING AN OFFICE FACILITY

As an office manager or supervisor you will have responsibility for all the administrative activities that enable an office to run smoothly, including the systems and procedures. In addition, you will be responsible for ensuring that facilities, equipment and resources are in place that meet the needs of the office's users, and that they are maintained and repaired effectively. You will also have to deal with staff issues including training, appraisal and recruitment, while maintaining an environment that is secure and meets health and safety requirements. This is an extremely important role in any organisation, and one that requires a wide range of skills and experience.

LEGAL REQUIREMENTS

Implicit

Not specifically stated but understood in what is expressed

The legal requirements relating to the management of office facilities will vary according to the type and size of organisation you work for. Contracts form the basis for business relationships. They can be oral or even **implicit**, but for clarity it's best to have them in writing. If you breach a contract, the other party will be entitled to damages. A binding contract must:

- include an offer and an acceptance
- include an obligation to pay or a promise to provide something in return
- be clear about what all parties are expected to do
- include an intention by both parties to be bound by the contract, even if it is just an oral agreement.

Some trades, such as the food industry and financial services providers, need specific licences in order to operate. Many businesses must also comply with certain environmental obligations, for example regarding the control and disposal of hazardous substances.

All businesses interact with the environment and should comply with the various regulations designed to protect the environment. It's not only large organisations that this applies to, as small organisations can also have a significant impact on the environment.

Good environmental management can help to:

- meet the organisation's legal obligations to prevent and reduce pollution
- save money by reducing production and waste disposal costs
- control environmental risks and reduce liabilities
- improve the organisation's position and confidence in the supply chain

- improve the organisation's relations and reputation with customers and create new business opportunities
- earn recognition for good environmental performance.

An environmental management system (EMS) is a framework that helps a company achieve its environmental goals through consistent control of its operations. This increased control aims to improve the environmental performance of the company, and is personalised to the company's business and goals. An effective EMS should:

- enable the organisation to manage compliance with environmental legislation and all environmental permits
- ensure all staff are competent to manage environmental risks and compliance
- use a plan–do–check–act (PDCA) methodology
- set specific environmental objectives and targets
- be 'owned' by senior management and checked to ensure it is fit for purpose.

Businesses can have a significant impact on the environment

Data protection legislation applies to almost all organisations. If you keep information about identifiable individuals, you may need to notify the Information Commissioner's Office (ICO), a simple and inexpensive process. Even if you are exempt from notification, you must still abide by the principles of the Data Protection Act 1998. The act applies to information on websites as much as to computer and paper records. There are eight enforceable principles of good practice concerning data. Data must be:

- fairly and lawfully processed
- used for limited purposes

- adequate, relevant and not excessive
- accurate
- kept only as long as necessary
- processed in line with the subject's rights
- not transferred to countries that don't have adequate protection
- secure – the responsibility for security rests with your organisation and even accidental disclosure of personal information could make you liable to pay compensation to the person concerned.

The Consumer Protection (Distance Selling) Regulations give certain rights to remote buyers

Organisations may only carry out data processing where one of the following conditions has been met:

- The individual concerned has given their consent.
- The processing is necessary to fulfil a contract with the person.
- It is to protect the person's vital interest.
- It is to comply with a particular law.
- It is in the legitimate interests of the business unless this adversely affects the individual.

It is a criminal offence to break the law on data protection. Organisations and their employees could face a fine, a custodial sentence or community service.

If your organisation sells goods or services by telephone, the internet or direct mail, the Consumer Protection (Distance Selling) Regulations give certain rights to remote buyers such as the right to cancel an order within seven days. You must make this clear to each customer in writing, at the latest by the time the goods have been delivered.

There are certain items that are exempt, which include holidays, perishable goods and personalised goods. Tapes, CDs, videos and computer software are also excluded unless they are returned unopened. If requested to, you must provide a refund within 30 days, whether the goods have been returned or not. There is no deadline for customers to return goods. You can charge for the cost of returning the goods but you must make this clear in writing at the time of purchase.

Organisations that employ staff have certain legal responsibilities and obligations to those staff. These are defined in legislation including the Equality Act, the Employment Rights Act, the Employment Relations Act and the Working Time Regulations, details of which can be found in chapter 4 of this book (Unit 320 B&A 59). Failure to meet these could result in legal action being taken.

- Make sure that all new employees are entitled to work in this country or you could face heavy penalties. For a list of the documents you can inspect to prove this, together with general guidance on employing workers from overseas, see the UK Visas and Immigration website (www.gov.uk/government/organisations/uk-visas-and-immigration).

- Have a contract of employment in place from the day all employees start work.
- To avoid leaving you open to claims for unfair dismissal, discrimination or breach of contract, you should take legal advice before altering **terms and conditions** of employment, making people redundant or dismissing them.
- To protect yourself, you should warn employees that any discrimination, sexual harassment and other illegal acts will not be tolerated.
- If your organisation employs five or more people, you must provide access to a pension scheme.
- If your organisation employs anyone, even on a casual part-time basis, you are legally required to have employer's insurance.

Terms and conditions

Arrangements laid down formally in an agreement or contract, or proposed by one side when negotiating an agreement

The Freedom of Information Act 2000 is relevant to the management of office facilities in the public sector. Details of this act are explained in Chapter 2 (Unit 318, B&A 57).

The Copyright, Designs and Patents Act exists to protect creative works like articles, poems, photographs, designs, songs and sculptures. You do not need to register copyright but you should be very careful when you copy material. Remember to seek permission to use other people's photographs or drawings. Copyright only applies to the original works, not copies, and only to the means of expression, not the concept itself. If someone writes an article then only the words, not the ideas expressed in it, are protected.

To protect an invention, you must apply for a patent. It is essential you do this before you have made details public anywhere. To protect a logo or a slogan, you must register it as a trademark. Some organisations take out intellectual property insurance to help pay for the cost of defending their intellectual property rights.

Other insurance can also be useful as a sensible business precaution:

- If you sell products, product liability insurance will protect you if someone is injured by a defect in your product.
- If you offer services or advice, consider adequate professional indemnity insurance. The effects of a mistake in a service or product you have provided can be out of all proportion to the initial error. Indemnity cover may be needed for years after the work has been done because it has to be in place when the claim is made. Many professional bodies actually require their members to take out adequate professional indemnity cover.

To ensure your organisation has effective means of debt control, you need to spell out your terms and conditions of trade and get your customers to agree to, and ideally sign them, when placing an order. Essential things to include in your terms and conditions are:

- Retention of title clause – under this, you retain ownership until payment. If your customer becomes insolvent before paying up, you may not be able to reclaim your goods without it.
- Payment terms – make it clear to your customers when you expect payment for goods or services.

SERVICES PROVIDED BY AN OFFICE FACILITY

The services provided by an office facility vary widely according to the type and size of organisation. A typical list of duties of an office manager or supervisor might include:

- monitoring the premises to ensure that it remains safe, secure and well maintained
- directing or co-ordinating the supportive services department of the organisation
- setting goals and deadlines for the department
- preparing and reviewing operational reports and schedules to ensure accuracy and efficiency
- analysing internal processes, and recommending and implementing procedural or policy changes to improve operations, such as supply changes or the disposal of records
- ordering, distributing and storing supplies
- planning, administering and controlling budgets for contracts, equipment and supplies
- overseeing construction and renovation projects to improve efficiency and to ensure that the premises meet environmental, health and security standards and comply with government regulations
- hiring and laying off clerical and administrative personnel
- overseeing the maintenance and repair of machinery, equipment, and electrical and mechanical systems
- managing the leasing of space
- participating in planning and design, including space and installation management
- carrying out staff training on procedures
- disposing of or overseeing the disposal of surplus or unclaimed property.

Typical services provided by an office facility include:

- document production
- audio transcription
- data entry
- photocopying and binding
- making travel arrangements
- invoicing
- bookkeeping and accounts
- document control
- filing and client records management
- stationery issue and stock control
- petty cash and expenses handling
- room booking and appointment making
- reception
- dealing with incoming and outgoing mail.

A wide range of services are provided by an office facility

In order to ensure that the wide range of services is provided efficiently, every office needs systems and procedures. As office manager or supervisor, you will need to put systems into place that enable the office to remain organised and run smoothly while remaining within the agreed budget. Procedures will be needed to cover, amongst other things:

- safe working procedures
- risk assessments
- fires, accidents and emergencies
- security of information and physical property
- resource use and stock control

- purchasing of equipment, consumables and service contracts
- equipment use, monitoring and maintenance
- sending, receiving and storing information
- staff movement and absence control
- progress reporting and productivity monitoring
- use of telephones, the internet and emails.

Whatever sort of office you are managing, one of its main functions will be to maintain proper records of the business carried out. You will need a working knowledge of the organisation's filing systems, regardless of whether it is electronic or manual. One of your responsibilities will be to ensure that these systems are kept up to date, accurate and secure. Records should be updated on a regular basis. If data cannot be added immediately it is received, it should be input at least daily. Out-of-date information is worse than no information at all.

Accounting systems are another priority area that must be kept on top of. It is very important that all sales, purchases, income and expenditure are recorded as soon as possible so that the management of the organisation has an up-to-date picture of the financial situation. Far-reaching decisions may be taken based on accounting information; if this information is incorrect, the decisions may be flawed.

If your office is responsible for maintaining personnel files, payroll and employee discipline and grievance records, these must also be maintained extremely accurately as they not only affect the pay received by employees but can also be used as evidence in case of any claim for unfair dismissal.

Effective use of systems and procedures depends on employees being well trained in operating them so they are clear about their own role and responsibilities within them. As office manager or supervisor you must ensure that all the staff in the office have clear job descriptions, and that these are updated whenever systems or procedures change or new tasks are introduced. Make sure that no individual is indispensable: if only one person – even if that person is you! – knows how a procedure is carried out or where certain information can be found, consider what would happen if that person was taken ill or decided to leave.

Maintenance of the facilities, equipment and resources that are required to operate the office, such as the office furniture, office equipment and stationery, are also part of the office manager or supervisor's responsibility. You need to ensure these are supplied and in working order so that the staff can carry out their tasks without interruption. Equipment is likely to include telephones, computer hardware (including monitors, keyboards and mice), printers, scanners, photocopiers, shredders, binding machines, fax machines and franking machines.

HANDY HINT

From time to time, walk through the office and sit at a desk normally occupied by one of the staff. Look at whether the staff have all the equipment they need to carry out their daily tasks close to hand and analyse whether the **ergonomics** for that member of staff are as good as they could be.

Ergonomics

The scientific study of people at work. The goal of ergonomics is to reduce stress and eliminate injuries and disorders associated with the overuse of muscles, bad posture, and repeated tasks.

ACTIVITIES

- Review the facilities and equipment in use in your office. Identify where there is a need to replace, upgrade or remove it. Create a plan to make more efficient use of these resources.
- Set up or update a maintenance schedule for the equipment in the office.

You must also ensure that the office is laid out in the most efficient way possible and that there are sufficient resources available. In a large organisation this may only require a request to be made to a purchasing department. In a smaller organisation, the office manager or supervisor may have to do the ordering themselves.

If you are dealing with suppliers yourself it pays to build good relationships with them. Saving money or improving the quality of products or services you buy will improve the efficiency of your organisation. Keep in regular contact with your suppliers. If new products become available, they will let you know. If there are changes to your needs, you will be able to discuss with them how they can be met.

You may need to deal with suppliers when managing an office facility

Some suppliers will offer a better deal if you give them an exclusive contract to supply products or services, but this could cause problems if they go out of business or you have concerns about their quality at a later date. Either way, you should place orders in good time to avoid supplies running out.

HANDY HINT

Try to avoid last-minute panics by maintaining proper stock control on products that you buy regularly.

MANAGING OFFICE RESOURCES

Office resources include materials, staff, information and equipment. An effective way of reducing your organisation's costs is to use office equipment efficiently, saving energy costs by reducing the amount of electricity consumed. By managing your office equipment carefully you can reduce the amount of energy it consumes by up to 70%. As well as saving money by reducing your energy costs, managing your use of equipment and improving efficiency can have the following additional benefits:

- longer working life for your equipment
- greater mobility – switching to laptops, for example, which use much less energy than desktop computers, can mean that staff become more flexible in where and when they work
- reduced need for mechanical ventilation and cooling as energy-efficient equipment and machines in standby mode run at lower temperatures
- lower carbon emissions with less impact on the environment.

There are steps you can take to reduce the amount of energy your office equipment uses. Most of these cost little or nothing to implement, take very little time and require no special expertise. Even the smallest adjustments to the way you manage and use your office equipment can add up to significant energy savings. Ways to reduce energy consumption include the following:

- Ensuring that computers and monitors are switched off when users are away from their desks for more than 10 minutes. Use power-saving settings to do this automatically wherever possible. Always switch off computers and monitors at the end of the day unless they need to remain on.

- Switching off all printers at the end of the day. A plug-in seven-day timer could help to make sure they are not left on out of hours. When printing, use the most energy-efficient mode possible for the job – reduced quality, black and white, and double-sided printing are more energy efficient. Avoid all unnecessary printing.
- Making sure that copiers are always switched off out of office hours. Enable all energy-saving standby features and encourage staff to do their copying in batches. Avoid all unnecessary copying.
- Upgrading to more energy-efficient equipment where appropriate.
- Setting up an equipment maintenance schedule – well-maintained equipment lasts longer and works more efficiently.
- Drawing up an office policy on energy efficiency and ensuring that it is followed.

It is important to allow yourself some time for planning. Avoid being so busy just keeping up that you don't have time to assess the need for change. Step back and look at the way the office works as if you had just been appointed manager or supervisor. Are things being done the way they are just because they always have been done that way?

MONITORING AND MANAGING WORKFLOWS

Managing workflows appropriately is an important part of an office manager or supervisor's responsibilities for a number of reasons. Workflow management is a way of overseeing the process of passing information, documents and tasks from one employee in an organisation to another. Through the proper use of systems, each employee will pass the work on according to a pre-determined procedure. As technology advances, much workflow management has become automated and takes advantage of software to make the process smoother.

The main advantage of workflow management is improved efficiency. By automating processes and establishing a procedure that is consistently followed, unnecessary steps are eliminated and every member of the team is fully aware of his or her responsibilities.

It also makes it easier to track employee performance. When a link in the chain is broken, it is easy to go back and find out where this occurred. Workflow management also standardises working methods, ensuring that every employee working at the same level is performing the same function.

If you decide to introduce changes to procedures, you must communicate that change to your staff and anybody else in the

ACTIVITY

Review your office's systems and procedures. Identify changes that would be beneficial and create a plan to implement them.

organisation that will be affected by it. Part of the decision whether to make changes to systems and procedures will be based on the ability of your staff to manage the new tasks required. You may have to re-arrange the staff into new teams, so look at both their individual work output and the interactions and relationships between them.

SUPPORT AND WELFARE FACILITIES

In large organisations there is usually a human resources department responsible for recruiting and training new staff. In smaller organisations this role may be delegated to the various individual departments. As office manager or supervisor, you may be involved in the task from the initial identification of a need for new staff right through to training the successful applicant in their duties.

Even in a large organisation, you will want to be involved in the employment policy that decides how new staff are selected and trained because you will be supervising, training and working with them on a daily basis. When adding to the staff under your supervision, take into consideration the skills of the staff already employed. If there is a weakness in their knowledge or abilities, look for a new recruit who can add strength in this area, even if it is not one of the direct requirements for the vacant post. Each new member of staff should add to the office's total capability.

It is important that office workers are provided with support and welfare facilities. These often include:

- toilets and hand basins, with soap and towels or a hand-dryer
- drinking water
- a place to store clothing
- somewhere to rest and eat meals away from their desk
- good ventilation – a supply of fresh, clean air drawn from outside or a ventilation system
- a reasonable working temperature, usually at least 16°c
- lighting suitable for the work being carried out
- enough room space
- suitable workstations and seating
- a clean workplace with appropriate waste containers
- occupational health support, such as counselling
- financial assistance
- legal advice
- a crèche
- staff discounts
- access to trade unions
- health and leisure schemes.

Office workers need facilities such as space to eat away from their desk

HANDY HINT

The comfort level of the employees during working hours should be given special consideration when designing workstations. Failure to do so can result in employees developing **musculoskeletal disorders** such as repetitive strain injury (RSI).

Musculoskeletal disorders

Musculoskeletal pain is pain that affects the muscles, ligaments and tendons, and bones

Support offered by the organisation to its staff might include help and guidance to anyone affected by personal, domestic or work-related problems, suggesting or exploring options to help progress the issue or arrive at a resolution. This might include:

- visiting staff who are on long-term sick leave
- providing practical support following a bereavement
- promoting healthy lifestyles and awareness/screening programmes
- providing advice and support for addictions such as gambling, alcoholism and drug dependence
- providing advice on retirement and preparation for the transition
- signposting other sources of specialist advice, information and support.

Line managers have an important role in assisting employers to pro-actively address work-related stress, and in doing so reduce the likelihood of employees suffering from this problem. Examples of issues you may want to consider include:

- whether stress may be a factor in relation to frequent or long-term absenteeism by individual employees
- how you will monitor and address potential sources of stress
- identifying what medical and other evidence is required to determine whether the employee may have a disability within the meaning of the disability discrimination act – if so, consider whether the employee is being treated less favourably for a reason related to the disability and whether there are reasonable adjustments that could be made
- reporting your concerns to appropriate senior personnel while maintaining any obligations of confidentiality.

Another issue that will inevitably arise when managing staff is conflict. Conflict resolution is an important part of your responsibilities. Knowing how to handle conflict will make life easier for yourself and your staff. Many organisations have a formal conflict management policy that lays down procedures for handling disagreements between team members. Try to resolve the issue by getting the parties together, finding common ground and agreeing on a compromise that everyone can live with. If this doesn't work, the formal policy will ensure that no conflict is ignored and allowed to affect the efficient working of the office.

HEALTH AND SAFETY IN A BUSINESS ENVIRONMENT

Assessment criteria

This section covers assessment criteria 2.1, 2.2 and 2.3

The Health and Safety Executive (HSE) say that everyone is entitled to work in environments that are safe for them to do so, and that customers, visitors and contractors are entitled to be protected from any risk to their health and safety while they are on the premises. There are a number of regulations that impose responsibilities on both you and the employer in respect of health and safety. Your employer's basic responsibility is to provide safe and healthy conditions and processes for you to work in, while your responsibility is to behave in a safe and responsible manner to protect from harm yourself, your colleagues, customers and visitors.

It is extremely important that everyone in the organisation is working in a healthy and safe way. Monitoring and reporting are vital parts of an organisation's health and safety culture. Management systems must allow senior management to receive both specific (ie following an incident) and routine reports on the performance of the health and safety policy. Much day-to-day health and safety information needs to be reported only at the time of a formal review, but only a strong system of monitoring can ensure that the formal review can proceed as planned and that relevant events in the **interim** are brought to the management's attention.

Interim

An interval of time between one event, process or period and another

The Health and Safety (First Aid) Regulations 1981 require employers to provide adequate and appropriate equipment, facilities and personnel to enable first aid to be given to employees if they are injured or become ill at work. It is important to remember that what comprises 'adequate and appropriate' will vary depending on the circumstances. A small organisation might only need to provide the bare minimum, but if the risk of injury is high this may not be the case and several personnel qualified in an appropriate first aid at work course may be necessary. Likewise, a large company with a low risk might be better served with a higher number of personnel appointed to take charge of first-aid arrangements.

The minimum requirement on any work site or office is a fully stocked first-aid kit and an appointed person. It is important to remember as well that the provision of first-aid cover is a constant requirement. If trained personnel are away, for example on holiday, then another person must provide the first aid cover.

Suggested numbers of first-aid personnel (reproduced from HSE information) are shown in the table.

Category of risk	Number employed at any location	Suggested number of first-aid personnel
Lower risk eg shops and offices	Fewer than 50	At least one appointed person
	50–100	At least one first aider
	More than 100	One additional first aider for every 100 employed
Medium risk eg light engineering and assembly work, food processing, warehousing	Fewer than 20	At least one appointed person
	20–100	At least one first aider
	More than 100	One additional first aider for every 100 employed
Higher risk eg most construction work, chemical manufacturing, extensive work with dangerous machinery	Fewer than 5	At least one appointed person
	5–50	At least one first aider
	More than 50	One additional first aider for every 50 employed

RESPONSIBILITIES IN THE WORKPLACE

The organisation must ensure that:

- appropriate importance is given to reporting both preventive information, such as progress of training and maintenance programmes, and incident data, such as accident and sickness absence rates
- audits of the effectiveness of management structures and risk controls for health and safety are carried out as often as necessary
- the impact of changes such as the introduction of new procedures, work processes or products, or any major health and safety failure, is reported as soon as possible
- there are procedures to implement new and changed legal requirements and to consider other external developments and events.

Organisations have policies and procedures on health and safety to ensure the well-being of staff, visitors and customers. It is important that you know and understand your organisation's policies and procedures. Always follow the legislation and carry out any responsibilities and specific policies that relate to your job role.

Everybody is responsible for minimising the risks to health and safety in the workplace. The factors to be taken into account when identifying health and safety risks include relevant legislation, regulations and organisational policies and procedures.

Untidy premises can cause health and safety risks

Following health and safety procedures correctly will help minimise risk. So will good housekeeping. This means keeping the workplace clean and tidy, removing and disposing of waste. All areas need to be kept clean as illness can spread as a result of dirty conditions. The premises need to be kept tidy or there will be a risk of falling over items left in aisles or slipping on spillages that are not dealt with immediately.

People with different responsibilities for the health and safety of the workplace will have different information and advice needs. Employees will need to know and understand the policies and procedures, their own responsibilities and how to assess their own risks. The health and safety officer will need to understand the legislation and regulations, government guidelines, how to carry out risk assessments, the reporting procedures, how health and safety is monitored, internal communication methods, and the management of the health and safety policy.

The organisation as a whole must understand the legislation and regulations, the importance of risk assessments, the reporting procedures and the resources required to carry out any actions to reduce risks. To communicate information on health and safety, the golden rule is not to use a single method of communication but to use multiple channels including:

- briefings via existing networks (team meetings etc)
- intranet bulletin boards
- email
- notice boards
- staff newsletters
- leaflets.

ACTIVITY

Carry out a risk assessment for your office covering risks to people and property, including equipment.

Effective monitoring of sickness absence and workplace health can alert the organisation to underlying problems that could seriously damage performance or result in accidents and long-term illness. The collection of workplace health and safety data can allow management to **benchmark** the organisation's performance against others in its sector. Appraisals of senior managers should include an assessment of their contribution to health and safety performance.

Benchmark

To provide a standard against which something can be measured or assessed

REVIEWING HEALTH AND SAFETY PERFORMANCE

A regular review of health and safety performance is essential. It establishes whether the health and safety principles of strong and active leadership, worker involvement, and assessment and review have been fixed in the organisation. It also tells the organisation whether its systems are effective in managing risk and protecting people.

Health and safety performance should be reviewed at least once a year. The review process should:

- examine whether the health and safety policy reflects the organisation's current priorities, plans and targets
- examine whether risk management and other health and safety systems have been reporting effectively
- report health and safety shortcomings and any effect of all relevant management decisions
- decide on actions to address any identified weaknesses and a system to monitor their implementation
- consider immediate reviews if major shortcomings are identified or an event takes place.

Larger public and private sector organisations need to have formal procedures for auditing and reporting health and safety performance. Their board should ensure that any audit is seen as a positive management and boardroom tool. It should have unrestricted access to both external and internal auditors, keeping their cost effectiveness, independence and objectivity under review. Various codes and guides, many of them sector specific, are available to help organisations report health and safety performance and risk management as part of good **governance**.

Governance

The process of governing a country or organisation

Management can make extra 'shop floor' visits to gather information for the formal review, and good health and safety performance can be celebrated at central and local level. Indeed, performance on health and safety is increasingly being recorded in organisations' annual reports to investors and stakeholders.

According to the HSE, sensible risk management is about:

- ensuring that workers and the public are properly protected
- providing an overall benefit to society by balancing benefits and risks, with a focus on reducing real risks – both those that arise more often and those with serious consequences
- enabling innovation and learning, not stifling them

- ensuring that those who create risks also manage them responsibly, and understand that failure to manage real risks responsibly is likely to lead to robust action
- enabling individuals to understand that, as well as the right to protection, they also have to exercise responsibility.

Sensible risk management is *not* about:

- creating a totally risk-free society
- generating useless paperwork mountains
- scaring people by exaggerating or publicising trivial risks
- stopping important recreational and learning activities for individuals where the risks are managed
- reducing protection of people from risks that cause real harm and suffering.

Risks are acceptable when managed properly

LEGISLATION AND REGULATIONS

All of the following pieces of legislation and regulations will have some impact on your job role, as they will affect the way you carry out your tasks, the equipment you use and your working hours, breaks etc.

HEALTH AND SAFETY AT WORK ACT 1974

There is a wide range of legislation and regulation that affects health and safety in a business environment. The major piece of legislation is the Health and Safety at Work Act (HASAWA), which imposes duties on both employees and employers.

Employees must:

- work in a safe and sensible way
- use equipment safely and correctly
- report potential risks
- help identify training needs.

Employers must:

- provide a safe work area
- provide clearly defined procedures
- ensure safe handling, storage and transport of stock
- train and supervise staff in health and safety matters
- maintain safe entries and exits in the building
- provide adequate temperature, lighting, seating etc
- ensure visitors are informed of any hazards.

REPORTING OF INJURIES, DISEASES AND DANGEROUS OCCURRENCES REGULATIONS 2013

The Reporting of Injuries, Diseases and Dangerous Occurrences Regulations (RIDDOR) require employers to take action in the following circumstances:

- Death or major injury to an employee or member of the public: notify the enforcing authority without delay and complete an accident report form within ten days.
- Accident causing an employee to be unable to work for more than three days: complete an accident report form within 10 days.
- Employee suffering a reportable work-related disease: complete a disease report form.
- Something dangerous happening that does not cause a reportable injury but clearly could have done: report immediately and then complete an accident report form within 10 days.

HANDY HINT

The HSE produces a list of the major injuries, dangerous occurrences and diseases that are reportable under RIDDOR.

MANAGEMENT OF HEALTH AND SAFETY AT WORK REGULATIONS 1999

The Management of Health and Safety at Work Regulations require employers with five or more employees to:

- carry out a risk assessment
- implement any measures identified as necessary
- appoint competent people to implement the measures
- set up emergency procedures
- provide clear information and training
- work together with any other employers sharing the same workplace.

HANDY HINT

Even if there are fewer than five employees in your organisation, it may be a good idea to have a written document outlining your general approach to health and safety.

ACTIVITY

Research the legislation relating to health and safety that applies in your workplace. This will include the Health and Safety at Work Act but the other legislation, such as RIDDOR, will depend on your workplace.

WORKPLACE (HEALTH, SAFETY AND WELFARE) REGULATIONS

The Workplace (Health, Safety and Welfare) Regulations aim to ensure that workplaces meet the needs of all members of a workforce, including people with disabilities. Where necessary, parts of the workplace, including in particular doors, passage ways, stairs, showers, wash basins, lavatories and workstations, should be made accessible for disabled people.

An accessible doorway

ACTIVITY

Look around your workplace and make a list of any areas that are not accessible to disabled people. Give the list to the person responsible for health and safety policy in your workplace.

THE HEALTH AND SAFETY (DISPLAY SCREEN EQUIPMENT) REGULATIONS 1992

The Display Screen Equipment Regulations apply to all who regularly use computers in their work and relate to workstations as well as equipment. They require employers to:

- assess all workstations for health and safety risks and to lower the risks as much as possible
- plan work activities to incorporate rest breaks at regular intervals
- arrange and pay for eye tests and to pay for spectacles or lenses if these are prescribed specifically for computer work
- provide health and safety training for users and retrain if the work station is changed or modified
- provide users with information on all aspects of health and safety that apply to them and the measures being taken to reduce risks to their health.

PROVISION AND USE OF WORK EQUIPMENT REGULATIONS 1998

The Provision and Use of Work Equipment Regulations require that equipment provided for use at work is:

- suitable for the intended use
- safe for use, maintained in a safe condition and, in certain circumstances, inspected
- used only by people who have received adequate information, instruction and training
- accompanied by suitable safety measures, eg protective devices, markings and warnings.

ACTIVITY

Look around your workplace and make a list of any equipment that is not suitable for its intended use. Give the list to the person responsible for health and safety policy in your workplace.

CONTROL OF SUBSTANCES HAZARDOUS TO HEALTH REGULATIONS

The Control of Substances Hazardous to Health (COSHH) Regulations require employers to control any substances that may damage the health of staff or customers, for instance bleach, ammonia and acid. Employers must:

- assess the risk from the hazardous substances
- decide how to prevent or at least reduce those risks
- control the exposure to the risks
- ensure employees are properly informed, trained and supervised.

ACTIVITY

Look around your workplace and make a list of any substances that may damage the health of staff or customers. Give the list to the person responsible for health and safety policy in your workplace.

ELECTRICITY AT WORK REGULATIONS

The Electricity at Work Regulations require that:

- all electrical systems should, so far as reasonably practicable, be of safe construction and maintained in that state
- work being carried out on or near systems to be carried out in such a manner as to avoid danger
- any protective equipment provided to be suitable and properly maintained and used
- no electrical equipment to be connected into a system if there is a chance that its strength and capability may be exceeded in such a way as to cause danger
- all electrical equipment that may be exposed to mechanical damage, the effects of the weather, natural hazards (animals, trees, plants etc), the effects of wet, dirty, dusty or corrosive conditions, flammable or explosive substances to be constructed or protected so that danger doesn't arise
- any conductor in a system (ie anything that conducts electricity) to either be insulated or protected in some other way from giving rise to danger
- suitable methods of earthing are used
- earthing conductors not to have their electrical continuity broken by anything that could give rise to danger
- all joints and connections to be suitable for safe use
- systems be protected from excess current
- all electrical equipment (except power sources themselves) to have secure and safe means of isolation from all sources of electrical energy
- suitable precautions to be taken to ensure that, once equipment is isolated so that work can be carried out on it, it cannot become electrically charged again while the work is in progress
- 'live' working only occurs when it is unavoidable and after suitable protective equipment has been provided
- the provision of adequate working space, safe access and adequate lighting to enable work on electrical equipment to be carried out safely
- anyone working on electrical systems where technical knowledge or experience is necessary to have the required knowledge and/or experience or be under suitable supervision.

HAZARDS AND RISKS

In order to understand what could pose possible health and safety risks in the workplace, the first thing to understand is the difference between a 'hazard' and a 'risk'.

A hazard is something that can cause harm, eg electricity, chemicals, working up a ladder, noise, a keyboard, a bully at work, or stress.

A risk is the chance, whether high or low, that any hazard will actually cause somebody harm.

For example, electricity cabling is a hazard. If it has been damaged by a sharp object, the risk changes and the exposed wiring places it in a 'high risk' category.

There are a wide variety of hazards that can arise in a business environment, including:

- Overuse or improper use of equipment, or poorly designed workstations or work environments, may cause posture problems and pain, discomfort or injuries to the hands and arms.
- Poor lighting can cause headaches or sore eyes.
- Lack of control over timing and frequency of incoming calls, or verbal abuse from customers, can cause stress.
- High noise levels for long periods could cause hearing problems.
- Poor headset hygiene could cause ear infections.
- Exposure to sudden loud sounds while using telephone equipment could cause shock.
- Call handlers may suffer voice problems, including voice loss.
- Staff and visitors may be injured if they trip over objects or slip on spillages.
- Handling heavy or bulky objects may cause injuries or back pain.
- Falls from any height can cause bruising and fractures.
- Using faulty electrical equipment can cause electrical shocks or burns.
- Electrical faults can lead to fires in which staff suffer from smoke inhalation and/or burns.

There will be actions that can be taken if hazards such as those listed are identified:

- Make sure you get breaks away from the screen.
- Report any pain suffered as a result of computer use.
- Report it if you feel unwell or uneasy about work issues.
- Access regular training on volume control.
- Modify working practices to minimise background noise.

ACTIVITY

Look around your workplace and make a list of any hazards. Give the list to the person responsible for health and safety policy in your workplace.

- Maintain stocks of ear pads.
- Investigate any report of acoustic shock.
- Clean voice tubes regularly.
- Ensure spills are cleared up promptly.
- Use correct manual handling procedures.
- Use stepladders correctly.
- Check electrical installations regularly.

It is everybody's responsibility to identify hazards and risks. If any risks are identified, they should be communicated to the person responsible for health and safety. Organisations will have at least one first aider or appointed person responsible for health and safety. Where the organisation has a health and safety officer, it is their responsibility to give advice and information on health and safety issues, ensure that training takes place, and make sure all necessary equipment and procedures are in place. They are also responsible for carrying out risk assessments.

The person nominated to take charge of health and safety must be a competent person, defined by the Management of Health and Safety at Work Regulations as someone with sufficient knowledge and experience to do the job properly. Remember, however, that *everyone* is responsible for the health and safety of themselves and others, safe use of equipment and reporting risks.

ACTIVITY

Make a list of the first aiders in your workplace, including the person responsible for health and safety policy.

RISK ASSESSMENTS

The HSE says: 'A risk assessment is nothing more than a careful examination of what, in your work, could cause harm to people.' Employers have a duty under the Management of Health and Safety at Work Regulations to carry out risk assessments to identify what hazards exist in a workplace, and how likely these hazards are to cause harm. They must then decide what prevention or control measures are needed. The frequency of scheduled risk audits will depend on:

- the level of risk
- legislation
- regulations
- organisational policies/procedures.

Precautions should be taken in unsafe working environments

Employers are responsible for carrying out the assessment and for any steps that they need to take to eliminate or control the risk. They should not only walk around the workplace and inspect for any hazards, but consult you and your colleagues about the hazards you face.

The HSE advises employers to follow five steps when carrying out a workplace risk assessment.

1 Identify the hazards, ie anything that may cause harm. Employers have a duty to assess the health and safety risks faced by the staff. They must systematically check for possible physical, mental, chemical and biological hazards. Common classification of hazards include:
    - Physical – lifting, awkward postures, slips and trips, noise, dust, machinery, computer equipment.
    - Mental – excess workload, long hours, working with high-need clients, bullying. These are also called 'psychosocial' hazards that affect mental health and occur within working relationships.
    - Chemical – asbestos, cleaning fluids, aerosols etc.
    - Biological – including tuberculosis, hepatitis and other infectious diseases faced by healthcare workers, home care staff and other healthcare professionals.
2 Decide who may be harmed and how. Identifying who is at risk starts with the organisation's staff but employers must also assess risks faced by agency and contract staff, visitors, clients and other members of the public on the premises. Employers must review work routines in all the different locations and situations where their staff are employed. For example, in contact centres workstation equipment must be adjusted to suit each employee. Employers have special duties towards the health and safety of young workers, disabled employees, night or shift-workers, and pregnant or breastfeeding women.
3 Assess the risks and take relevant action. Consider how likely it is that each hazard could cause harm. This will determine whether or not they should reduce the level of risk. Even after all precautions have been taken, some risk usually remains. Employers must decide for each remaining hazard whether the risk remains high, medium or low.
4 Make a record of the findings. Organisations with five or more staff are required to record in writing the main findings of the risk assessment. This record should include details of any significant hazards noted in the risk assessment and the action taken to reduce or eliminate risk. This record provides proof that the assessment was carried out and gives the basis for a later review of working practices. The risk assessment is a working document. You should be able to refer to it, so it should not be locked away in a cupboard.
5 Review the risk assessment to ensure that the agreed safe working practices continue to be applied (ie that the management's safety instructions are respected by supervisors and line managers) and to take account of any new working practices, new machinery or more demanding work targets.

The basic rule is that employers must adapt the work to the worker. The key aims of risk assessment are to:

- Prioritise the risks – rank them in order of seriousness, focusing on significant rather than trivial hazards.
- Make all risks small – the two main options are to eliminate the hazard altogether or, if this is not possible, control the risk so that harm is unlikely.

The Management of Health and Safety at Work Regulations set out the following safety management guidance for employers for tackling risks. The basic approach is also known as a hierarchy of control:

- Substitution – ie try a risk-free or less-risky option.
- Prevention – eg erect a machine guard or add a non-slip surface to a pathway.
- Re-organise work to reduce exposure to a risk – a basic rule is to adapt the work to the worker. Ensure chairs and display screen equipment are adjustable to the individual, and plan all work involving a computer to include regular breaks. For monotonous or routine work, introduce work variety and greater control over work. For instance, in call centres introduce work variety by providing work off the phones and varying the type of calls handled.
- As a last resort, issue personal protective equipment (such as appropriate eye protection, gloves, special clothing or footwear) to all staff at risk and make sure they are trained in when and how to use this equipment.
- Provide training in safe working systems.
- Provide information on likely hazards and how to avoid them.
- Provide social and welfare facilities – eg washing facilities for the removal of contaminants, a rest room.

The HSE says risk should be assessed 'every time there are new machines, substances and procedures, which could lead to new hazards'. If a new job brings in significant new hazards, then that job should be fully risk assessed. If there is high staff turnover, then the way new staff do their work should be checked against the risk assessment and training provided in safe working practices, if necessary.

EMERGENCIES

Your organisation should have a procedure in place that explains your role in the event of a fire or other emergency. This procedure will cover:

- how you should raise the alarm
- how to evacuate the building
- where the fire exits are
- where to go when you have evacuated the building
- where to find fire extinguishers
- how and when to use them.

The procedure will differ from organisation to organisation but there are some basic things to know wherever you work. Make sure you have received adequate training in the procedures. Before an emergency happens, know the procedures above by heart as if an incident occurs you will not have time to look for the instructions to refresh your memory.

HANDY HINT

The basic rule in an emergency is: 'Get out, call the emergency services out, and stay out.' No personal belongings or property are worth losing your life for.

If you discover a fire, operate the nearest fire alarm. (If there isn't one, shouting 'Fire! Fire!' is usually pretty effective.) Make sure you keep your escape route clear and know whose job it is to call the fire brigade. If it's your responsibility to call the fire brigade, dial 999 and follow the instructions the emergency operator gives you. Direct any customers and visitors to the nearest fire exit and shut doors and windows in any room where there is a fire. *Only if you have been trained and the fire is small enough*, tackle the fire using the fire equipment available.

Of course, fire is not the only emergency you may come across. In most organisations, bomb threats are dealt with in a similar way to fires, but again find out what *your* company policy is, learn it and follow it.

There is also the possibility of a medical emergency involving staff, visitors or customers. The important thing in this situation is to know who the first aiders are and to get them to the patient as quickly as possible. You can do serious and possibly permanent damage trying to help when you have not had the proper training.

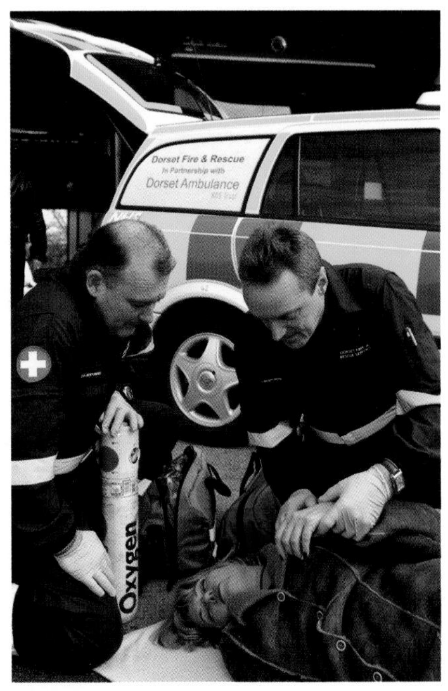

In a medical emergency, first call the first aider and then an ambulance if needed

Assessment criteria

This section covers assessment criteria 3.1, 3.2, 3.3, 3.4, 3.5 and 4.5

TAKING MINUTES AT MEETINGS

Organisational requirements will probably dictate that minutes are taken at formal meetings, while at some meetings this will be compulsory due to a legal requirement under the Freedom of Information Act 2000 for information in relation to certain organisations to be accessible to the public. The act applies to all public authorities within the United Kingdom including:

- government departments
- the Houses of Parliament
- the Northern Ireland Assembly
- the Welsh Assembly
- the armed forces
- local government bodies
- National Health Service bodies
- schools, colleges and universities
- police authorities
- companies wholly owned by the Crown, a public authority or a government department.

Exemption

Permission or entitlement not to do something that others are obliged to do

Intelligence services

An organisation that gathers information about the secret plans or activities of an adversary or potential adversary

There are, however, some **exemptions** to the above list, including the **intelligence services** and information that could compromise security and defence forces.

In effect, public authorities have 20 working days to respond to an information request. To reduce the number of requests for similar information, public authorities also have a duty to release important information such as annual reports and accounts as a matter of routine.

Obviously, in order to be able to meet requests for information it is important that accurate records are kept of meetings at which decisions are made that may affect members of the public. Minutes meet both the organisational and legal requirements for the accurate recording of decisions and the discussions that led to them.

There are also legal requirements for some other meeting minutes, even of organisations not on the list above. For instance, the Companies Act requires a company to record minutes of all meetings of its directors. The minutes must be kept for at least 10 years. Failure to make and keep minutes is a criminal offence applying to every officer of the company that is in default. Minutes also provide written proof that the organisation is functioning as it should and may be used as evidence in legal proceedings.

In order to correctly record the discussions at a meeting, you need to understand some terms that are commonly used in meetings. A list of these can be found in the table opposite.

USEFUL TERM

Ad hoc 'For the purpose of', as for example when a temporary sub-committee is set up especially to organise a works outing

Adjourn To suspend a meeting until a later date

Adopt minutes Minutes are 'adopted' when accepted by members and signed by the chairperson

Advisory Providing advice or suggestion, not taking action

Agenda A schedule of items drawn up for discussion at a meeting

Apologies Reasons given in advance for inability to attend a meeting

Articles of association Rules required by company law that govern a company's activities

Attendance list In some meetings a list is passed round to be signed as a record of attendance

Bylaws Rules regulating an organisation's activities

Casting vote Some committee chairpersons may use a 'casting vote' to reach a decision if votes are equally divided

Chairperson Leader or person given authority to conduct a meeting

Chairperson's agenda Based on the meeting agenda but also containing explanatory notes

Collective responsibility A convention by which all meeting members agree to accept and support a majority decision, even if they disagreed with it during the discussion

Committee A group of people, usually elected or appointed, who meet to conduct agreed business and report to a senior body

Consensus Agreement by general consent, no formal vote being taken

Constitution A set of rules governing the activities of an organisation

Convene To call a meeting

Decision Resolution minutes are sometimes called 'decision minutes'

Eject To remove someone (by force if necessary) from a meeting

Executive Having the power to act upon taken decisions

Ex officio Given powers or rights by reason of office

Guillotine Cut short a debate – usually in parliament

Honorary post A duty performed without payment, eg honorary secretary

Intra vires From Latin, within the power of the committee or meeting to discuss, to carry out

Lie on the table To leave an item to be considered instead at the next meeting

Lobbying A practice of seeking members' support before a meeting

Motion The name given to a proposal when it is being discussed at a meeting

Mover Someone who speaks on behalf of a motion

Nem con From Latin, literally, 'no one speaking against'

Opposer One who speaks against a motion

Other business Either items left over from a previous meeting or items discussed after the main business of a meeting

Point of information The drawing of attention in a meeting to a relevant item of fact

Point of order Proceedings may be interrupted on a 'point of order' to draw attention to a breach of rules or procedures

Proposal The name given to an item submitted for discussion (usually in writing) before a meeting takes place

Proxy Literally 'on behalf of another person' – proxy vote

Quorum The number of people needed to be in attendance for a meeting to be legitimate and so commence

Refer back To pass an item back for further consideration

Resolution The name given to a 'motion' which has been passed or carried, used after the decision has been reached

Seconder One who supports the 'proposer' of a motion or proposal by 'seconding' it

Secretary Committee official responsible for the internal and external administration of the committee

Secret ballot A system of voting in secret

Shelve To drop a motion that has no support

Sine die From Latin, literally 'without a day', that is to say indefinitely, eg 'Adjourned sine die'

Standing committee A committee that has an indefinite term of office

Standing orders Rules of procedure governing public sector meetings

Table To introduce a paper or schedule for noting

Taken as read To save time, it is assumed the members have already read the minutes

Treasurer Committee official responsible for its financial records and transactions

Ultra vires From Latin, beyond the authority of the meeting to consider

Unanimous Everyone being in favour

TYPES OF MINUTES

There are different types of minutes which can be taken. If you are taking minutes of a particular meeting for the first time, look back at previous meetings or ask the **chairperson** of the meeting which type is required:

Chairperson
The person running a meeting

- Resolution minutes – record the decisions taken but do not detail any discussion about the topic.
- Narrative minutes – include a summary of the main points of the discussion, which are usually quite detailed, and the decisions taken.
- Action minutes – briefly report proceedings and name the person delegated to undertake a course of action.

TAKING MINUTES

When keeping records of information discussed in a meeting, there may be issues of security and confidentiality. Care should be taken not to leave minutes of meetings where they may be read by people not involved in the meeting. As the minute taker, you should record the meeting in the agreed organisational format; it is usually the chairperson's responsibility to deal with any issues before the minutes are circulated.

Whether you are an experienced minute taker or taking minutes for the first time, it is important to prepare each time. Decide whether you are going to use pen and paper, a laptop, a tablet or a digital recorder, and check that your chosen equipment is in working order. Always take a spare pen or pencil with you; if all other equipment fails you will still be able to keep up. Familiarise yourself with the agenda so that you know what is coming next.

HANDY HINT

Always have a spare pen or pencil with you – even if using a recorder, a pen will be useful for making notes.

When taking minutes it is important that you can hear everything that is said, so you must listen carefully and remain focused. If you allow yourself to become distracted, even momentarily, you may miss something that proves to be vital.

If you are taking **verbatim** minutes, you will probably be recording the discussion on audio equipment or using shorthand, as it will otherwise not be possible to record every word that is said. You will need to have a method of noting who is speaking when, if recording the meeting, as you may not be able to recognise the individual voices when **transcribing** the recording. Using the speaker's initials is a useful way, unless of course you have two people with the same initials, in which case you might use an alternative style (eg Sue Smith and Sharon Stone might become 'SSm' and 'SSt').

Verbatim

Word for word

Transcribe

To make a written copy of something

Shorthand is a system used to transcribe quickly

TAKING NOTES

If you are taking resolution or narrative minutes, your notes should record the discussion in such a way that your minutes give a precise account of the points made for and against a proposal and the reasons given in support of those points. Remember, you are not trying to record every word spoken, only a summary of what was said.

It is a good idea to leave a line between each line of notes taken. This will allow you to add in further comments if the chairperson decides to go back to an item after the meeting has moved on.

Motions, **amendments** and **resolutions** must be recorded word for word, to prevent any dispute later. Record the name of the person who proposed the motion, who seconded it and the result of the vote. Where a decision leads to an action point, record who has been made responsible for carrying out the action and any timescale agreed.

Motion

A proposal put forward for discussion at a meeting

Amendment

An addition or alteration to a motion

Resolution

A firm decision to do something

Minutes should enable anybody who was not at the meeting to understand what decisions were made, what alternatives were considered and the reasoning behind the decision.

Although minute takers are usually not actively participating in the meeting, it is essential that you understand what is taking place sufficiently to accurately record the discussion. If you do not understand something that is said and you feel that this will affect the accuracy of the minutes, ask the chairperson for clarification. Address all requests for clarification directly to the chairperson; do not get drawn into discussion with the other attendees.

ACTIVITIES

- Study the table of terms listed on pages 83–84. Find out which are used in meetings at your organisation and learn their meanings.
- Attend a meeting and take notes – this could be a meeting at work or outside work. Produce a set of minutes from your notes and check with the official meeting minutes, if available, or the chairperson to make sure your minutes have recorded the meeting accurately.

PRODUCING MINUTES AND RECORDS OF MEETINGS

Type up your notes as soon as possible after the meeting. The longer you wait, the more difficult it will be to remember what your notes mean. The structure, style, tone and language used in the completed minutes will probably be set by the organisation's house style, but should always be written using professional language. The important points are that minutes should be:

- consistent in the way they are written
- written in plain English
- accurate
- concise
- grammatically correct.

It is important that the minutes are **objective**, recording the facts rather than your view of them, and focus on action points rather than the discussion that led to them. They must include the:

- title or purpose of the meeting
- names of the people who attended
- details of the proceedings
- agreed actions
- allocated responsibilities for agreed actions
- agreed attachments and/or appendices.

Write minutes in the past tense (eg 'Mrs Christian said that ...') and indicate where any action is required and who by. Many organisations will use a column to the right of the text for this. Check the accuracy of the minutes using a spell checker but also proofread them to look for common errors not picked up by spell check, such as 'right' and 'write'. Number the pages and remember to create an appendix for any additional documents.

When you have drafted the minutes, ask the chairperson to check them before circulating them. This will avoid the need to send out a new set of minutes if the chairperson spots an error. Send copies of the approved minutes to everyone who attended the meeting, those who sent their apologies and anyone else who is expected to take any action as a result.

Occasionally, someone will request a change to the wording of the minutes. This should be noted so that it can be discussed at the next meeting during the agenda item 'Approval of the minutes of last meeting'. If it is agreed that an alteration should be made, this will be done before the chairperson signs off the minutes as correct.

Signed off copies of the minutes should be filed together with a copy of the actual notes taken and the final version of any documents and reports that were considered at the meeting.

COMMON MISTAKE

If you get too interested in what is being said, you might forget to record it.

Using language that is more formal than necessary and making the minutes unintelligible to people reading them.

Objective

Based on facts rather than thoughts or opinions; free of any bias or prejudice caused by personal feelings

HANDY HINTS

- You do not need to record any irrelevant comments made, only those that refer directly to the agenda item.
- Make a seating plan at the start of the meeting, noting the names of attendees, or send round a register asking attendees to sign – this will help you to record who said what.
- Record those who arrive late or leave early.
- Develop your own abbreviations for common phrases, names and places – the less you have to write the better you will be able to pay attention.

ACTIVITY

Minutes must be written in the past tense. Write up these notes as minutes:

- Imran Tahir says that Tuesday will be acceptable as a deadline.
- The production figures will be produced tomorrow.
- Everybody present agrees that the deadline is achievable.
- Brian James said: 'My assistant will stand in at the next meeting as I am on holiday'.
- Point 4 on the agenda is carried forward to the next meeting.

CHAIRING, LEADING AND MANAGING MEETINGS

Assessment criteria

This section covers assessment criteria 4.1, 4.2, 4.3, 4.4 and 4.5

Meetings are held in organisations for a wide variety of purposes. Some are formal but many more are informal. Informal meetings include departmental meetings, team briefings, progress meetings and working parties.

FORMAL MEETINGS

Formal meetings usually fall into one of a number of categories:

- Shareholder meetings – public limited companies are required to hold a meeting at least once a year where all shareholders are invited to attend. Their purpose is to give shareholders the opportunity to question directors and vote on resolutions. Private limited companies are no longer obliged to hold AGMs, but are able to hold shareholder meetings if they wish to and meetings can be instituted by the directors at any time, or by members representing 10% of voting shares (5% if it is more than 12 months since the members met). Companies may still need to hold a meeting in certain circumstances, since they will not be able to dismiss a director or an auditor before their contracted term of office expires by written resolution. Since the AGM requirement has been abolished, private company meetings are now all on 14 days' notice unless the articles say otherwise. Members can agree to hold a meeting on short notice as long as there is a 90% consensus (although the articles can specify a higher percentage of up to but not exceeding 95%).
- Board meetings – these are regular meetings between the directors at which decisions are taken on the strategy to be followed by the organisation.
- Management meetings – these are regular meetings held by senior managers to decide how the strategy of the organisation is to be put into action on a practical level.
- Team meetings – at these, decisions made at management meetings are cascaded by team leaders to the members of staff who will be directly involved in putting them into practice.
- Committee meetings – there may be committees formed within the organisation to oversee particular areas of activity. In a commercial organisation their responsibilities will usually be confined to areas such as health and safety or staff welfare, but in a public organisation such as a local authority committees are powerful groups responsible for areas of policy, such as planning or transport.

A chairperson is responsible for running formal meetings

Every formal meeting has a person nominated to run the meeting. In different organisations this person may be known as the chairman or chairwoman, the chair or the chairperson. Attendance at some meetings is mandatory, but meetings where people have a choice whether to attend or not can attract a disappointing turnout. In order to **optimise** the number of people attending:

Optimise
To make something such as a method or process as good or as effective as possible

- Set an end time (and stick to it) – more people will attend your meetings if they are confident they can fit it in to their busy schedule.
- Make the objective of the meeting clear – if anyone in the meeting does not understand the purpose of a meeting, they won't come back. Set an objective in advance and repeat it, writing the meeting objective at the top of the agenda.
- Explain why this specific meeting is important – people understand that meetings in general are important but they need to be informed what's special about this particular meeting.
- Focus on the **engagement** of existing attendees first and then seek new ones – getting people interested and contributing is more important than getting new people to attend. Ensure that everyone who attends feels their presence at the meeting has contributed in some way. In a small meeting this might mean everyone introducing themselves and giving a point of view. In a larger meeting this might include getting everyone to vote on some issue or other.
- Keep reminding people – while your meeting might be the most important thing happening from your point of view, for the attendees it is often just one thing in a very busy schedule. Send meeting reminders by email or text message. Don't be afraid to remind people that the event is still on, they rarely mind! An old marketing adage called 'the rule of seven' states that people need to hear your message seven times before they take action.
- Keep the structure of each meeting the same – maintaining a structure for each meeting helps people engage with it because they know what to expect each time
- Understand and explain the benefits of attendance for the attendees – it might be clear to you why you need a meeting but very often the benefit is not clear for the attendees. Spend some time to **articulate** what's in it for them.

Engagement
The feeling of being involved in a particular activity

Articulate
To express thoughts, ideas or feelings coherently

All meetings will need planning and organising. In most cases they will need a notice to be sent to attendees, an agenda, a chairperson's agenda, minutes, reports, briefings and correspondence. They will usually also need:

- a chairperson, who is responsible for making sure that the meeting is conducted correctly
- a secretary, who is responsible for recording the meeting
- in some cases a treasurer, who is responsible for reporting on financial issues.

There will also be resources needed, such as audio/visual equipment, pens, pencils and paper, and refreshments. Send out invitations to attend as far in advance of the meeting as possible. At this time also send a map showing the location of the meeting, nearby car parks and the nearest railway station, together with directions to the venue. A week before the meeting send an agenda and copies of any meeting papers to those who indicated they would be attending.

The agenda of a meeting sets out in a logical order what is to be discussed at the meeting. The first three items are usually apologies for absence, the minutes of the last meeting and matters arising. The last two items are always any other business ('AOB') and the date of the next meeting. The actual business of the meeting is sandwiched between the first three and the last two items. Copies of any documents needed are sent with the agenda.

RESPONSIBILITIES OF THE CHAIRPERSON

In many cases the chairperson will have been involved in the initial planning of the meeting and will be well aware of its purpose, but there will be occasions when they will need to be briefed on the particular stances or viewpoints of the attendees. The chairperson's responsibilities during the meeting are to:

- start the meeting on time
- clarify roles and responsibilities
- establish ground rules and guidelines
- participate as an attendee
- have the final say in votes, if necessary
- follow the agenda and keep the meeting focused on agenda items
- retain the power to stop what's happening and change the format
- encourage accountability
- summarise key decisions and actions
- record recommendations and allocate responsibilities for specific tasks
- make the most of the experience of those people present, asking questions to draw out people's experience
- allow time to hear experts' points of view but allocate time with clear directions
- for important issues when time is limited, set up a sub-committee to collect facts, review the situation and prepare recommendations to be considered at the next meeting
- close the meeting on time.

They also have responsibilities to help the minute taker by:

- agreeing the items to be included on the agenda
- following agenda items in sequence and informing the minute taker of any departures from the agreed agenda
- summarising specific points, decisions or courses of action agreed for each specific agenda item before moving on to the next item
- providing specific guidance to the minute taker on what to record for a particular agenda item where lengthy discussion has occurred or a complex issue has been discussed
- taking time to review the minutes when they are drafted.

Delegated

Authority given to somebody else to act, make decisions or allocate resources

Other formal responsibilities within meetings are held by the treasurer and secretary. The treasurer will be responsible for reporting on financial matters while the secretary will often be the minute taker, although sometimes this function will have been **delegated**. The secretary may be responsible for ensuring the required documentation and any correspondence to be discussed or referred to at the meeting is available.

Assessment criteria

This section covers assessment criteria 5.1, 5.2, 5.3 and 5.4

SUPERVISING AN ADMINISTRATION TEAM

ALLOCATING WORK

Some people think that good managers are born with leadership skills but, while there are some whose personality lends itself to having good leadership qualities, most people have to learn management skills, usually through a combination of education, a desire to obtain a supervisory role and their own character.

In order for administration teams to work effectively, it's important to use budgets and targets which each person individually and the team collectively can be measured against. Budgets are explained in greater detail in Chapter 4 (Unit 320, B&A 59). Setting and achieving targets is not only vital for any team to ensure that everybody is working to the same overall objectives, but it also serves many additional purposes. Setting targets ensures each member of the team understands where they and the other team members fit into the overall picture, and how their individual targets contribute to team and organisational targets.

It is also important to clarify the role of each team member so that they can focus on what they need to do. Understanding their own responsibilities within the team gives each member a commitment to their own responsibilities and targets and to those of the team as a whole.

When allocating work to a team and delegating particular tasks to individual team members, it may be useful to hold a team meeting to communicate:

- what the team is required to achieve
- why the team is required to achieve it
- how the team is going to achieve it
- by what date and time the team is required to achieve it
- what each member of the team is required to contribute as individuals and how they will achieve it.

This will clarify for the team members what the targets are and how they are going to achieve them. This is also the time when the allocation of individual tasks can be discussed and when team members with particular skill sets can wherever possible be allocated suitable tasks.

Team members need to know their own responsibilities and targets and those of the team

COMMUNICATION

Communicating through regular team meetings is another important part of the success of an administration team in achieving its targets. This enables the team to discuss any potential problems or difficulties that they face. Team meetings are also an opportunity to explain any adjustments to the targets and to consider any tasks that may require more attention than others.

Teamwork and setting and achieving goals will be important to your career progression. You will rely on the skills and talents of others and your ability to delegate effectively. Two important leadership qualities that can't be taught are trust and respect. To be an effective office manager or supervisor you must have the trust and respect of the rest of the team. You must be able to demonstrate honesty and integrity in order to gain their respect.

If you are not dedicated to your work you cannot expect your team to be. Effective management skills include the ability to be able to inspire, even if that means rolling up your sleeves and getting stuck in yourself. You need to be confident in order to inspire confidence in the rest of the team. Even in times of uncertainty, you need to be able to offer re-assurance to others and to maintain a cool head.

DELEGATION

If you're leading an administration team, you need to look at the overall picture to draw out the key elements of the task and break it down into smaller parts. It's also vital to be able to delegate particular responsibilities within the overall task to the various members of the team in a clear-cut way, so that each member is clear about what is expected from them.

Good managers learn the personalities of the individual team members thoroughly. You need to understand what each member's strengths and weaknesses are and what skills and talents each of them possess. This is vitally important when handing over tasks to individuals. Ideas and input should be encouraged from the rest of the team and their opinions should be valued.

You also need a good understanding of what motivates each individual and which members respond better to a stick and which ones require more of a carrot. People like to know where they stand and what is expected of them so, while changes do occur that might require changing direction at short notice, keep things as simple and straightforward as possible so that team members know where they stand and what is expected of them.

Autonomy

Functioning independently, without supervision

It is important that you are able to delegate tasks to members of your team knowing that they will carry them out effectively without you having to supervise too closely. Most people produce their best efforts when given **autonomy** to work on their own initiative. Delegation does not mean you are no longer responsible for the completion of the tasks, however. You will need to monitor the individual's work to check that standards and deadlines are being met. If you find that someone is not meeting the requirements, you should help them to improve. Discuss with them the reasons for the shortfall and ways to close the gap. Avoid blaming, shaming or threatening them.

There are nine steps to successful delegation:

1 Define the task. Confirm in your own mind that the task is suitable to be delegated and meets the criteria for delegating.

2 Select the individual or team. Decide your reasons for delegating to this person or team and what you are going to get out of it.

3 Assess ability and training needs. Check that the other person or team of people is capable of doing the task and understand what needs to be done. If not, you can't delegate.

4 Explain the reasons the job or responsibility is being delegated and why to that person or people. Explain its importance and relevance and where it fits in with the overall scheme of things.

5 State the required results that must be achieved. Clarify understanding by getting feedback from the other person or people. Decide how the task will be measured and make sure they know how you intend to decide that the job is being successfully done.

6 Consider the resources required. Discuss and agree what is required to get the job done. Consider people, location, premises, equipment, money, materials, other related activities and services.

7 Agree the deadline by which the job must be finished. If it is an ongoing task, set review dates and agree when reports are due. If the task is complex and has parts or stages, set the priorities. Confirm understanding of the previous points with the other person or people, getting ideas and interpretation. As well as showing you that the job can be done, this helps to reinforce commitment. Methods of checking and controlling must be agreed with the other person or people. Failing to agree this in advance will cause monitoring to seem like interference or lack of trust.

8 Support and communicate. Think about who else needs to know what's going on, and inform them. Involve the other person in considering this so they can see beyond the issue at hand. Do not leave the person to inform your own peers of their new responsibility. Warn the person about any awkward matters of politics or protocol. Inform your own line manager if the task is important and of sufficient profile.

9 Feed back on results. It is essential to let the person know how they are doing and whether they have achieved their aims. If not, you must review with them why things did not go to plan and deal with the problems. You must absorb the consequences of failure and pass on the credit for success.

HANDY HINT

The less interesting tasks should not necessarily always be the responsibility of the most junior member of staff. It is de-motivating if these are the only tasks they are allowed to do. Share them around and give inexperienced staff the opportunity to learn the more interesting aspects of the job.

Delegation isn't just a matter of telling someone else what to do. There is a wide range of varying freedom that you can confer on the other person. The more experienced and reliable the other person is, the more freedom you can give. The more critical the task, the more cautious you need to be about extending a lot of freedom, especially if your job or reputation depends on getting a good result. Take care to choose the most appropriate approach for each situation.

It's important to ask the other person what level of authority they feel comfortable being given. If you ask, you can find out for sure and agree this with the other person. Some people are confident; others less so. It's your responsibility to agree with them what level is most appropriate so that the job is done effectively and with minimal unnecessary involvement from you. Involving the other person in agreeing the level of delegated freedom for any particular responsibility is an essential part of the 'contract' that you make with them. Take time to discuss and adapt according to the situation the agreements and contracts that you make with people regarding the delegated tasks, responsibility for them and the level of freedom.

Be creative in choosing levels of delegated responsibility and always check with the other person that they are comfortable with your chosen level. People are generally capable of doing far more than you imagine. The rate and extent of responsibility and freedom delegated to people is a fundamental driver of organisational growth and effectiveness, the growth and well-being of your team members, and your own development and advancement.

The following examples of different delegation levels progressively offer, encourage and enable more delegated freedom. Level 1 is the lowest level of delegated freedom (basically none); Level 10 is the highest level that can rarely be found in organisations.

- Level 1 – 'wait to be told', 'do exactly what I say' or 'follow these instructions precisely'. This is instruction and there is no delegated freedom at all.
- Level 2 – 'look into this and tell me the situation – I'll decide'. This is asking for investigation and analysis but no recommendation. The person delegating retains responsibility for assessing options before making the decision.
- Level 3 – 'look into this and tell me the situation – we'll decide together'. This has a subtle important difference from Level 2. This level of delegation encourages and enables the analysis and decision to be a shared process, which can be very helpful in coaching and development.
- Level 4 – 'tell me the situation and what help you need from me in assessing and handling it, then we'll decide'. This opens up the possibility of greater freedom for analysis and decision making, subject to both people agreeing this is appropriate. Again, this level is helpful in growing and defining coaching and development relationships.
- Level 5 – 'give me your analysis of the situation (reasons, options, pros and cons) and recommendation – I'll let you know whether you can go ahead'. Asks for analysis and recommendation but you will check the thinking before deciding.
- Level 6 – 'decide and let me know your decision, but wait for my "go ahead" before proceeding'. The other person is trusted to assess the situation and options, and is probably competent enough to decide and implement too, but for reasons of task importance or competence, or perhaps externally changing factors, you prefer to keep control of timing. This level of

delegation can be frustrating for people if used too often or for too long, and in any event the reason for keeping people waiting, after they've inevitably invested time and effort, needs to be explained.

- Level 7 – 'decide and let me know your decision, then go ahead unless I say not to'. Now the other person begins to control the action. The subtle increase in responsibility saves time. The default is now positive rather than negative. This is a very liberating change in delegated freedom. (This approach can also be used very effectively when seeking responsibility from above or elsewhere in an organisation, especially one that is strangled by indecision and bureaucracy, by saying, for example, 'Here is my analysis and recommendation; I will proceed unless you tell me otherwise by [date]'.
- Level 8 – 'decide and take action – let me know what you did (and what happened)'. This delegation level, as with each increase up the scale, saves even more time. This level of delegation also enables a degree of follow-up by the manager as to the effectiveness of the delegated responsibility, which is necessary when people are being managed from a greater distance or in a more 'hands-off' style. The level also allows and invites positive feedback by the manager, which is helpful in coaching and development.
- Level 9 – 'decide and take action – you need not check back with me'. The most freedom that you can give to another person when you still need to retain responsibility for the activity. A high level of confidence is necessary, and you would normally assess the quality of the activity after the event according to overall results, potentially weeks or months later. Feedback and review remain helpful and important, although the relationship is more likely one of mentoring, rather than coaching.
- Level 10 – 'decide where action needs to be taken and manage the situation accordingly – it's your area of responsibility now'. The most freedom that you can give to the other person and not generally used without formal change of a person's job role. It's the delegation of a strategic responsibility. This gives the other person responsibility for defining what changes to projects, tasks, analysis and decisions are necessary for the management of a particular area of responsibility, as well as the task, project or change itself, and how the initiative or change is to be implemented and measured, etc. This amounts to delegating part of your job, not just a task or project. You would use this utmost level of delegation, for example, when developing a successor, or as part of an intentional and agreed plan to devolve some of your job accountability in a formal sense.

Some people think that delegation and abdication amount to the same thing but this is not true. Delegation is where one person appoints another to act as a chosen representative on his or her behalf. Abdication, on the other hand, is the act of giving up power, either by abandoning it or resigning from the post.

Training is an important part of quality management

QUALITY MANAGEMENT

Quality management ensures that the products or services provided by an organisation are consistent. It has four main components:

- quality planning
- quality control
- quality assurance
- quality improvement.

It concentrates on product and service quality and the means of achieving these aims.

Several quality management techniques have been developed in recent years. These include:

- Six Sigma – the elements that make up the Six Sigma process are:
  - define the opportunity
  - measure the performance
  - analyse the opportunity
  - improve performance
  - control performance
  - transfer best practice to spread the learning to other areas of the organisation.
- Total quality management (TQM) – its elements are:
  - a long-term commitment to continuous improvement
  - a philosophy of zero errors/defects to change the culture to 'right first time'
  - train people to understand customer/supplier relationships
  - do not buy products or services on price alone – look at the total cost
  - recognise that improvement of the systems must be managed
  - adopt modern methods of supervising and training – eliminate fear
  - eliminate barriers between departments by managing the process – improve communication and teamwork
  - eliminate goals without methods, standards based only on numbers, barriers to pride of workmanship and fiction – get facts by studying processes
  - constantly educate and retrain – develop experts in the organisation
  - develop a systematic approach to manage the implementation of TQM.
- Business process re-engineering – its elements are:
  - organise around outcomes, not tasks
  - identify all the processes in an organisation and prioritise them in order of redesign urgency

  - integrate information processing work into the real work that produces the information
  - treat geographically dispersed resources as though they were centralised
  - link parallel activities in the workflow instead of just integrating their results
  - put the decision point where the work is performed, and build control into the process
  - capture information once and at the source.
- Lean systems – the elements of lean systems are:
  - Gaining a true understanding of how things work so you can constantly improve, reduce waste and increase efficiency.
  - Reducing **buffer storage** to the absolute minimum, which makes everything connected: if one point in the system breaks down, everyone is very rapidly also affected.
  - Paying attention to **bottlenecks**, including when 'up stream' to suppliers and 'down stream' to customers.
  - Being able to rapidly change the system to work on different products.
  - Having flexible, multi-skilled people who can perform such changes.
  - Having systems and management that prompts such a capable and motivated workforce.
- The theory of Constraints – the principles of this are:
  - Identify the current constraint (the single part of the process that limits the rate at which the goal is achieved).
  - Exploit – make quick improvements to the constraint using existing resources, ie make the most of what you have.
  - Subordinate – review all other activities in the process to ensure that they are aligned with and truly support the needs of the constraint.
  - Elevate – if the constraint still exists, consider what further actions can be taken to eliminate it. Normally, actions are continued at this step until the constraint has been broken. In some cases, capital investment may be required.
  - Repeat – the five steps are a continuous-improvement cycle. Therefore, once a constraint is resolved the next constraint should immediately be addressed. This step is a reminder to never become complacent – aggressively improve the current constraint and then immediately move on to the next constraint.

One or more of these techniques will help you to manage and improve the performance of your administrative team.

Buffer storage

An element used between two different forms of storage

Bottleneck

Delays caused when one part of a process or activity is slower than the others and so hinders overall progress

ACTIVITY

Research the various techniques described above in greater detail and consider which is/are appropriate to supervising your team.

MONITORING PERFORMANCE

Regular monitoring is a good way of maintaining best practice and ensuring that staff get the details right. With regular quality monitoring, you can prevent bad habits from creeping in, helping the team maintain high standards. It is not necessary to go hi-tech; in many cases simply observing what the employee is doing is sufficient. Remember, some monitoring is better than no monitoring. Set realistic targets and achieving them will be motivating, paving the way to other more ambitious goals.

Techniques to monitor and manage workflows and identify the need for improvements in team outputs and standards include:

- setting guidelines
- team meetings
- observation
- checking work products
- checking records and logs
- monitoring and analysis of errors
- progress reporting
- delegation
- target setting
- feedback
- performance review
- analysis of outputs and deadlines met.

When managing the performance of an administrative team, it is important to set 'SMART' targets. SMART targets are:

- Specific – the target is clear, unambiguous, straightforward and understandable.
- Measurable – the target is related to quantified or qualitative performance measures.
- Achievable – the resources are available to meet the target.
- Realistic – the target is linked to business needs.
- Time-bound – the target includes a completion date and review dates.

By aligning each individual's key performance indicators (KPIs) with the organisation's and team's KPIs, employee performance can be linked to organisational success. For instance, if the organisation's KPI is to reduce the number of customer complaints by 20%, the individual's KPI might be to increase the number of satisfactory complaint resolutions by 15%.

Winning staff engagement and involvement from early on in the monitoring process is essential. When monitoring is first introduced, there's a tendency to think it will be critical. On the other hand, where a monitoring system has been in place unchanged for a long time, staff may start to take it for granted.

Monitoring that is **collaborative** rather than **prescriptive**, inclusive rather than authoritarian, is likely to lead to more acceptance and co-operation. Most team members find it helpful to know what the organisation expects of them and why their work is important to the team and its customers.

Collaborative

Involving people or groups working together to produce something

Prescriptive

Establishing or adhering to rules and regulations

Performance appraisals and reviews will identify the employee's current level of performance, strengths and weaknesses, training and development needs, and potential while rewarding their contribution to the organisation and motivating them. Feedback can be delivered one-to-one, remotely or through group sessions where the team shares and spreads best practice. Whatever method is selected, the important thing is that there is an opportunity for individuals to contribute to the discussion. Not only does this encourage their buy-in to the process, but their comments and suggestions are often extremely insightful. Bear in mind that staff are sometimes harder on their own and colleagues' performances than their supervisors would be.

Feedback can be delivered one-to-one, remotely or through group sessions

Progress and status reporting is used by employees to communicate recent performance and upcoming plans on a project or objective. The information contained in the progress status report helps managers and cross-departmental teams stay co-ordinated with employee activities, while being a critical element in how teams map progress against company goals and individual objectives.

Subjective

Based on somebody's opinions or feelings rather than on facts or evidence

As well as internal monitoring, it's also helpful to compare your performance with others, especially the competition. Internal checks will give you a more **subjective** picture, which could be misleading. For a truly objective result, you need external benchmarking. Benchmarking is the continuous search for and adaptation of significantly better practices that leads to improved performance by investigating the performance and practices of other organisations. Benchmarking goes beyond comparisons with competitors to understanding the practices that lie behind the performance gaps.

There are many benefits to benchmarking. It:

- provides realistic and achievable targets
- prevents organisations from being industry led
- challenges operational complacency
- creates an atmosphere that encourages continuous improvement
- allows employees to visualise the improvement, which can be a strong motivator for change
- creates a sense of urgency for improvement
- confirms the belief that there is a need for change
- helps to identify weak areas and indicates what needs to be done to improve.

Benchmarking must be a continuous process, with its extent and scope dependent on the resources that the organisation has available. It may involve analysing errors or analysing output and consistency of meeting deadlines.

Staff recognition rewards the most important outcomes people create for your organisation

Reward high-quality work through mechanisms such as 'employee of the month' awards and staff excellence certificates, or highlight it in your staff newsletter and intranet site. If customers are pleased with the service, pass on their messages. Staff recognition is not just a nice thing to do for people, it is a communication device that reinforces and rewards the most important outcomes people create for your organisation. When you recognise people effectively, you reinforce the actions and behaviours you most want to see people repeat. An effective staff recognition system is simple, immediate and powerfully reinforcing.

When you consider staff recognition processes, you need to develop recognition that is equally powerful for both the organisation and the employee. You must address some important issues if you want the recognition you offer to be viewed as motivating and rewarding by your staff and important for the success of your organisation:

- You need to establish criteria for what performance or contribution constitutes 'reward-able' behaviour or actions.
- All staff must be eligible for the recognition.

- The recognition must supply the employer and staff with specific information about what behaviours or actions are being rewarded and recognised.
- Anyone who then performs at the level or standard stated in the criteria receives the reward.
- The recognition should occur as close to the performance of the actions as possible, so the recognition reinforces behaviour that the employer wants to encourage.
- Don't design a process in which managers select the people to receive recognition – this type of process will be viewed as favouritism or talked about as 'it's your turn to get recognised this month'.

If you attach recognition to real accomplishments and goal achievement as negotiated in performance development planning, make sure the recognition meets the above stated requirements. For the process to be a success, the challenge of individually negotiated goals is to make certain that accomplishing them is viewed as similarly difficult by the employee and the organisation. People also like recognition that is random and that provides an element of surprise.

COMMON MISTAKE

If you are always praising staff, it ceases to mean much. If you never praise them, they will become de-motivated.

HANDY HINT

Offer praise to encourage staff and to reward good work. If someone is struggling with a task, praise them when they get it right.

ORGANISING EVENTS

Assessment criteria

This section covers assessment criteria 6.1, 6.2, 6.3, 6.4 and 6.5

Events are different from meetings. They will be larger, last longer, involve more people and sometimes even be open to the public. They don't just happen, they have to be planned and organised in great detail. The event organiser will need a wide range of skills including communication, negotiation, project management, budget management, staff management, public relations and interpersonal skills. The measure of successful event organisation is that people attending the event are completely unaware of the amount of planning that has gone into it.

Organising the event ends on the day the event takes place. Co-ordinating the event takes over at this point. Co-ordinating an event involves making sure that everything runs smoothly on the day. You may be a full-time event co-ordinator or this may be a part of your job that happens only occasionally. You may be co-ordinating an event that you have organised yourself or you may be liaising with the organiser.

TYPES OF EVENT

There are a large range of different types of event, each of which has different features.

EXHIBITIONS

Exhibitions, or trade shows, are promotional opportunities for manufacturers and producers to exhibit their products and talk to potential customers. They range from small, chamber of commerce sponsored events to national conferences held in convention centres. They are an opportunity to introduce your organisation's products or services to their targeted audience.

Unless the event has some history, it will be difficult for the people selling space to give you a good idea on the number of attendees, and they definitely wouldn't be able to give you any idea of the number of **qualified buyers** that will come through the event.

Qualified buyer

An individual or company who is in the market and displays some evidence of being financially able to buy

Whether the event is new or established, ask some questions before you commit your organisation to attend the event. Find out how they are marketing the event and whether the exhibit area is free or only available to paid conference attendees. There will be many more attendees if the exhibit area is free but they might not be qualified buyers. These people are more likely to be unqualified prospects looking to see what is new and what their competition is doing, or people attempting to sell things to exhibitors.

If the event appeals to you but you are unsure of likely attendance figures, you will be taking a risk that qualified prospects won't be there and it might just be a learning experience for you. If you aren't sure whether you should be an exhibitor or not, consider going to the event as an attendee first. You can network among other attendees to see if there is interest in what you offer and decide whether or not you want to participate in the future.

Before you book space at the exhibition or trade show, find out exactly what you're paying for. An exhibit space may just be a six-foot table, a booth made of pipe and curtaining, with a draped table and a couple of chairs. It might be a space that can accommodate – or it might even require – a freestanding booth that you buy or rent. Find out exactly what you get and whether electricity and telecommunications are included if you need them in your exhibit. Ask how many staff members are allowed in your booth and if you get free passes to the event. Find out if any marketing, sponsorship or advertising is included. Don't forget to factor in the cost of travel and staff time.

In most cases, sponsors or hosts of the event, past exhibitors and people buying the largest booth spaces get to select their location first. If you're a new exhibitor, ask what the layout of the space will look like. Remember that areas with the most traffic will be at the front, near the entrances. If you are stuck at the back or far corners of the room, you can still make the show work for you if you have the budget. Have entertainment in your booth or offer a fabulous promotional item that everyone will want. Make sure it's something that is very visible when carried or worn so other attendees can see it and ask where they got it. Also make sure you have people work for this item by watching a presentation or completing a questionnaire or survey, and get their contact information: don't just give things away free.

Trade shows are an opportunity to exhibit products and meet potential customers

Some shows don't allow you to actually sell things in your exhibit area. If this is the case, you will only be allowed to gather contact information so that you can follow-up later. This type of event may not be for you if you rely heavily on people buying your products on impulse. If, however, you establish relationships before selling and expect a longer sales cycle, you could do well in this environment.

Consider the staff you'll need to keep someone at your booth at all times during exhibition hours. If the event doesn't have scheduled free time or if there isn't time dedicated for attendees to visit exhibits, you'll be fighting with speakers to get the attention of the audience and the speakers usually win. If you decide to become an exhibitor, you'll want to make sure attendees have plenty of time to visit the exhibit area to learn about you.

It doesn't do any good to get qualified prospects if the organisation doesn't have the time to follow up after the show. There should be a timeline and strategy in place for contacting prospects and potential business partners for follow up.

CONFERENCES

Conferences are among the most important events for event organisers to be involved in. They may be held in venues ranging from meeting rooms in hotels to large conference centres.

Conferences may be held in a variety of venues, such as hotels or conference centres

Considerations when selecting venues include:

- Cost – during difficult economic times, many organisations are reducing the size of their conferences. Many companies are relocating conferences to smaller cities that offer cheaper rates. Some are hosting conferences on their own premises rather than hosting them at conference centres. Smaller organisations are taking advantage of the facilities at universities in their area to save on cost.
- Convenience – a gathering of sales people from a northern organisation is more likely to be held in Manchester than in London. This reduces the cost for the attendees and planners. Even if a venue has an excellent conference room, if there are not enough hotels in town for all of the attendees, it does not make sense to hold it there. While many attendees would be willing to drive from several miles to attend, many would not.
- The conference room at the venue – if you need to make a presentation on a large screen, having the screen and a way to project those images available in the room is hugely important. You may have to pay extra for the convenience of not having to provide your own screen and projector. The acoustics and seating arrangements also factor in the room set up.

Meeting room ready for an AGM

There are many different types of conferences. While all share some similarities, there are some differences:

A training conference

Academic conferences may be held on a university campus

- Business conferences may be AGMs, held for shareholders to announce the company's results for the past year and to plan the company's future. Aside from AGMs, if an organisation has many sites around the country, the management teams will get together to talk about the organisation's future and to share best practice. This may be the only time the management teams are in the same location. Often these conferences are held in the company's headquarters.
- Training conferences – large organisations will hold these several times a year. This gives everyone the opportunity to learn new information and share best practice with their colleagues. Some training conferences are presented by a training organisation and will be open to people from different organisations. These conferences require a classroom type of setting and easy access to restaurants if lunch and dinner are not included in the session.
- Academic conferences can be held for two main reasons: to announce research results or to present newly published information. Many of these conferences are held on the campus of a large university.
- Internet conferences connect delegates together through the internet, rather than making them have to physically travel to a venue in order to interact. They have grown in popularity as travel

costs have increased while budgets have not. Even though they may seem as simple as just getting online, these conferences require planning – particularly if the participants are in different time zones.

Internet conferences require careful planning

Conference planning involves covering every little detail, from making sure there are enough water glasses on each table to making sure the sound system works. These tasks may be delegated to several people but are overseen by the event organiser, who carries a huge responsibility.

ACTIVITY

You have been tasked to organise a conference in 12 months' time. Write a rough timetable covering all the areas that will need organising.

PRODUCT LAUNCHES

Product launches are an essential component of the marketing mix of large companies. They give the public and the media a chance to hear everything about the product. Product launch events introduce the product to investors and other partners. Often new products are launched at the annual shareholder meetings. This gives the shareholders a chance to see and perhaps even test the product before it is introduced to the general public. However, if the product is a major new addition to the organisation's range, the company may want to create a huge event and the shareholders may find out at the same time as the media and the company's customers.

Marketing kiosks can be used to launch a product

Product launches to introduce the product to old and new customers may not be formal events. For example, a company announcing a new soft drink may set up a kiosk at a major sporting event or large fair. These events require just as much planning as setting up a major event. Space has to be reserved, displays have to be set up and staff have to be hired.

Product launches to introduce the product to the media could be in the form of a press conference. If you are planning a product launch where the media is invited you must make sure there is room for photographers, both stills photographers and film cameras. They must have an excellent view so that they can capture the action. Prepare a 'press kit' that contains information about the product and the company.

If you are given the task of handling the market introduction of a new product, you have a huge responsibility. Some of the things to consider are:

- Venue – most product launch events happen in big cities or in cities where the company is located. Sometimes these launches are held in big conference centres so that there is room for the shareholders and the media. However, some product launches are held in the boardroom of the organisation. The venue depends on how big the company is, how big the product is and how much money the company wants to invest in the market introduction.

- Timing – usually the introduction of a new product, such as a new toy or game console, coincides with the Christmas season. New soft drinks may be launched during a big sporting event like the Wimbledon tennis fortnight or the football World Cup. Millions of people watch these events and announcing the new product and airing commercials during these events will create interest.

If the client wants food at the event, you have a lot of decisions to make. Will it be a buffet or a full-course meal? What time of day will the new product launch event be held? What kind of food will be best for the attendees? How much food should be ordered? Will waiting staff be needed?

The small details may not seem important, but they could make or break an event. Can you imagine launching a new product and half the attendees having to stand because there are not enough chairs? Most product launches include an information pack that is given to the guests. These packs need to be ready and there need to be enough for all the attendees. The organiser is responsible for making sure the small details are handled well. Product launches are some of the most exciting events for any organiser but these events are also the most stressful. The key, as it is for any event, is in proper planning.

ACTIVITY

Your organisation has decided to hold a product launch to which the media are to be invited. Research suitable venues and obtain estimates of the cost. Write a note to your line manager suggesting the most appropriate venue, with reasons.

TEAM-BUILDING EVENTS

Team-building events or away days can increase overall employee performance, promote co-operation among team members and across teams, improve job satisfaction, and help to broaden the understanding of organisational goals and objectives. If they are improperly designed or administered, on the other hand, they can be completely pointless.

The events should serve as small-scale versions of the problems and solutions that staff face at work, and the challenges of the events should relate to the struggles they are challenged with on a daily basis. If an important current team challenge is, for example, adapting to a new organisational structure, matching exercises involving small, specialised teams working together to achieve a common goal would be a good idea.

Remember that physical endurance, strength and dexterity are not likely to be the major attributes of team members. Fitness and physical ability should, therefore, not play a major role in team-building events. Consider the members of the team and set the level of physical assertion necessary low enough so that each team member can participate satisfactorily. Physical activities, especially outdoors, can be memorable and successful as long as everyone can be included.

Often, team-building exercises are administered as stand-alone events, but they should be viewed as the opening episode in a continuing drive towards success. Don't create events that are too taxing or too mindless. In an effort to ensure that employees have fun while completing the team-building exercises, some organisers make them too light and silly, while some create events that are unduly draining, emotionally or otherwise. Try to strike a balance so that events aren't too funny or too difficult, as either of these extremes will undermine the main message or messages of the event.

Team-building events can help improve employee performance

Consider hiring professionals to create and administer the exercises. Depending on your cost and time constraints, and the complexity of the exercises, professional consultants can help to identify the message, facilitate the event and implement the feedback and measurement components afterwards.

AWARDS CEREMONIES

Awards ceremonies may be organised to recognise people's performance and make people aware that good work gets rewarded. They show the general public and other staff that the organisation is aware of outstanding accomplishments. The recognition motivates others to strive for excellence, as being rewarded for doing well is one of the biggest incentives anyone can receive.

If you are asked to organise an awards ceremony, agree the budget. This will help determine the menu, the number of guests, the venue for the event and other details that involve spending money. Decide where to hold the ceremony. Think about what kind of event you're going to hold and then find a venue to match. Your organisation may have a recreation centre or a presentations room. If not, you will need to rent a room somewhere else. Consider whether you are going to serve food and what you need in the room. Think about how big the venue needs to be. A big hall will look empty if there are only a few people in it, but a small one will limit how many people you can have.

Awards ceremonies are used to celebrate achievement

The physical award should fit the action being recognised, the person and the occasion. Possible types of award include pins, statuettes, certificates, plaques, framed recognition citations and gifts.

Bear in mind the surprise element. Is the recipient going to be told in advance that they are going to receive an award? Surprises can be fun, but you don't want the recipient to have a heart attack from shock before reaching the podium to accept the award!

When considering the number of guests, include the immediate guests and their own guests, family and friends. You'll probably want to serve refreshments, and the size of the event and the resources the venue offers will help decide what kind of food you serve. For example, you will not be able to serve a sit-down dinner at a venue with no kitchen.

When considering refreshments, you can either plan it yourself or get help from a caterer. Doing it yourself can save money, but remember that you have to plan, buy, prepare and serve the food and clean up, all of which the caterers would do. On the other hand, you're paying the caterer for a pre-established number of people, whether those people show up or not.

You may need people to set up the venue, serve the food, put the water glass close to the speakers, serve the guests and clean up afterwards. You may need to hire support staff to help or leave this to the caterers.

No matter how small the ceremony, you don't want people tripping over tables or sitting with their backs to the podium. If the ceremony is large, then you need to consider who will sit where and with whom. Also consider who needs to be close to the podium.

Decorating the venue will depend to a large extent on the tone you want the ceremony to take. Silly balloons and festive noise-makers would be inappropriate for a sober, dignified ceremony. Consider the following decorations for a formal awards ceremony:

- flowers
- balloons
- bows
- tablecloths
- centre pieces
- pictures on the wall
- banners
- posters
- plants
- candles.

Finally you will need to consider:

- Who is going to actually present the awards? A choice could be made depending upon the recipient's job or accomplishment. It could be a colleague, the person who received good service, or the recipient's spouse, parent or child. Whoever it is, you need to contact that person in advance and allow them time for preparation. If necessary, arrange a rehearsal to fine-tune the length and tone of speeches.
- Who is going to speak first?
- How are you going to start the ceremony?
- When will it end?
- At what time during the ceremony will the award be presented?

The presentation schedule doesn't have to be followed to the minute but you need to know who will speak and in what order so that you can print a programme for the guests. Also, people should know how much time they have to present their speeches and comments. If you expect everyone to take about three minutes and someone takes thirty, it will not only risk boring the audience but can throw out the timings of the whole event and change the feeling of it. The clearer you can be about timing, the more likely you are to get close to what you want.

WORKSHOPS

Workshops are a flexible and effective method of training, learning, development, change management, team building and problem solving. If you are organising a workshop, before arranging it you should consider and agree its aims. It might be useful to invite suggestions from delegates beforehand regarding the workshop's subjects and aims to make the most of commitment and **empowerment**.

Empowerment

To give somebody a greater sense of confidence or self-esteem

Adapt the content and structure of workshops to the particular situation. Consider what you or the delegates are seeking to achieve. Establish and agree a measurable output or result that represents the aims and then think how to structure the workshop.

It is often a good idea to have the delegates use flipcharts and coloured marker pens, hanging the sheets around the walls, rather than using modern technology media. This enables delegates to be far more dynamic and creative. Encourage people to use creative methods that are appropriate for their personal styles and learning styles:

- visual, spatial, creative people enjoy working with flipcharts, colours, sticky notes etc
- people-centred individuals and teams enjoy human interaction, such as role plays, discussions, mutual interviews etc
- logical, numerate, process-oriented people are happier with more structured planning tools and computers.

Think about the equipment required for different types of workshop

Think about the sort of people in the workshop groups and provide the tools, materials and methods that they will be comfortable using.

CONSULTATION FORUMS AND ADVICE SESSIONS

Consultation is a process by which the public's input on matters affecting them is sought. Its main goals are to improve the efficiency, transparency and public involvement in large-scale projects or laws and policies. It usually involves:

- Notification – publicising the matter to be consulted on.
- Consultation – a two-way flow of information and opinion exchange.
- Participation – involving interest groups in the drafting of policy or legislation.

Public consultation is typical of countries such as the United Kingdom, Canada, New Zealand and Australia, though most democratic countries have similar systems. But consultation can become regarded as ineffective if it's considered to be cosmetic consultation done for show and not for true participatory decision making.

If you are asked to organise a consultation event, you need to consider:

- ensuring the consultation method is appropriate for your target audiences
- taking advice from members of the target audience to ensure that the consultation method is appropriate
- ensuring the consultation exercise is well publicised in a variety of media to attract your target audience
- explaining clearly from the outset what you are consulting on and what the options are
- ensuring information is available in the right format, eg other languages
- ensuring venues are fully accessible for the target audience
- ensuring the venue is appropriate, eg community buildings such as schools, day centres, council offices
- ensuring the layout is appropriate, eg chairs 'in the round' rather than the audience sat facing a top table
- the need to provide translators, interpreters or sign language interpreters
- whether the timing is appropriate for your audience
- the need to provide crèche facilities
- providing transport for those who need it, or offering to pay transport costs
- providing refreshments
- providing any other incentives for attendance
- who the key stakeholders are in the exercise
- ensuring that all the groups that are likely to be affected, both internal and external, are involved.

A consultation event

At the end of the event, remember to thank the participants and tell them how and when you will be feeding back the results. Ensure that the results of the consultation exercise are widely communicated in a variety of media.

SEMINARS

Seminars are a popular source of academic, professional or technical instruction, presenting information to diverse audiences. They may be private or public, part of a series or a single event, commercial or informative, lecture- or dialogue-based. They are less formal than academic lectures, allowing audience members to interrupt with opinions or discuss results.

Planning for a seminar should begin several months in advance by developing a theme. Is the seminar ground breaking, **philosophical** or technically orientated? Who is the target audience? Select the niche market carefully.

Philosophical

Concerned with or given to thinking about the larger issues and deeper meanings in life and events

When choosing a venue, remember that different seminar styles require different facilities. The higher the status of the seminar attendees, the more prestigious the venue must be. Additionally, the size of the location needed is dependent upon the estimated attendance figures.

Paid seminars typically attract more people than free seminars. This is because people believe that paid seminars have academic integrity, educational value and increased expectations.

Your organisation may be able to find sponsors to help fund the event as seminars are an effective method for organisations to promote their business. For instance, a car manufacturer's seminar has already assembled a niche market, so local car dealerships and garages have a guarantee of brand positioning.

Different seminar styles require different facilities

COMMON MISTAKE

Don't assume a free seminar will attract more people than one where they have to pay to attend.

PROBLEMS AND RISKS

Whatever type of event you are organising, it is important to consider the problems that might arise and the risks associated with these types of event. Contingency planning is a systematic approach to identifying what could go wrong in a situation. Rather than hoping that everything will turn out well, you should try to identify what might go wrong and be prepared with plans, strategies and approaches for avoiding or coping. Difficulties that have a low probability of happening can often be the ones that have the biggest impact if they do.

The aim of contingency planning is not to identify and develop a plan for every possibility but to think about the major risks and possible responses. Organisers who have given thought to contingencies and possible responses are more likely to achieve the client's objectives.

You need to consider:

- what may occur
- the worst-case scenario
- what would cause the greatest disruption
- what happens if delays occur
- what happens if key people leave the organisation.

You will need to take into account the resources that are required by the particular event, which may include:

- accommodation
- catering
- equipment
- car parking.

HANDY HINT

Order as many items (including speakers!) as early as possible early. Speakers' schedules fill up quickly, and equipment orders may take up to eight weeks if your item is not in stock.

You will also need to consider any special requirements that attendees might have, such as wheelchair access, hearing induction loops or dietary restrictions.

ACTIVITY

Carry out a risk assessment for an event. Make a contingency plan to cover the risks identified.

You can then carry out a risk assessment for the event. The risk assessment will be unique to that event and will take into account the venue itself, the marketing and media attention attached to the event, any high-risk attendees, and the size and location of the event.

The risk assessment should also take into account all the potential risks at the event which may include:

- Fire – it will put checks in place regarding placement of chairs, aisles and access to emergency exits. It will also look at eliminating any potentially highly combustible material.
- Theft – large events are prime targets for theft. Unfortunately, theft has to be a major concern for any event that draws crowds of people.
- Political activists/demonstrators – this may be anybody with a grudge against the company that is organising or participating in the event, and may include ex-employees or current employees.

Identify risks associated with each activity and consider each of the following:

- Physical risks – injury, death, travel, food-related illnesses etc.
- Reputation risks – the risk of damage to the reputation of the whole organisation and/or the reputation of the department responsible for the event.
- Emotional risks – reactions of attendees, sensitive subject matter, potential controversy etc.
- Financial risks – costs, poor budgeting etc.
- Facilities risks – the safety of the facilities for your participants or attendees, the maintenance and clean-up of the facilities etc.

Assess each risk for the probability of it happening and the seriousness of the consequences. Make decisions about how to manage each risk identified. You can accept, modify, transfer and/or eliminate each risk based on your assessment. Share your plans and risk management actions with your client and plan your event according to those decisions.

CHOOSING A VENUE

Once you have shortlisted suitable venues that have the necessary facilities, you will be in a position to compare costs. Ask each venue for a quote, making sure that they provide information on whether the rate offered is a 24-hour per delegate rate or a room-hire rate plus accommodation. Ask whether prices are negotiable or whether a discount is available if a certain number of attendees are involved.

When you receive the quotes, consider the following:

- whether a deposit is required and when
- what their policy is on cancellation refunds
- when final payment is required
- whether the total cost is within the budget you have agreed for the event.

Unless you have held similar events at a particular venue previously, do not make assumptions that the offered rooms will provide adequate facilities – check them out for yourself. There are a huge number of issues that you will want to be confident of before the day of the event; 'firefighting' problems immediately before or even during the event is never satisfactory.

When you have considered all the variables, you can select the right venue for the event. Perhaps the most important area of choosing a venue is the availability of the most suitable layout for the event. Different types of layout are used for different types of event:

- theatre-style layout
- classroom layout
- boardroom layout
- horseshoe layout
- banquet – cabaret layout.

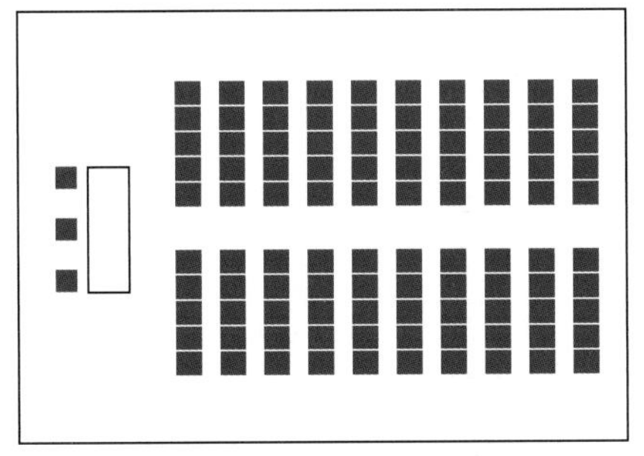
Theatre

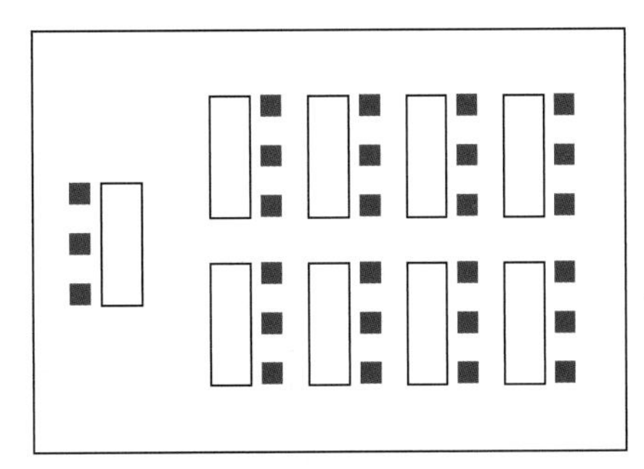
Classroom

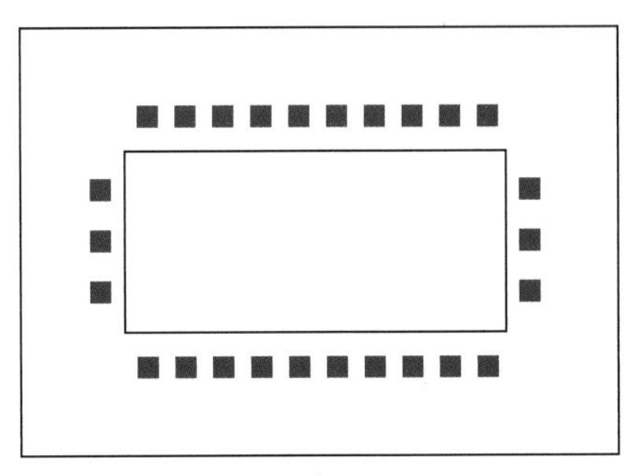
Boardroom

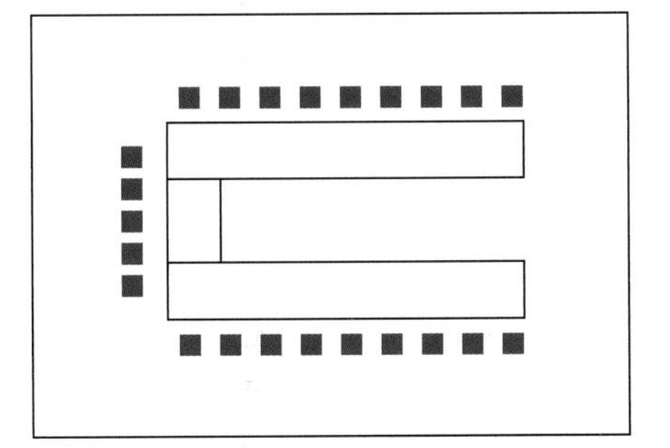
Horseshoe

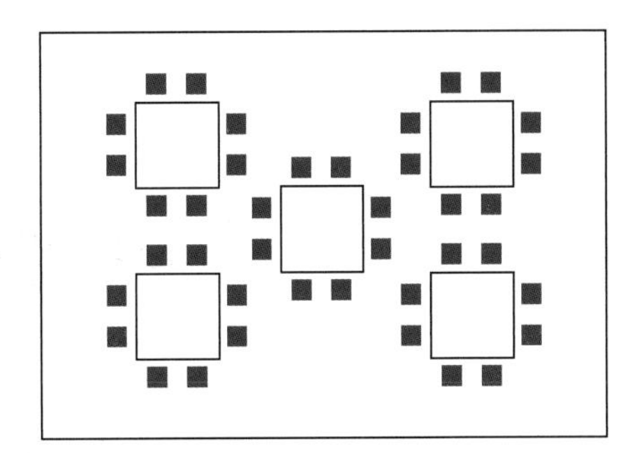
Banquet – Cabaret

Make sure the layout you require is available and that the room or rooms will be laid out in the required way before attendees arrive.

Once the venue is decided, you can start to arrange the event. Develop an event plan listing all the tasks that need to be completed along with target completion dates. Most major events take up to 12 months to arrange, while some types of event require even longer. You should put the following milestones into your diary.

Twelve months before the event:

- confirm the venue
- invite speakers
- advise the venue of the estimated numbers.

Six months before the event:

- confirm the programme
- invite attendees
- agree catering requirements
- confirm room layouts
- confirm equipment requirements.

Two months before the event:

- acknowledge responses from attendees
- follow-up unanswered invitations
- visit the venue
- send reminders to invited speakers.

One month before the event:

- assemble any resources required
- recheck arrangements.

Two weeks before the event:

- confirm the final details
- arrange pre-registration so attendees only have to give their name on arrival.

One week before the event:

- confirm final numbers to the venue
- work out seating plans.

You may be able to delegate some of these arrangements to other members of staff but remember to monitor that they have been carried out correctly. When the day of the event arrives, it will be too late to find out that someone has forgotten to make sure there is somewhere for attendees to park.

HANDY HINTS

- If the venue you select is previously unknown to you, ask for the names of other organisations that have held similar events and check their experience of the venue. Visit the venue in person and check out the facilities offered and the level of customer service.
- By building good contacts, such as with event-hosting venues, guest speakers and within your own company, you can accomplish the different aspects of the event more easily and in less time.

ON THE DAY OF THE EVENT

Arrive well before the start time so that you can check that all the arrangements are in place. You will need to liaise with the venue to make sure that all the client's requirements have been met.

Check arrangements, such as catering, are in place before the event begins

Your responsibilities will include checking that the catering has been organised for the agreed times. If a sit-down meal is included in the event, delegates may have been asked to indicate their choices for each course prior to the day. If not, you will need to confirm the deadline for providing this information to the catering staff and ensure that delegates are asked for their preferences in plenty of time.

If a buffet is to be provided, you will need to check where it is to be set out and at what time, and that any special dietary requirements that you have been advised of have been catered for.

If the event is taking place at a venue that you are not familiar with, you will need to check where the toilets are and what provision there is for smokers. You will also need to know where fire exits are situated, where the assembly point is and whether there is a fire alarm test scheduled during the event, so that you can pass this information on to the attendees.

You should re-assure yourself that you know how to raise the alarm should an emergency arise, who to contact if first aid is required, and where disabled access and exits are situated. Lastly, check that all the equipment and resources that have been requested for the event are in place and working.

If there are guest speakers or presenters booked for the event, you should run though their arrangements with them. If they are providing resources of their own, such as computer disks or USB sticks containing their slides, make sure they are compatible with any hardware being provided by the organiser or the venue. This should have already been checked before the event but it is well worth making sure that there will be no problems before it is too late to take any necessary action.

Greet your delegates as they arrive

If delegates are staying overnight, check whether pre-registration has been organised so that arriving delegates have only to give their names to reception in order to receive their room key. If rooms are not ready at the time that delegates arrive, make sure there is locked storage available for their luggage. Delegates will not want to have to carry suitcases with them during the day if they have arrived by taxi.

You will need to carry out all of these checks before the first delegates arrive, as you should be available to greet them and welcome them to the event. You can then check whether they have any questions or previously unstated requirements, show them where to sign in, where the cloakroom is, where they can find refreshments and where they need to go for the main event.

If delegate packs are provided, you can direct the delegates to the area where they are being distributed, together with any identity badges and a seating plan. The actual handing out of packs and badges should have been delegated to another member of the team, leaving you free to deal with the delegates' needs on arrival.

ACTIVITY

Arrange to attend an event and help greet arrivals, directing them as necessary. Ask the event organiser for a witness testimony describing how you carried out the task.

When the event is under way, check the delegate list against the arrivals and follow up on non-arrivals that you have booked accommodation for. You will need to advise the venue as soon as you can of any accommodation that will no longer be needed, as the cancellation charge can be reduced if they are able to resell it.

This is also a good time to check whether all the contracted provision has been provided, both between you and the venue and between you and the client. If anything is missing, you will be able to investigate whether it can still be supplied or if payments will need to be adjusted in line with the agreed terms and conditions.

While the event is in progress, you need to be available to everybody. Your role is to handle any difficulties as they arise and, wherever possible, foresee them so they can be prevented. The delegates, and your client, are looking forward to an event that appears to proceed without any effort. It is your efforts that will make this happen.

Arrange for the reception area to advise you of late arrivals so that you can meet them and escort them into the event with a minimum of disruption. Keep at least one step ahead of each planned stage of the event. Check that refreshments will be available before they are due. Check that speakers have everything they need before their slot begins.

HANDY HINT

There will be countless calls on you – be patient and cheerful.

Deal with any problems that arise quickly and efficiently. The list of potential problems is as long as the list of delegates but the most likely, and the most serious, will include problems with catering. If refreshments and, even worse, meals are not provided on time and to the expected standard, this will have a major effect on the delegates' views of the whole event.

You will have been checking with the catering staff at regular intervals so should be aware of any timing issues with enough notice to work around them. Quality issues, on the other hand, may not arise until the food is actually served. If a delegate with a particular dietary requirement's needs have not been met, you will have to use your initiative to make sure that they are adequately refreshed and take the matter up with the caterers later. Check that their requirements were made known to the caterers before laying the blame for the problem on them. You need the caterers' co-operation during the event and it will not help if you criticise them for failing to fulfil a requirement that you had not made them aware of.

Another regular cause of problems is equipment failure. A common saying is that 'anything that can go wrong, will go wrong'. While this may be overly pessimistic, the fact is that you should always be prepared for equipment to fail and for this to happen at the most inconvenient time. Wherever possible, have a standby piece of equipment available. If the equipment has been supplied by the venue as part of the contractual agreement, they should have a back-up available, but it is worth checking.

A problem that is difficult, if not impossible, to solve to everybody's satisfaction is the question of heating, lighting and ventilation. If you have 10 people in a room you will have 11 opinions on whether it is too hot, too cold, too bright, too dim, too stuffy or too airy. You can only provide facilities that meet the health and safety requirements and are working efficiently. In general, the more assertive delegates will get their way and others will put up with it.

Delayed speakers can usually warn you by phone

The last problem that occurs regularly is the failure of speakers to arrive. This will usually be caused by transport problems. If they are travelling by public transport, delayed speakers will usually have the opportunity to warn you about their problems, so at least you have some time to deal with it by rescheduling if possible.

Where speakers are travelling alone by car and are held up by unexpected delays, they may not be able to let you know as they may not be in a position to use their mobile phones legally. In these situations you can only apologise to delegates for their non-arrival and suggest moving on to the next item.

AFTER THE EVENT

When the event is over, your work as event co-ordinator is far from finished.

Your first task will be to clear and vacate the venue. Delegates who have stayed overnight will be checking out and you need to be available to help resolve any issues. The joining instructions should have made it clear whether all, some or none of the delegates' expenses were being met by the organisers. If delegates leave without settling their accounts the venue may hold the organisation running the event responsible rather than the individual, as they are much easier for the venue to deal with.

Once all the delegates have left, deal with the equipment. If it has all been provided by the venue, check that there has been no damage caused to it during the event, to avoid any disputes later. If it has been hired from a separate supplier you will need to organise its safe return. If you have supplied it yourself you will need to pack it away safely. Confirm with your venue contact that everything is completed before leaving the site.

Your next task is to forward any papers, documents or activities resulting from the event to delegates. You may have received sales enquiries during the event that you will either deal with yourself or pass on to the sales department. These should receive priority. If records of activities that occurred during the event are to be circulated, consider whether people who were invited but unable to attend will need copies.

An important task will be to reconcile the accounts for the event to the original budget. You won't be able to finalise this until you have received all the invoices for the hire of the venue, the hire of equipment, catering, accommodation, speakers' fees and expenses. The true cost of the event will also include the cost of preparing for the event, postage costs, your travel costs and an amount for your time.

If your total costs exceed your budget, you will need to analyse the reasons in order to ensure that you can stay within budget for future events. Some of the areas to consider are:

- whether anything provided for the event was, in hindsight, unnecessary
- whether it is possible to introduce some form of sponsorship to cover some of the expenses
- whether an increase in the charge you make to the organisation putting on the event, or the individuals attending, is possible.

If your total costs were significantly below budget, you will want to look at the response the event received from the attendees before congratulating yourself on saving money. If you cut corners, the clients may decide to use someone else to put on future events so that they feel they have received value for money.

Your final task is to evaluate the event. Invite the client and the team responsible for delivering the event to a meeting to discuss what went well and what could have been improved. Organise this as soon after the event as possible, as other tasks and responsibilities will soon cloud people's memories. Have an agenda prepared so that the meeting can remain focused. Topics you will be seeking feedback on may include:

- the venue
- any entertainment
- food and beverages
- timeline for communications, invitations etc
- invitations and other printed materials
- table arrangements
- staff assignments
- registration on arrival
- checkout on departure
- general event flow and timing
- opportunities for improvements
- successes and failures at the event.

Before the evaluation meeting, contact as many of the attendees as possible and ask for their feedback. This could be done most economically by email or, where small numbers are involved, a short telephone interview will gather important feedback. The questions you would like answers to may include:

- What did you like best about the event?
- What did you like least?
- Was the event too short, too long or just right?
- How would you rate the food and beverage?
- Do you think the entertainment was appropriate for the event?

To complete the evaluation process, make files or binder sections for the materials you have created, including:

- the financial report
- minutes of the evaluation meeting
- a list of problems and possible solutions
- interview notes
- a copy of the survey to guests and a summary of responses you received.

Organise them within the event files or binder you will be archiving. These will be important files to consider when making initial plans for future events. Be sure to back up any electronic files (including your software database) to a disk or flash drive.

HANDY HINT

Event evaluation can be challenging but is essential to future success. Using this process will give your next event a valuable boost.

ACTIVITY

Create a file containing all the information on a completed event that will be useful for organising future events.

CASE STUDY
OFFICE MANAGER

Rachel works as an office manager in a business school, where she manages eight staff. She completed her business management degree part time while working.

Her role involves managing staff, conducting appraisals, supervising all the office work, delegating tasks, planning for future workflows and projects, budgeting, client liaison and meetings. The most rewarding parts of the role are seeing a project through to completion, working directly with students and clients, and seeing how team members progress and develop.

Rachel started as an administrator, applying for the position because of the reputation of the employer, the entry-level wages and a well-structured career path. After two years the office manager position became vacant and was advertised internally. After applying, Rachel was invited to an interview and was also required to sit some clerical tests. She feels that her success was partly due to the experience she had already gained in the team, but more importantly it was due to her effort to keep up to date with training and her willingness to take on extra responsibility by managing projects.

Rachel completed her business management degree part time. She received one afternoon per week off work to attend lectures. Although the degree was not a requirement of her post, it will be necessary when she applies for more senior positions. Rachel feels the subject of her study is relevant to her post as it has given her a background in areas including human resource management and business management.

In the future, Rachel would like to progress to managing a whole section in the school and, ultimately, the school itself.

UNIT 319 (B&A 58): TEST YOUR KNOWLEDGE

Learning outcome 1: Understand how to manage an office facility

1. Name two legal requirements that relate to the management of office facilities.
2. List the typical services provided by an office facility.
3. List the office resources that have to be managed.
4. Explain the importance of managing workflows.
5. Explain why welfare facilities are important.

Learning outcome 2: Understand health and safety in a business environment

1. Name the legislation that relates to the use of computer screens.
2. Describe an employee's responsibilities for health and safety.
3. Describe your organisation's emergency procedures.

Learning outcome 3: Understand how to take minutes of meetings

1. Give an example of a meeting at which you would record verbatim minutes.
2. Describe the legal requirements that apply to minute taking.
3. Explain why it is important that minutes are accurate and grammatical.
4. Explain terms that are commonly used in meetings.
5. Describe how you would make notes during a meeting to ensure that all relevant points have been recorded.

Learning outcome 4: Understand how to chair, lead and manage meetings

1. List two types of formal meetings.
2. Describe the role of the chairperson in a meeting.
3. Explain the importance of working in partnership with the chairperson when taking minutes.
4. Explain what you would do if you required clarification of a point during discussion of an agenda item.

UNIT 319 (B&A 58): TEST YOUR KNOWLEDGE

Learning outcome 5: Understand how to supervise an administration team

1 Why are targets important in managing workloads?

2 What is the difference between delegation and abdication?

3 Describe the quality management techniques used in your organisation.

4 Explain the techniques used in your organisation to identify the need for improvement.

Learning outcome 6: Understand how to organise events

1 Describe three different types of event layout.

2 Describe the sources of information for an event held in your organisation.

3 Describe the purpose of a contingency plan.

4 Describe the types of resources that may be needed during an event.

5 Explain how the brief and a budget for events are agreed.

CHAPTER 4

UNIT 320 (B&A 59) PRINCIPLES OF BUSINESS

There are a few basic principles that are essential to the success of any business, whether it's a multinational or run by one person. These are:

- Get organised – you will spend less time looking for things.
- Control stress – remain calm and you'll be more effective.
- Research – there are a whole range of books available on how to be successful.
- Be passionate – if you're not, then work will become hard.
- Budget – when you are in control of your finances, you can stop stressing about money and focus on what makes you successful.
- Value your health – you will become more successful if you take care of yourself and look more presentable.
- Embrace selling – even if you have nothing to do with sales, you are still selling yourself.
- Satisfy customers – go over and above what you say you will do, and customers will remember you for it.
- Network – collect people's contact information and store it in a database.
- Maintain cash flow – this principle is more for business owners and managers than for employees, but it is crucial to keep money coming in.
- Achieve a work/life balance – remember what is important and do things that you enjoy outside of work.

In this unit you will cover the following learning outcomes:

1 understand business markets
2 understand business innovation and growth
3 understand financial management
4 understand business budgeting
5 understand sales and marketing.

Assessment criteria

This section covers assessment criteria 1.1, 1.2, 1.3 and 1.4

BUSINESS MARKETS

Different types of organisations will have different characteristics including:

- purpose
- finance
- ethos
- structure
- customers
- ownership.

These characteristics will be explored in this chapter.

There are three basic types of market systems:

- free market
- command market
- mixed market.

FREE MARKET

In a free market, resources and industries are owned completely by private individuals. In this system, two parties enter into an agreed exchange that is mutually beneficial. A free market system is driven by the goal of profit, which is determined mostly by consumer demand. The government plays only a remote role, ensuring only that the market remains stable.

Exchanges in a free market system can be as simple as buying and selling a cup of tea. The tea shop is owned completely by the merchant, but the customer has the power to shape the business through providing repeat business or by going to a competitor. The competition encourages all tea shops in the area to have competitive pricing or to offer a clearly superior product.

The market system has many benefits but also some drawbacks, including:

- possible shortages and surpluses due to market fluctuations
- income differences that can lead to a society of very rich and very poor people, with few in between
- public services such as defence, health care and education that are used by everyone but towards which not everyone pays an equal share of the costs.

COMMAND MARKET

The command market is also known as the 'planned economy' or 'planned market'. It works through central planning by a government that owns all the resources and controls all aspects of the economy, including:

- what and how much is produced
- financial compensation to workers
- prices of products and who can receive them.

This type of market usually operates in **communist** countries. The benefits of a true command market system include a similar standard of living for all citizens, with little homelessness and no inflation due to government price controls, but this common standard of living tends to be the lowest, not the highest, standard. The command system has a number of drawbacks, including:

- limited product selection
- needs determined by a central planning authority that aren't truly compatible with what the society requires or wants
- restriction of personal freedom.

The command market system can end up damaging the economy through **stagnation**. When workers don't own the resources and receive the same amount of compensation regardless of what they do, there is no incentive to improve existing products or make innovations. This can lead to loss of technological and financial progress.

Communist

A political theory or system in which all property and wealth is owned in a classless society by all the members of that society

ACTIVITY

Find examples of a free market economy and a command market economy. Give advantages and disadvantages of each.

Stagnation

Failure to develop, progress or make necessary changes

MIXED MARKET

The third type of market is the mixed market. Most countries operate an economy somewhere between a free market and a command market economy. In a mixed market there are various types of market operating alongside each other.

Competitive markets

Competitive markets have multiple buyers and sellers. In a perfectly competitive market:

- no individual supplier has a dominant market share
- standardised or similar products are supplied by each supplier
- customers have full information about prices and trends
- all sellers in the market, whether new or existing, have equal access to technology and other resources
- there are no barriers to entry into the market or exit
- the market is open to external competition.

A competitive market serves as a benchmark for other real-world markets.

Monopoly markets

A monopoly or monopolistic market is one that has only one seller that has the independence to raise and lower prices without affecting the demand for its services and products. Monopolies serve the needs of sellers but are harmful to customers. They are characterised by:

- an absence of economic competition
- technological superiority
- no substitutes for the goods sold (ie customers do not have an alternative)
- a seller having full control of market power, with the ability to lower and raise prices without losing clients or customers.

Monopolies can form for a variety of reasons, including:

- a firm having exclusive ownership of a scarce or essential resource, as with Microsoft's original dominance of the Windows operating system for PCs, it has monopoly power over this resource and is the only firm that can exploit it
- government granting a firm monopoly status, as with the Post Office which was given monopoly status by Oliver Cromwell in 1654
- producers having **patents** over designs or copyright over ideas, characters, images, sounds or names, giving them exclusive rights to sell a good or service, such as a songwriter having a monopoly over their own material
- following the merger of two or more firms – such mergers are subject to close regulation and may be prevented by the government if the two firms have a combined market share of 25% or more.

Patents

A set of exclusive rights granted to an inventor for a limited period of time

The Post Office was given monopoly status by Oliver Cromwell in 1654

Monopsony markets

A monopsony is a type of market in which a single powerful buyer controls and affects market prices. Multiple sellers offer goods and services, but there is only a single buyer who has exclusive control of market power and can bring the prices of goods/services down. A pure monopsony is rare, and is most often found in the context of a large employer in a small town having a monopsony on the available work force. Examples of monopsony purchasers include:

- major employers in a small town, such as a car plant, a major supermarket or the head office of a bank
- nursing homes as employers of care assistants
- the government as the major purchaser in the teaching profession or in the NHS
- local authorities for example in refuse collection, street-cleaning and in running council nursing homes and local libraries

- agencies, which employ thousands of people in the hotel, catering and cleaning industries
- the farming sector, which employs huge numbers of people on temporary terms during the peak harvesting season.

The farming sector employs people on temporary terms during peak harvesting season

Oligopoly markets

An oligopoly market is characterised by a limited number of competing sellers who sell similar or different products. Sellers compete with each other through aggressive advertising and improved service delivery. An oligopoly sets barriers to entry and makes it difficult for new sellers to enter the market. Barriers include:

- patent rights
- financial requirements
- legal barriers.

Tobacco companies and airlines are examples of oligopolies.

Oligopsony markets

An oligopsony market has few buyers but multiple sellers. A duopsony is a type of oligopsony that has two buyers. The buyers affect each other's buying action. An example of an oligopsony is the market for cocoa. There are three large firms that purchase the majority of cocoa bean production around the world. These three firms therefore control most of the world's cocoa supply. The sellers of cocoa beans must compete to receive business from one or more of these three firms. The three firms therefore have an extraordinary amount of power over the sellers and can dictate where the cocoa beans are grown, how they are grown, how they are sent and how they are sold.

ACTIVITY

Carry out research to identify further examples of monopolies, monopsonies, oligopolies and oligopsonies.

An example of an oligopsony is the market for cocoa beans

TYPES OF ORGANISATION

The economy of the UK can be divided into three main sectors:

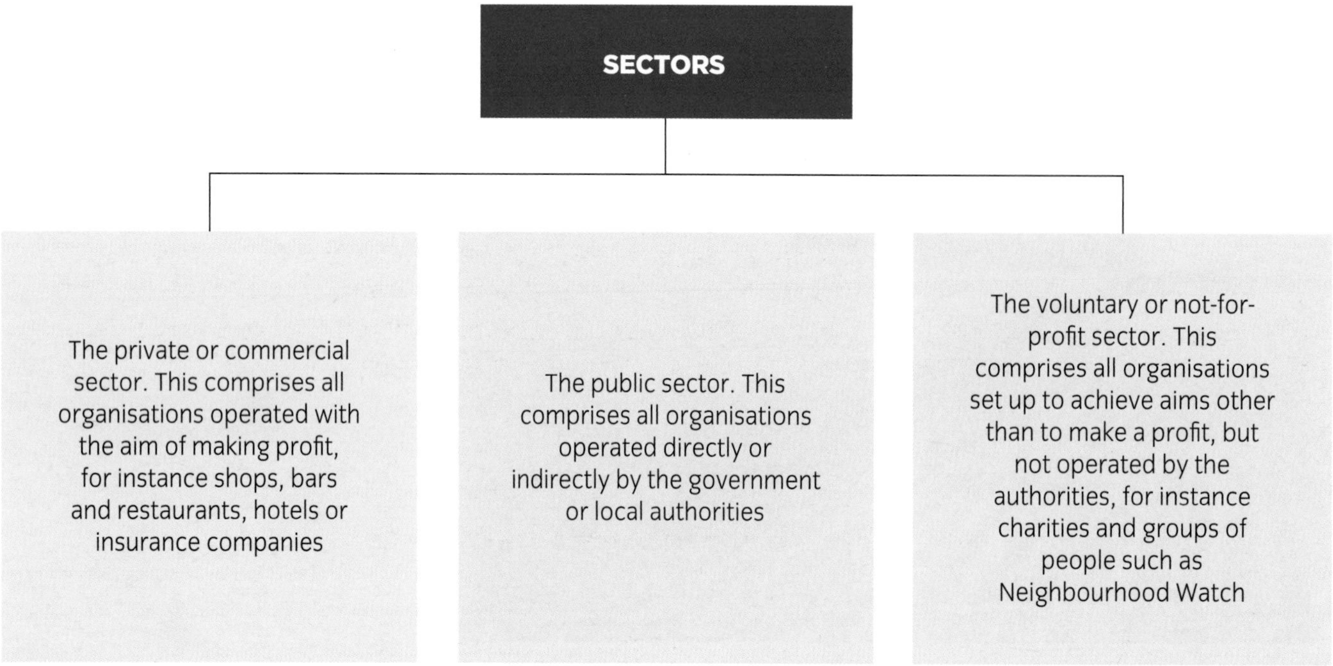

SECTORS

The private or commercial sector. This comprises all organisations operated with the aim of making profit, for instance shops, bars and restaurants, hotels or insurance companies

The public sector. This comprises all organisations operated directly or indirectly by the government or local authorities

The voluntary or not-for-profit sector. This comprises all organisations set up to achieve aims other than to make a profit, but not operated by the authorities, for instance charities and groups of people such as Neighbourhood Watch

THE PRIVATE OR COMMERCIAL SECTOR

Organisations that are set up to make a profit may be any of the following.

Sole traders

This means the business is owned by one person, who takes all the financial risk of operating the business in return for all the profits. Sole traders are personally responsible for any losses the business makes, bills for things they buy for the business (like stock or equipment) and keeping records of the business's sales and spending.

Sole traders must register with HM Revenue and Customs (HMRC) as soon as they can after starting the business. Sole traders must send a self-assessment tax return every year, pay Income Tax on their profits, pay National Insurance, and register for VAT if they expect the business's takings to be above a threshold that the government sets each year.

Partnerships

Two or more people own the business and share the risks and profits. The partners may own equal or unequal parts of the business, and the risk and profit is shared proportionately. Profits are shared between the partners and each partner pays tax on their share of the profits. Partners are personally responsible for their share of any losses the business suffers, and for bills for things bought for the business such as stock or equipment.

A partner doesn't have to be an actual person. For example, a limited company counts as a 'legal person' and can also be a partner in a partnership.

To set up as a business partnership, a 'nominated partner' must be chosen to be responsible for keeping business records and managing tax returns. The nominated partner must register the partnership with HMRC. When they do this, they will automatically register personally for self-assessment. The other partners must register individually.

The nominated partner must send a self-assessment tax return for the partnership every year, and all the partners must send a personal self-assessment tax return every year, pay Income Tax on their share of the partnership's profits, and pay National Insurance. The partnership will also have to register for VAT if they expect its takings to be above the threshold.

Corporations

Corporations may be public limited companies or private limited companies. A limited company is an organisation that you can set up to run your business. It's responsible in its own right for everything it does and its finances are separate to the owners' personal finances. Any profit it makes is owned by the company, after it pays Corporation Tax. The company can then share its profits.

Every limited company has members or shareholders who own shares in the company and elect a board of directors. The company's directors are responsible for running the company. The directors often own shares, too, but they don't have to.

Because the shareholders of a company limited by shares are distinct 'legal persons' quite separate from the limited company itself, the direct liability of such shareholders to outsiders with whom the company has dealt is nil. However, such shareholders may indirectly be liable up to the limit of the amount which they have agreed to pay the limited company for their shares and which remains unpaid.

Shares in limited companies can be bought and sold. *Public* limited companies have 'floated' and have their value listed on a stock exchange, so the shareholders in these companies regularly change. In contrast, shares in *private* limited companies are traded privately, the shares aren't listed and so they change hands less frequently. Some of the profits are distributed to the shareholders as dividends, based on the number of shares they hold.

Limited companies must be set up with Companies House and let HMRC know when the company starts business activities. Every financial year, the company must put together statutory accounts, send Companies House an annual return, send HMRC a Company Tax Return, and register for VAT if they expect their takings to be above the threshold.

Co-operatives

Co-operatives are owned by their members, who may be employees or customers. Profits are distributed to members based on their salary (if they are employees) or spend (if they are customers). In legal terms, co-operatives usually take on the form of one of the types of corporation described above.

Franchises

A franchise exists when firms that already have a successful product or service enter into a relationship with other businesses to operate under the franchiser's trade name, and usually with the franchiser's guidance, in exchange for a fee. Some of the most popular franchises include Subway and McDonalds. The legal form of a franchise can be any of those described above.

A clothes shop is an example of a profit-making organisation

THE PUBLIC SECTOR

The public sector consists of:

- government departments such as the Home Office, the Foreign and Commonwealth Office and the Treasury
- non-ministerial government departments such as the Office for Standards in Education (Ofsted), Her Majesty's Revenue and Customs (HMRC) and the Charity Commission
- executive agencies such as the Food and Environment Research Agency, the Rural Payments Agency and the Maritime and Coastguard Agency
- non-departmental public bodies (NDPBs) such as the Environment Agency, Sport England and the Royal Commission on Environmental Pollution

- local authorities such as county councils, district councils and unitary authorities
- public corporations such as the Audit Commission, the BBC and the Civil Aviation Authority
- trusts such as the BMA Medical Educational Trust and the many NHS Trusts.

Public sector organisations differ in terms of purpose, size, budget, service provided, customers, governance, values and ethics. For instance:

- the stated purpose of the Home Office is control of immigration and passports, drugs policy, counter-terrorism and the police
- the Charity Commission regulates registered charities in England and Wales and is responsible for maintaining the register of charities and making charities accountable
- the Rural Payments Agency provides rural payments, rural inspections and livestock tracing, and enforcing the size and shape of vegetables and fruit sold in shops by warning and advising businesses
- the Royal Commission on Environmental Pollution advises the government on environmental pollution
- local authorities provide public services such as schools, social services, public transport, council housing, leisure facilities, planning, recycling and refuse collection.

COMMON MISTAKE

People often speak of public bodies as being funded by 'government money' but in reality there is no such thing: it is taxpayers' money that funds all government spending.

THE VOLUNTARY OR NOT-FOR-PROFIT SECTOR

Organisations that are run for purposes other than to make a profit are often run in much the same way as profit-making organisations. The difference is that their purpose is to raise money to promote a cause. Often they are run by volunteers, although paid staff may be employed for their expertise in fundraising or carrying on the business operations of the organisation. Among the not-for-profit organisations are:

- Charities – these are often registered with the Charity Commission, or in Scotland with the Office of the Scottish Charity Regulator, and must conform with strict criteria in order to operate as registered charities.
- Community interest companies (CICs) – these are social enterprises set up to tackle a wide range of social and environmental issues. Their surpluses are re-invested for the benefit of the community.
- Trade unions – these are organisations of workers that negotiate wages, working conditions and health and safety rules for their members. Their income is derived from members' subscriptions and used for the benefit of members.

ACTIVITY

Research the organisation you are working in. What is its purpose? How did it start/evolve into the organisation it is today?

The British Heart Foundation is an example of a not-for-profit organisation

INDUSTRIES

Organisations can also be characterised by their position in the supply chain. Different types of organisations include:

- Extractive industries – these produce raw materials through mining, quarrying, dredging, and oil and gas extraction. Mining is the extraction of metals and solid fossil fuel in either an underground mine or in an above ground mine, known as a surface mine, 'open-cast mine', 'open-pit' or just 'pit'. Quarrying is the extraction of aggregates and industrial minerals above ground. Dredging is the extraction of marine aggregate underwater. Oil extraction is the extraction of liquid fossil fuel and gas extraction is the extraction of gaseous fossil fuel.
- Manufacturers – these produce merchandise for use or sale using labour and machines, tools, chemical and biological processing, or formulation. Raw materials are transformed into finished goods on a large scale. These goods may be used for manufacturing other more complex products or sold to wholesalers.
- Wholesalers – these sell goods or merchandise to retailers, industrial, commercial, institutional, or other professional business users or to other wholesalers.
- Retailers – these sell goods and services to an end-user. Retailing can be done in either fixed locations such as stores or markets, door-to-door or by delivery. An increasing amount of retailing is done using online websites via electronic payment.
- Service providers – these provide consulting, legal, real estate, education, communications, storage, processing and other services.

TYPES OF MARKET

A market is anywhere where buyers and sellers come together to **transact** with each other. The traditional image of a market is a place where buyers and sellers come together in one place. This still happens: the UK has many towns that are referred to as 'market towns', so called because they host a town-centre market on regular dates throughout the year. Car boot sales are another classic example of a physical market in action.

Transact

To conduct or carry out something such as business

There are two main categories of physical market:

- Local markets where customers are a short distance from suppliers. These are often used for the sale of fresh and locally sourced products and the delivery of locally supplied services. The car boot sale is a great example of a local product market. The use of local services such as the local high street or retail park is another example, where consumer goods are sold to people who tend to live nearby. Businesses operating in local markets enjoy several advantages. They are physically closer to their customers so are better placed to understand local cultural issues and traditions. It is also easier to develop relationships with local customers, to engage in market research and to respond quickly to changes in the market. The main disadvantage to operating in local markets is that the market size may be relatively small.
- National markets, where customers are spread throughout the country or over a large area. The same product or service is offered to customers through many locations in the country. For example, there are branches of Sainsbury's, McDonald's and Greggs in almost every town and city.

Local markets are often used to sell fresh and locally sourced products

However, the buyer and seller don't have to be in the same physical place in order to conduct transactions with each other. A much larger number of markets are now electronic. Businesses find their customers using electronic media, including the internet, mobile telephones, television and email. Transactions are completed electronically with the delivery method depending on the nature of the product sold. For example, items bought and sold on eBay, Amazon or iTunes, or bought from a catalogue by making a phone call, are all examples of transactions in a market, although the buyers were not physically in contact with the sellers.

The key points about electronic markets include:

- They provide an easier way for start-ups to enter a national market, particularly if the business has identified a small **niche** segment of that market.
- They tend to be highly competitive on price since it is quite easy for customers to search for products from a variety of suppliers and to compare the best prices available.
- Start-up costs tend to be lower compared with entering a physical market.

Niche

A specialised part of a market

Markets can also be sub-divided into 'consumer' and 'industrial' markets.

Consumer markets are markets for products and services that are bought by individuals for their own or family use. Goods bought in consumer markets include:

- Fast-moving consumer goods (FMCGs) – these are high-volume, low unit-value, fast-repurchase products. Examples include ready meals, baked beans and newspapers.
- Consumer durables – these have low volume but high unit-value. Consumer durables include 'white goods' such as fridge-freezers, cookers, dishwashers and microwaves, and 'brown goods' such as DVD players, games consoles and personal computers.
- Soft goods – these are similar to consumer durables except that they wear out more quickly and therefore have a shorter replacement cycle. Examples include clothes and shoes.
- Services – such as hairdressing, dentistry and childcare.

Industrial markets involve the sale of goods between businesses and are not aimed directly at consumers. Industrial markets include those:

- selling finished goods such as office furniture and computer systems
- selling raw materials or components such as steel, coal, gas and timber
- selling services to businesses such as waste disposal, security, accounting and legal services.

INTERACTIONS

Businesses interact with each other in a variety of ways. These include:

- Supply chain transactions – The Council of Supply Chain Management Professionals (csmp.org) defines supply chain management as follows:

  > Supply chain management encompasses the planning and management of all activities involved in sourcing and procurement, conversion, and all logistics management activities. Importantly, it also includes co-ordination and collaboration with channel partners, which can be suppliers, intermediaries, third-party service providers, and customers. In essence, supply chain management integrates supply and demand management within and across companies. Supply chain management is an integrating function with primary responsibility for linking major business functions and business processes within and across companies into a cohesive and high-performing business model. It includes all of the logistics management activities noted above, as well as manufacturing operations, and it drives co-ordination of processes and activities with and across marketing, sales, product design, finance and information technology.

  A typical supply chain begins with the ecological, biological, and political regulation of natural resources, followed by the human extraction of raw material, and includes several production links (eg component construction, assembly, and merging) before moving on to several layers of storage facilities of ever-decreasing size and increasingly remote geographical locations, and finally reaching the consumer.

- Logistics – this is the management of the flow of goods between the point of origin and the point of consumption, and usually involves the integration of information flow, material handling, production, packaging, inventory, transportation and warehousing.
- Advertising – this involves making the public aware of products and services through paid announcements in newspapers and magazines, via radio or television, on billboards, etc.
- Collaboration on loyalty rewards, discounts and joint promotions to share the cost and rewards of sales promotions.

COMPETITION

Competition prompts invention as companies try to beat each other by creating new products and services to attract customers and increase sales. In turn, innovation benefits customers as companies produce better products and services. Innovation may cause changes in society and raise standards of living. Technological breakthroughs such as the airplane, car, phone and personal computer are inventions that resulted from competition and raised living standards.

Competition also causes companies to look for ways to reduce manufacturing costs to increase their profits. The savings benefit customers who eventually pay lower prices as manufacturing costs drop.

Businesses also conduct market research to identify consumer needs that their competitors may not be fulfilling and to develop products and services that meet these customer needs.

ACTIVITY

Research a situation where two or more organisations are in direct competition. What benefits has this competition brought to the customers of the organisations?

Competition among businesses also drives economic growth. New consumer electronic devices and advances in communications cause economies to grow worldwide. For example, changes in the technology industry encourage innovation and quickly expand consumers' product choices. Companies lower product prices to stay competitive as consumer demand grows for the newest electronic devices.

An organisation's goals may be shaped by the market in which it operates. A business is bound to fail unless it has a reasonable understanding of its target market. The business needs to understand:

- the needs and wants of its customers, and how these differ
- the buying behaviour of customers – why, what and how they buy
- the ways in which a market is split up into market segments to serve different customer needs
- the nature of demand in the market, how prices are set and the factors that influence demand
- the size and growth rate of the overall market and its segments
- the proportion of market demand that is taken by competitors, known as market share.

Organisations' goals can also be shaped by:

- Climate change – if this proves to be a genuine phenomenon, it will affect the goals of many organisations. It is predicted that the earth's climate will rise by 3°C over the next 100 years which could result in:
  - sea levels rising
  - global food supplies reducing

  - 3 billion people suffering increased water stress
  - 290 million people being exposed to the risk of malaria
  - tropical rain forests disappearing due to water shortages.

  The social, environmental and economic costs associated with this could be huge.

- Resource scarcity – this is becoming a central issue on the policy agenda for many governing bodies. The European Union is pushing for resource efficiency and trade policies that favour international open markets. In the US, the Dodd–Frank Act is forcing companies to become transparent about how they use so-called 'conflict minerals'. Producing countries are starting to protect their interests with export taxes and trade restrictions – for example, China has imposed trade barriers for some metals to protect its domestic industries.
- Urbanisation – prior to 1950 the majority of urbanisation occurred in the more economically developed countries. Rapid urbanisation took place during the period of industrialisation in Europe and North America in the 19th and early 20th centuries. Many people moved from rural to urban areas to get jobs in the rapidly expanding industries in towns and cities. Since 1950 urbanisation has slowed and now some of the biggest cities are losing population as people move away from the city to rural environments. This is known as counter-urbanisation.
- Ageing population – over the last 30 years the average life expectancy in the UK for men has risen from 69 to 79.5, while for women it has risen from 76 to 82.5. Within 20 years, it's expected that one in four UK adults will be pensioners. An ageing population has effects on healthcare, care services and pensions.
- The economy – some argue that recessions speed up the process of economic **churn**. Downturns in the economy leave boarded-up windows on the high street, but when people have less money to spend, entrepreneurs see an opportunity to give them what they want more cheaply or efficiently. Downturns may also encourage people to reinvent themselves as entrepreneurs.

Churn

A measure of the number of individuals or items moving out of a collective group over a specific period of time

LEGAL OBLIGATIONS OF A BUSINESS

It is impossible to cover in detail all the legal obligations of a business in a book such as this. Small businesses need access to a reliable source of information such as the Citizens Advice Bureau, their local Chamber of Commerce or trade organisations, while larger businesses will employ experts to ensure they are complying with all the legislation and regulations that apply to their particular organisation.

The legal structure of the organisation can have significant long-term implications for the running of the business. As we have seen earlier in this chapter (see page 128), there are three main legal structures that organisations can operate as:

- sole trader
- limited company
- partnership.

ACTIVITY

Research the reasons for the legal structure of the organisation you work in.

A sole trader arrangement is the easiest to establish, although sole traders assume significant personal risk.

Industries whose actions could result in risk to members of the public, or who deal with hazardous materials, may need a licence. A catering or hospitality business, such as a pub or restaurant, will almost certainly require a licence. Businesses will need to be licensed if they serve alcohol, and may also need to register with their local authority for food standards and health and safety oversight. There are also various licence requirements for music and entertainment.

Business owners assume a range of important health and safety responsibilities. They have a duty of care for anyone who might be affected by the business. This might include members of the public (both inside and outside the premises), employees and visitors.

HANDY HINT

Some businesses need professional indemnity insurance. If they provide a service to other companies and something goes wrong which causes them to lose money or customers, they could sue you. This is what professional indemnity insurance will protect against.

For businesses that take on staff, employers' liability insurance is a legal requirement. They run the risk of a significant fine for every day that they are uninsured, as well as being vulnerable to compensation claims from employees who suffer injury or illness as a result of their work.

Business owners also have a number of legal obligations to the taxman. These vary depending on the legal structure of the business but all have to file at least one annual return, and for businesses with staff the paperwork burden increases significantly. Companies must comply with the Companies Act 2006 and if your annual turnover exceeds the registration threshold you are legally obliged to become VAT registered. There are significant penalties for those that fail to register in time.

Organisations are bound by the Data Protection Act, which is covered in more detail in Chapter 2 (Unit 318, B&A 57), and also have legal obligations in respect of their relationships with their employees.

HEALTH AND SAFETY LEGISLATION

There is a wide range of legislation and regulation that affects health and safety in a business environment. The major piece of legislation is the Health and Safety at Work Act (HASAWA), which imposes duties on both employees and employers.

Employees must:

- work in a safe and sensible way
- use equipment safely and correctly
- report potential risks
- help identify training needs.

Employers must:

- provide a safe work area
- provide clearly defined procedures
- ensure safe handling, storage and transport of stock
- train and supervise staff in health and safety matters
- maintain safe entries and exits
- provide adequate temperature, lighting, seating etc
- ensure visitors are informed of any hazards.

EMPLOYEE-PROTECTION LEGISLATION

There are regulations to protect employees from being unfairly treated. These include:

- The Employment Relations Act – which covers among other things:
  - the recognition of trade unions
  - maternity/paternity leave and time off for dependants
  - the right to be accompanied at disciplinary and grievance hearings.
- The Employment Equality (Age) Regulations – which make it illegal to treat an employee less favourably because of their age in:
  - recruitment
  - promotion
  - terms and conditions
  - redundancy and dismissal.
- The Employment Rights Act – which includes sections on:
  - fair dismissal
  - complaints to a tribunal
  - reasonable notice
  - written contracts
  - rights to time off
  - flexible working
  - redundancy payments
  - compensation for lost earnings
  - time off for public duties, ante-natal care and training
  - dismissals related to health and safety
  - 'whistleblower' protection.

- Working Time Regulations – which impose an obligation on employers to ensure that employees:
  - work an average of no more than 48 hours per week calculated over a 17-week period including working lunches, job-related travel and time spent on business abroad
  - have an 11-hour continuous rest period between working days
  - have a continuous 24-hour period off work each week
  - have a break of 20 minutes if the day is more than six hours long.
- The Employment Act – which includes sections on:
  - paternity leave and pay
  - maternity leave and pay
  - adoption leave and pay
  - dispute resolution.
- The National Minimum Wage Act – which applies to anyone who has a contract to do work personally, other than for a customer or a client. Those working through agencies and home workers are also included. The Secretary of State can make exclusions, as has been done for au pairs and family members in a family business, among others. The hours that are used in a national minimum wage calculation do not include time when the worker is on industrial action, travelling to and from work, or absent, but a worker who is required to be awake and available for work must receive the minimum rate. This does not prevent use of 'zero hour contracts', where the worker is guaranteed no hours and is under no obligation to work.
- The Human Rights Act – adapted parts of the European Convention on Human Rights and allows workers to sue their employers for breaches of their rights, but only if that employer is a public authority. Employees are entitled to their privacy and cannot be discriminated against for any aspect of it. Employers have the right to monitor employees for health and safety or security issues but cannot do this at all times, and staff are entitled to see what is filed away about them. All public authorities have a drug misuse policy in place, but employers cannot test for drugs or alcohol without express consent, which may be given when employees signed their contract of employment. Any random testing must be genuinely random, although employers can test certain employees by virtue of their particular job, for instance if they are a driver or a heavy-machinery operator.

In addition, the Equality Act gives protection from unlawful discrimination in relation to the following protected characteristics:

- age
- disability
- gender re-assignment

- marriage and civil partnership
- pregnancy and maternity
- race
- religion and belief
- sex
- sexual orientation.

The following pieces of legislation are absorbed into the Equality Act:

- The Equal Pay Act – made it illegal to offer different pay and conditions to men and women who perform the 'same type of work', which was defined as work of equal value in terms of effort and skill.
- The Race Relations Act – made it illegal to treat employees differently because of their race, colour, nationality or ethnic origins.
- The Sex Discrimination Act – made it illegal to treat employees differently because of their gender.
- The Disability Discrimination Act – made it illegal to discriminate against disabled people in the areas of employment, access to goods, facilities and services, and management, buying or renting land or property.

BUSINESS INNOVATION AND GROWTH

Assessment criteria

This section covers assessment criteria 2.1, 2.2, 2.3, 2.4 and 2.5

Organisations change in order to grow, improve performance and, in the private sector, remain competitive. Change may be initiated by external forces beyond the control of the organisation. For example, alterations in the **demographics** of the customer base, levels of unemployment, inflation and technology can all affect the way organisations carry out their work. Failure to react to these changes will leave the organisation struggling to keep up.

Demographics

Groups of people characterised by age, income, sex, education, occupation, socio-economic group etc

Organisations themselves have a lifecycle of creation, expansion, contraction and decline. Successful organisations look for ways to extend the expansion phase and delay the contraction phase of this cycle. Extending the expansion phase may be accomplished through:

- mergers – where the organisation joins with another to create a new entity
- acquiring new companies – where the organisation absorbs another
- new ownership – where the organisation itself is taken over
- relocation of the organisation to a new site – which may be closer to customers, more efficient to operate or help create an improved image.

Changes that may initiate the contraction phase include:

- loss of revenue and rising costs
- legislative changes that affect the operation of the organisation
- economic changes that affect the purchasing power of the customers
- political changes, which particularly affect public- and voluntary sector organisations.

WHAT IS AN INNOVATION?

An innovation is a product, service or idea that is perceived by customers as new. There are different levels of innovation. Reducing the level of salt or sugar in an existing breakfast cereal is a *continuous* innovation in that it creates a small change to an existing product with little market impact, while an innovation like the personal computer, which caused great social impact, is a *discontinuous* innovation. A business with an innovative strategy uses both continuous and discontinuous innovation to stay one step ahead of the competition.

The adoption process of a new product or service begins with customer awareness, leading to trial usage and ending in regular use. Over time the adoption process resembles a bell curve, as shown in the diagram.

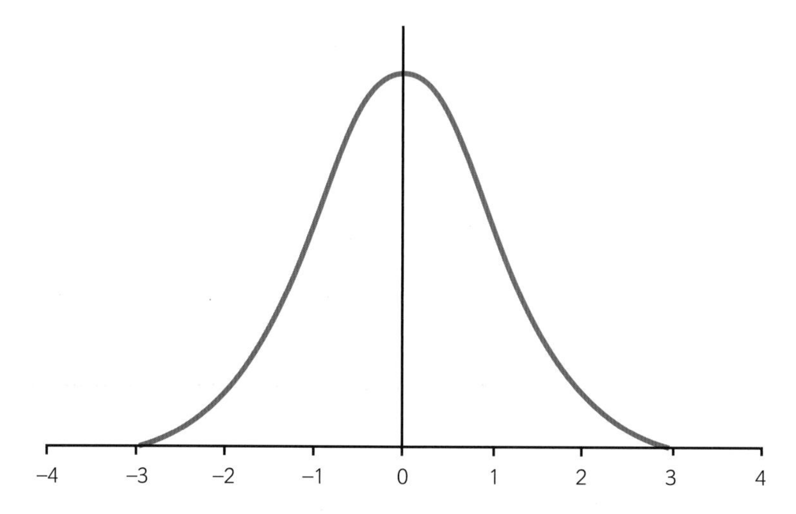

The bell curve is formed by:

- Innovators – a customer who is among the first within a market to adopt an innovation. According to the bell curve model of diffusion, innovators are the first 2.5% of the consumers in a market to adopt an innovation.
- Early adopters – customers who are among the earliest to adopt an innovation, after the innovators, and represent 13.5% of the market.

- The majority of consumers – the first part of the mass market to purchase is the 'early majority'. Although rarely leaders, these consumers usually adopt new ideas before the average person and they represent 34% of the market.
- Late adopters – the 'late majority' also represents 34% of the target market. This group of people is usually sceptical of change and will adopt an innovation only after a majority has tried it.
- Laggards – the laggards represent 16% of the target market and are the last to purchase. They are usually price conscious, suspicious of change, tradition bound and conservative by nature.

The adoption of a new product or service begins with customer awareness

Diffusion is the process by which a new product or idea attracts the attention and interest of a market and is gradually adopted by the many individuals making up that market. Unlike individual adoption decisions, diffusion is influenced by communication about a product between an ever-widening group of customers and is affected by the social dynamics of the group.

ACTIVITY

Identify a new product or service introduced by your organisation and trace its adoption process.

USING MODELS OF BUSINESS INNOVATION

There are a number of different innovation models that provide a framework for identifying the ideas most likely to create sustained growth. Characteristics to look for when deciding on an innovation model include:

- simplicity – the model should be easy to understand and use
- descriptive – there should be sufficient detail to enable explanation, comparison and/or imitation
- assessable – the model should enable measurement and the evaluation of alternatives
- predictive – when model assumptions are true, the model should provide probabilities for described outcomes
- timely – the model should provide assessments, measurements and insights that enable innovation opportunities in a timeframe that will lead to success.

Timeliness can be particularly challenging. Innovation requires decisions for change which are often resisted, so a good model should provide the information, insight and needed motivation for internal change before external changes can disrupt the company. Premature change can also be ineffective if environmental conditions are not ready to support the change being promoted. An effective model will detect environmental readiness for change adoption, enabling acceptable returns for innovation investments.

The linear innovation model can be summarised as:

Basic research → Applied research → Development → Production and diffusion

The continuing use of this model is attributed to its simplicity. Innovation research has generated additional models that attempt to address the deficiencies seen in the linear model. Attempts have been made to acknowledge sources of ideas that can help generate value, recognising that some highly successful innovations have not been the direct result of application of scientific or technology advances.

Variations of the linear model have been developed that include:

- Technology push – this has a small change from the linear model where 'marketing and sales' is added after 'production'.
- Market pull – this variant suggests that research and development is responding to a market need, resulting in this modification to the earlier model:

  Market Need → Development → Production → Sales

- The phase gate model – this modifies the linear model by recognising that there are feedback loops and time variations between steps, and establishes readiness criteria for moving between major phases of innovation development. Phase gate approaches are often represented by a funnel approach.
- The connect and develop model – developed by Procter and Gamble in the 1980s, this model addresses the increasing cost of keeping all research and development within the company, representing an example of open innovation. In this model, parts of research and development come from outside the company as a result of networking and partnerships.

Detecting the need for change, or finding new places to generate growth, can present significant challenges for any organisation. Having an innovation model that facilitates and promotes understanding of how things change could make the difference to the long-term survival of the business. An effective model:

- provides a conceptual framework and promotes innovation thought
- aids faster identification of new sources of innovation
- facilitates better timing for market introduction
- helps find innovation opportunities aligned with timeframes needed for the business
- reduces the likelihood of competitive disruption
- increases return on innovation investment
- improves ability to anticipate needed innovation
- sustains competitive advantage and enables long-term growth.

An innovation model is a key element in creating competitive advantage and is critical for sustained growth in the business environment.

Models of business innovation include:

- Reviewing systems – there are four steps in developing an innovation system:
    - review formal and informal systems and processes
    - interview key stakeholders and staff members
    - understand the requirements and resources required
    - identify the key outputs required.
- Customer value propositions – which include the benefits that a customer receives from doing business with a particular seller. This addresses not only basics such as price but also related issues such as quality of service and support, prompt delivery and the relationship that is established between the customer and the supplier.
- Innovation ecosystems – there are three main components of an organisation's innovation ecosystem; mix of innovation types, structure (process, capabilities, culture, funding), and metrics and tracking. The right mix depends on the business and their innovation needs. There are three hierarchical levels of innovation within the business innovation ecosystem:
    - Core innovation – in most businesses the largest amount of effort in terms of time and resource will be given over to ideas and innovation within this category. These are typically more incremental improvements to existing products or services to optimise the delivery, return and experience for the existing customers.
    - Adjacent innovation – innovation involves an increasing level of risk as the business moves away from the core. This type of innovation can be very complex and result in high failure rates. It can involve taking existing products to new markets or, more commonly, developing value-added products or services to existing core propositions.
    - Transformational innovation is the highest risk of all the innovation categories. It can take up a huge amount of time, even be a distraction, and often be costly. Organisations will be looking for new products and services or new markets. This type of innovation is more popular with early stage and highly innovative businesses.
- Social innovations – social innovations are new products, services and models that simultaneously meet social needs more effectively than alternatives and create new social relationships or collaborations. Social innovations meet social needs of all kinds, from working conditions and education to community development and health, to extend and strengthen civil society

- Unique selling points (USPs) – in creating a USP look at what your competitors are doing and decide how you can differentiate yourselves from them. Ask 'What do you want to be known for?
    - quality
    - value
    - service
    - selection
    - no-risk purchase
    - lifetime guarantee.

You might want to be known for all of these things yet it's important you pick one out which makes the biggest statement about your company or product and which your competitors cannot rival.

The government has schemes to help promote innovation

SUPPORT AND GUIDANCE

Support and guidance for business innovation comes in part from the UK government, which spends billions of pounds each year buying goods, works and services and uses this huge purchasing power to encourage companies to develop and advance new technology-based products and services.

UK government programmes to support business innovation are shown in the table.

Programme	Description
The Small Business Research Initiative (SBRI)	A programme that uses open competitions from government departments and public bodies to find innovative solutions to public sector problems. Winners are awarded a staged, fully funded research and development contract to develop new commercial products or services. Any organisation can submit an application to an SBRI competition, although they are especially suitable for small- to medium-sized enterprises (SMEs).
Forward Commitment **Procurement** (FCP)	This encourages the public sector organisations to engage with suppliers by providing credible information about their future requirements and purchases. It lowers the risk of failure for companies in their most risky period (between developing a product or service and selling it) which encourages them to be innovative rather than safe.

Procurement
The process of buying supplies or equipment for a government department or company

Programme	Description
Joint public–private procurement compacts	The Department for Business, Innovation & Skills (BIS) and the Prince of Wales UK Corporate Leaders Group have launched three low-carbon procurement compacts. Compacts are partnerships between government and the third sector that commit the government to be a customer of low-carbon products and services. They are an invitation to suppliers of all sizes, particularly SMEs, to seize the opportunities available. The compacts are in the areas of heat and power from renewable bio-methane, low-carbon transport, and zero-carbon catering. The initiative aims to significantly reduce UK emissions and demonstrate to other organisations that low-carbon solutions can work.
EU innovation procurement projects	The UK is a partner in a number of projects that support networks of procurers across Europe around a common theme, such as healthcare or transport. Public sector procurement is used to create markets for innovative, more-environmentally sustainable products and services while raising the quality of public services. Projects include developing demonstration pilots that test and develop the tools created and enable the spread of best practice.
UK Innovation Investment Fund	The government has invested £150 million creating the UK Innovation Investment Fund (UKIIF). They have also raised £180 million in private investment, giving the fund a total of £330 million to invest in businesses. The UKIIF is a venture capital fund that invests in growing small businesses, and new businesses working in digital, life sciences, clean technology and advanced manufacturing. Rather than investing directly in companies, the UKIIF pays into a fund that is used by venture capitalists who have the expertise to invest in business.

The Welsh government also has programmes to support innovation

Similarly, support and funding is available to businesses in Wales to encourage innovation. An integrated innovation support package is available from the Welsh government, which encourages and enables organisations to:

- invest in research and development (R&D) in order to harness the commercial opportunities of innovation and research
- work with universities and other academic institutions to exploit commercially directed research
- adopt a more focused approach, tackling the barriers to investment in R&D and innovation.

The support is delivered through a team of highly experienced innovation specialists, design managers, manufacturing managers and intellectual property specialists, all of whom have extensive industrial experience. Support can be given to assist with:

- new product development
- design and manufacturing
- managing intellectual property (IP) rights
- research and development projects
- commercialisation – access to markets
- sourcing and accessing SMART Cymru research, development and innovation (RD&I) funding from the Welsh government and other UK and European schemes.

Scottish funding comes through SMART: SCOTLAND

The Welsh government can provide financial assistance at key stages of the innovation process, including:

- for the research and development of new, technically innovative products and processes with good commercial potential
- towards preparing proposals to obtain European Framework funding for R&D
- to allow businesses and academia to travel abroad to meet potential R&D partners
- to Wales's academic institutions to facilitate closer collaboration with businesses.

In Scotland, SMEs can access grants from SMART: SCOTLAND. The grant helps organisations to undertake technical feasibility studies and R&D projects that have a commercial endpoint. A feasibility study is carried out at an early stage of an R&D project to see if the new product or process will work in the real world. The Scottish government can support up to 75% of the eligible costs. Studies must last between 6 and 18 months, and the maximum grant is £100,000. One third of the grant is paid upfront when the project starts.

Research and development projects aim to develop a pre-production prototype of a new product or process. Support is available at up to 35% of the eligible project costs. Projects must last between 6 and 36 months, and the maximum grant is £600,000. The grant is paid quarterly in arrears and minimum total project cost is £75,000.

In Northern Ireland, Invest NI is the economic development agency. Its role is to grow the economy by:

- stimulating entrepreneurial activity
- increasing exports and trade
- promoting research, development and innovation
- attracting new investment to and within Northern Ireland.

The Northern Ireland Assembly provides support through Invest NI

Invest NI offers a single point of contact for support and expert advice. It offers programmes to support business research and development, increase the commercialisation of science and ideas, and actively promote innovation, invention and knowledge exchange. Support includes:

- innovation advice
- grants for R&D
- innovation vouchers
- design service
- proof of concept fund
- venture capital funds
- technology transfer
- a collaborative R&D support service
- advice on intellectual property, patents etc
- centres of excellence.

There are also regional authorities throughout the UK that provide support and guidance for business innovation.

PRODUCT OR SERVICE DEVELOPMENT

There are seven steps involved in developing a product or service from being an idea to being a product or service that will contribute to the organisation's growth.

1. Idea generation – the first step of new product development requires gathering ideas. Many market research techniques are used to encourage ideas including running focus groups, encouraging customer comments and suggestions, and brainstorming with creative thinkers sharing ideas.
2. Screening – the ideas generated are evaluated to recognise the best options. Rough estimates are made of an idea's potential in

terms of sales, production costs, profit potential, and competitors' response if the product is introduced. Acceptable ideas move on to the next step.

3 Concept development and testing – feedback is obtained from customers, distributors and employees. Focus groups are arranged where the ideas are presented in the form of storyboards or a mock-up of the idea. Information obtained may include:
   - likes and dislikes about the concept
   - level of interest in purchasing the product
   - likely frequency of purchase
   - price points to determine how much customers would be willing to spend on the product.

4 Business analysis – at this point the process becomes very dependent on market research as efforts are made to analyse the viability of the product ideas. The key objective at this stage is to forecast market size, production costs and financial projections for sales and profits. The organisation must decide if the product will fit within their overall mission and strategy.

5 Product and marketing mix development – marketers begin to build a marketing plan for the product. The customer experiences the real product as well as other aspects of the marketing mix, such as advertising, pricing and distribution options. Favourable customer reaction helps the decision to introduce the product and also provides other valuable information, such as estimated purchase rates and understanding how the product will be used by the customer. Reaction that is less favourable may suggest the need for adjustments to elements of the marketing mix. This step is used to gauge the feasibility of large-scale, cost-effective production for manufactured products.

6 Market testing – the most common type of market testing makes the product available to a selective small segment of the target market (eg one city), which is exposed to the full marketing effort. In some cases, especially with consumer products sold at retail stores, the marketer must work hard to get the product into the test market by convincing distributors to agree to purchase and place the product on their store shelves. In more controlled test markets, distributors may be paid a fee if they agree to place the product on their shelves to allow for testing.

7 Commercialisation – if market testing displays promising results, the product is ready to be introduced to a wider market. Some firms introduce or roll-out the product in waves, with parts of the market receiving the product on different schedules. This allows the company to ramp up production in a more controlled way and to fine tune the marketing mix as the product is distributed to new areas.

THE BENEFITS, RISKS AND IMPLICATIONS OF INNOVATION

For a change that has financial implications for the organisation, there has to be a compelling business case. A business case looks at the cost of the change and weighs that against the benefits that the organisation will gain. If the benefits outweigh the costs, the return on investment (ROI) is positive and the change will be approved.

The formula for calculating return on investment is:

$$\frac{\text{Net project benefit}}{\text{Project costs}} = \text{ROI}$$

$$\text{ROI} = \frac{\text{Benefits of project} - \text{Project costs}}{\text{Project costs}} \times 100$$

In this formula:

- 'Benefit of project' is based on the project's purpose – the purpose could range from increasing sales to reducing the cost of handling customers. Organisations usually estimate that making certain changes to the business, installing new software, making processes more efficient etc will yield a particular project benefit that has a financial amount associated with it.
- 'Project costs' includes hard costs, such as hardware and software, as well as what are sometimes termed 'soft costs'. Soft costs, for example, can include items such as the salaries for the time period people are on the improvement project. Salaries are important to include because the time employees spend on the improvement project should be seen as a cost to the organisation. The longer the project takes, the longer employees will be away from their primary job, whether it is sales, marketing or manufacturing. If they are working on an improvement project, they cannot spend the same amount of time they normally would on their regular job. While the model for many accounting systems has not shifted, research shows that these so-called soft costs are actually as or more important to a project's success than the hard costs. The argument is that, as a result, these costs should no longer be termed soft costs because they have a defined, **bottom-line effect**.

The psychological impact of change, and the implications of change for the way in which staff are managed, can be viewed as a four-stage transitional model.

Bottom-line effect

The effect on the net profit or loss

STAGE 1: SHOCK AND RESISTANCE

Change can be difficult to deal with

Expected behaviours:

- Change generates resistance.
- Status quo seems preferable, even if not ideal itself.
- Fear of the unknown prevails.
- Reluctance to lose familiar rituals, practices and colleagues.
- Feelings of inadequacy emerge as people confront new roles and demands.
- Feelings of resentment at loss of old relationships and practices in imposed change.
- Status and authority seem under threat.
- Perception of rewards and opportunities of advancement under threat.
- People may 'opt out' of trying to understand.
- Evidence of resistance may show itself in the form of anger, sadness, anxiety, withdrawal, indifference, 'bloody mindedness', excessive caution, apathy, 'yearning for the past', low effort and productivity, grievances.

Management responses:

- Listen, and allow resistance and resentment to be expressed rather than be 'bottled up'. People like to be able to go home and say, '... and what's more, I told 'em so!' – they need a safety valve.
- Communicate the maximum amount of information as a counter to rumour, misinformation (deliberate or otherwise) and anxiety.
- Explain the reasons for change and allow individuals to engage in discussion about this – they need a sense of purpose.
- Seek the views and ideas of staff on implementation of change to engender 'ownership'.
- Recognise that dependency needs of individuals become greater for a while.
- Be seen by, and be close to, affected staff, offering them support, reassurance, evidence of caring, recognition of their needs and fears, recognition of their contribution.

STAGE 2: CONFUSION

Expected behaviours:

- Beginnings of acceptance having 'got it off their chests'.
- Assumption of new roles and development of new relationships will begin.
- Requests for information and clarification.
- Negative behaviour still includes fear and confusion when others are seen to be coping better and doing well out of the change; when some aspects of change are still not going very well and when pace of change reinforces perceptions of loss of control and ability to cope.
- Positive behaviour now includes seeking clarification of what is expected of the group and others; identification and expression of issues for discussion with managers and a readiness to recognise new opportunities.

Management responses:

- Continue to communicate and listen.
- Continue to involve staff as much as possible.
- Be clear about objectives – people need to see where things are going.
- Explain new work roles and clarify expectations.
- Re-state objectives and expectations at intervals for reinforcement.
- Place the highest possible emphasis on guiding and developing staff to learn new ways of doing things; form new relationships; establish new routines and acquire new knowledge and skills.
- Distinguish between attitudes and behaviour. Attitude cannot be changed to order – negative attitude can be tolerated to a degree if behaviour is consistent with the objectives of the change.
- Display clear understanding of the change and commitment to it – there cannot be a chink in your armour.
- Provide strong leadership.

STAGE 3: INTEGRATION

Expected behaviours:

- Optimism begins to replace depression.
- Job satisfaction re-emerges.
- Anxiety decreases.
- New working relationships become established.
- There is an awareness of behavioural expectations.
- A sense of competence and self-worth returns.

- More looking ahead than dwelling on the past.
- Productivity is improving.

Management responses:

- Continue to involve staff in the change process.
- Continue to communicate all possible information.
- Continue to listen.
- Continue to provide guidance and support.

STAGE 4: ACCEPTANCE

Expected behaviours:

- Contributions are being recognised.
- Individuals no longer feel threatened.
- Working relationships have been reconstructed and are largely harmonious.
- New, effective channels of communication have been established.
- Managers can once again distribute their attention between individuals, the team and the task.
- Productivity is optimal.

Management response:

- Remind yourself that any special efforts made in the first three stages now need to be sustained.

Managers are subject to the same reactions, resistances and strains. Some types of innovation, such as restructuring or downsizing, can put considerable strain on the leaders of an organisation. A major concern regarding change is the stress it imposes on those undergoing the change. Managers, because they have obligations to their staff, not only have to deal with change as employees but also need to carry some of the concerns of their staff. In the case of downsizing, the stress levels can be extremely high because the manager is charged with conveying very upsetting information.

Stress is part of the job, but in times of change it is critical that you recognise that it may cause you to act in ways that are less effective than usual. As with anything connected with change, the major concern is not short term but long term. If your stress levels result in a marked loss of effectiveness, the risk is that a vicious cycle will be set up, where ineffective leadership results in creating more long-term problems, which increases your stress, which reduces your effectiveness even more.

A common response to unpleasant change is to ignore the situation. Avoidance can take many forms. Most commonly, the avoiding manager plays only a minimal role in moving the organisation forward. After announcing the change and doing the minimum required, the manager hides from the change, through delegation or attending to other work. This tactic involves treating things as 'business as usual'.

The outcomes of this tactic can be devastating. By avoiding situations, the manager abdicates any leadership role when staff need it most, during and after significant change. In addition, the avoidance results in the manager becoming out of touch with the people and realities of the organisation. While avoidance serves a need for the manager in the short term, it destroys the manager's credibility and results in poor decisions. The long-term consequence of such action is that the organisation tends to deteriorate in terms of morale, effectiveness and productivity.

Sometimes the manager deals with change by denying its impact. Usually, the denying manager takes a very logical approach to change. Decisions get made, systems are put in place or new procedures are developed. Unfortunately, this logical approach denies the impact of change on the people in the organisation. The denying manager tends to refuse to understand 'what the big deal is' and shows little empathy with employees in the organisation. As with avoidance, the denying tactic tends to lower the manager's credibility and destroy any personal loyalty on the part of employees.

FINANCIAL MANAGEMENT

Assessment criteria

This section covers assessment criteria 3.1, 3.2 and 3.3

Viability

The long-term survival of an organisation and its ability to have sustainable profits over a period of time

The financial **viability** of an organisation is important to its investors, staff and stakeholders because it demonstrates the organisation's ability to generate sufficient income to meet its operating expenses and financial obligations, as well as providing the potential for future growth. Reviewing the current performance level and financial position of the business and considering the future will determine its financial viability.

To assess the financial viability of a business, the following questions should be asked:

- Is the business currently performing better or worse than it has in the recent past?
- Is the business generating enough income to support its needs?
- Can the business pay its creditors (people and other organisations that it owes money to) on time?
- Does the business need to borrow money to keep going?
- Could the business survive if unexpected events occurred that negatively affected sales?

- If the business is not currently profitable, do you see it becoming profitable in the future?
- How long can the business continue operating while making a loss?
- Considering all of the money, resources and effort put into operating the business, is it worthwhile continuing into the future?

COMMON MISTAKE

The organisation's bank balance does not, on its own, indicate the financial viability of the organisation.

Business owners usually acquire a general level of knowledge about running a business by operating their own venture. However, their knowledge may be limited and may not be sufficient to meet the complex needs of operating a successful business. It can be helpful to seek advice and assistance from professional advisers.

Professional business advisers work with their clients' businesses to provide specialised skills and knowledge in specific aspects of business operation. They also help ensure that all the business's obligations, requirements and entitlements are being met, and can help them obtain and manage their financial resources.

Professional advisers include:

- Accountants – offer advice and services on business planning, record keeping, preparation of financial statements, taxation compliance, estimating financial projections and determining future funding requirements.
- Bankers – provide advice and assistance on loan facilities, loan products, loan applications, cash flow management, risk management, money management, investment options etc.
- Solicitors/lawyers – offer legal services relating to issues such as contracts, leases, taxation, disputes, litigation, intellectual property, debt recovery etc.
- Insurance brokers – give advice on risk identification, risk assessment, risk minimisation, cost-effective insurance options, lodging insurance claims etc.
- Financial planners – help with developing financial strategies, tax planning, retirement planning and investment advice.
- Management consultants – advise on areas including human resource management, training, marketing and operations.

ACTIVITY

List the financial advisers used by your organisation and the contribution they make to the management of the organisation.

In addition to these professional business advisers, advice can be obtained from government agencies and advisory services. Many provide free information and assistance covering a range of business issues including business planning, finance, marketing, employment, legal and regulatory compliance etc.

Studies overwhelmingly identify bad financial management planning as the leading cause of business failure. All too often, management is so caught up in the day-to-day tasks of getting the product out the door and struggling to collect payments to meet the payroll that they do not plan. Often managers understand their products but not the financial statements or the bookkeeping records. Success is achieved only by focusing on all factors affecting a business's performance. Focusing on financial management is essential to the survival of the business.

Growth can be funded in only two ways: with profits or by borrowing. If expansion exceeds the capital available to support higher levels of debtors, stock, fixed assets and operating expenses (see the next section on *Financial terms* for definitions), a business's development will be slowed or stopped entirely by its failure to meet debts as they become payable. This can lead to insolvency, which will result in the business's assets being liquidated (sold off) to meet the demands of the creditors. The only way to avoid this is by planning to control growth.

After projecting reasonable sales volumes and profitability, management should use a cash flow budget to decide how these projected sales volumes translate into the flow of cash in and out of the business during normal operations. Where additional stock, equipment or other physical assets are necessary to support the sales forecast, it must be determined whether or not the business will still generate enough profit to sustain the growth forecast.

Often, businesses simply grow too rapidly for internally generated cash to support the growth. If profits are inadequate to fund the growth forecast, the business must either make arrangements to borrow working growth capital or slow down its growth to allow internal cash to catch up and keep pace with the expansion. This need must be anticipated well in advance to avoid interrupting the business's operations.

Insolvency results in the business's assets being sold off to meet the demands of creditors

FINANCIAL TERMS

It is useful to understand financial terminology:

Accruals income or expenditure that was due in an accounting period but was not received or paid by the end of the period.

Acid test a company's ability to pay its short-term debts.

Asset anything owned by the company that has a monetary value.

Asset turnover a measure of operational efficiency that shows how much revenue is produced per £ of assets available to the business.

Audit an independent assessment of the finances of the organisation by a qualified person.

Balance sheet one of the three essential measurement reports for the performance and health of a company, along with the *profit and loss account* and the *cash flow statement*. The balance sheet is a 'snapshot' in time of who owns what in the company, and what assets and debts represent the value of the company. The balance sheet equation is basically: capital + liabilities = assets.

Bank reconciliation a method of confirming that an organisation's accounting records agree with those of the bank as shown in the bank statement.

Break-even point in time or in number of units sold when forecasted revenue exactly equals the estimated total costs, where loss ends and profit begins.

Budget an amount of money that it is planned to be spent on a particularly activity or resource, usually over a trading year, although budgets can also apply to shorter and longer periods. An overall organisational plan contains budgets within it for all the different departments and the costs held by them.

Capital employed the value of all the resources available to the company, typically comprising share capital, retained profits and reserves, long-term loans and deferred taxation. In other words, this is the total long-term funds invested in or lent to the business and used by it to carry out its operations.

Capital gain the amount by which an asset's selling price exceeds its initial purchase price. For most investments sold at a profit, capital gains tax is payable.

Cash flow the movement of cash in and out of a business from day-to-day direct trading and other non-trading or indirect effects, such as capital expenditure, tax and dividend payments.

Cash flow statement one of the three essential reporting and measurement systems for any company. The cash flow statement provides a third perspective alongside the *profit and loss account* and *balance sheet*, and shows the movement and availability of cash through and to the business over a given period.

Cost of debt ratio the amount of interest charged on a debt over a given period, expressed as a percentage of the average outstanding debt over the same period, or the cost of interest divided by the average outstanding debt.

Cost of goods sold (COGS) the directly attributable costs of products or services sold, usually comprised of materials, labour and direct production costs. Sales COGS = gross profit. Effectively the same as cost of sales (COS).

Cost of sales (COS) cost of sales is the value, at cost, of the goods or services sold during the period in question, usually the financial year. Uses the formula: opening stock + stock purchased closing stock.

Creditor a person to whom money is owed by a debtor; someone to whom an obligation exists.

Current assets cash and anything that is expected to be converted into cash within 12 months of the balance sheet date.

Current ratio the relationship between current assets and current liabilities, indicating the liquidity of a business, ie its ability to meet its short-term obligations. Also referred to as the *liquidity ratio*.

Current liabilities money owed by the business that is generally due for payment within 12 months of the balance sheet date, for instance creditors, bank overdraft and taxes.

Debtor another person or organisation that owes your organisation money; someone who has the obligation of paying a debt.

Depreciation the sharing of the cost of a large capital item over an agreed period, based on its life expectancy or when it is expected to be out of date. For example, a piece of equipment costing £10,000 and with a life of five years might be depreciated over five years at a cost of £2,000 per year.

Dividend a payment made per share by a company to its shareholders, based on the profits of the year but not necessarily all the profits, arrived at by the directors and voted on at the company's annual general meeting.

Equity the remaining value or interest of investors in assets after all liabilities are paid.

Expenditure money spent in generating sales or in maintaining an asset.

Fixed assets assets held for use by the business rather than for sale or conversion into cash, for instance fixtures and fittings, equipment and buildings.

Fixed cost a cost that does not vary with changing sales or production volumes, for instance building lease costs, permanent staff wages, rates and depreciation of capital assets.

Gearing the ratio of debt to equity, usually the relationship between long-term borrowings and shareholders' funds.

Goodwill any extra money paid when acquiring a company that exceeds that company's net tangible assets value.

Gross profit or loss sales less cost of goods or services sold.

Income the monetary payment received for goods or services, or from other sources such as rents or investments.

Liabilities general term for what the business owes. Liabilities are long-term loans of the type used to finance the business and short-term debts or money owing as a result of trading activities.

Liquidity ratio indicates the company's ability to pay its short-term debts by measuring the relationship between current assets against the short-term debt value. Uses the formula: current assets ÷ current liabilities.

National Insurance compulsory state-run social security scheme based on contributions from employees and employers. It provides medical and financial assistance, including pensions, to people who are ill, retired or unemployed.

Net assets (also called *total net assets*) total assets, fixed and current, minus current liabilities and long-term liabilities that have not been **capitalised**, for instance short-term loans.

Net current assets current assets minus current liabilities.

Net profit or loss profit or loss after deducting all operating expenses. This contrasts with the term *gross profit or loss* which normally refers to the difference between sales and direct costs of the product or service sold.

Operating expense any expense incurred in running a business, such as in sales and administration, as opposed to an expense incurred in production.

Overhead an expense that cannot be attributed to any one single part of the company's activities.

Profit and loss account *(P&L)* one of the three principal business reporting and measuring tools, along with the *balance sheet* and the *cash flow statement*. The P&L is essentially a trading account for a period, usually a year, which shows profit performance.

Reserves the accumulated and retained difference between profits and losses year on year since the company's formation.

Return on capital employed (*ROCE*) a percentage figure representing profit before interest against the money that is invested in the business. Calculated as: profit before interest and tax ÷ divided by capital employed × 100.

Revenue the income generated from the sale of goods or services, or any other use of capital or assets, associated with the main operations of an organisation before any costs or expenses are deducted.

Share capital the balance sheet's nominal value paid into the company by shareholders at the time the shares were issued.

Shareholders' funds a measure of the shareholders' total interest in the company represented by the total share capital + reserves.

Turnover annual sales volume net of all discounts and taxes.

Value added tax (VAT) a consumption tax that is applied at each stage of production based on the value added to the product at that stage.

Variable cost a cost that varies with sales or operational volumes, for instance materials, fuel and commission payments.

Working capital current assets less current liabilities, representing the required investment continually circulating to finance stock, debtors and work in progress.

Assessment criteria

This section covers assessment criteria 4.1 and 4.2

Capitalised

An asset that is regarded as a capital asset when determining Income Tax liability

ACTIVITY

Relate the financial terms listed to activities within your own organisation.

BUSINESS BUDGETING

There are three types of budget produced in most organisations: master budgets, capital budgets and operational budgets.

MASTER BUDGETS

The master budget is a one-year budget planning document covering all other budgets. It coincides with the financial year of the firm and may be broken down into quarters and into months. If the master budget is to be an ongoing document, rolling from year to year, then normally a month is added to the end of the budget to facilitate planning. This is called continuous budgeting.

The master budget is a comprehensive budget planning document. It usually has two parts, the operating budget and the capital budget. The operating budget shows the income-generating activities of the firm, including revenues and expenses. The capital budget shows the inflows and outflows of cash and other elements of the firm's financial position.

CAPITAL BUDGETS

Capital budgeting is used to decide whether or not an investment is worthwhile. Organisations may have several opportunities to use their available capital and must measure the potential of each opportunity before choosing between them. They might be trying to decide whether to buy new equipment to expand production on an existing product, or whether to invest in research and development for a new product.

The three main methods of taking this measurement are:

- Internal rate of return (IRR) – this is a percentage used to compare a capital investment against other kinds of investment. Dividing the expected profit by the expected expenditure will calculate a percentage of return. The organisation will look at their other projects and determine its own minimum acceptable percentage of return, or its 'hurdle rate'. If the IRR is higher than the hurdle rate, the project is worth pursuing.
- Net present value (NPV) – this method determines how much cash will flow in as a result of the investment and compares that against the cash that will flow out in order to make the investment. Using this method, organisations also take into account the present and future value of money. Because of inflation, money earned in the future is worth less than the same amount of money would be today. Therefore, NPV calculates all of the inflows and outflows over time, takes inflation and foreign exchange rates into account, and calculates the final benefit to the organisation.

- Payback period – this method calculates how long it will take to recover the investment in a project. If it will take one year to make back the investment from revenues from a new product, the payback period is '1'. The payback period method is out-dated and falling into disuse because it has some significant drawbacks. It doesn't take into account the time value of money, and tends to favour products that make most of their money up front rather than those that build momentum and can produce cash inflows over a longer period.

In reality, most organisations use more than one technique to help them with capital budgeting decisions. There are a number of minor methods, such as profitability index and sensitivity analysis, that can also be employed when making decisions. Since each method looks at the investment from a different perspective, it is best to employ multiple analyses and take the opportunities that all the techniques show has the best return.

OPERATIONAL BUDGETS

An operational budget gives a picture of where a business is currently and where it expects to be in the near future

The operational budget gives a clear financial picture of where the business is currently and where it expects to be in twelve months' time, through financial forecasts and details of investment in the business. It translates aims and objectives into financial terms so that the business can manage its financial resources effectively and meet its legal requirements in terms of accounting and tax.

Operational budgets provide a framework for responsibility and control by considering growth areas, competitors, cash flow and profit. They are usually created annually and give organisations:

- sound financial information
- greater focus
- ability to anticipate problems
- confidence in decision making.

There are four key steps in developing an operational budget:

1. Use historical information – collect all the historical information that is available on income and expenditure as this is an indication of likely future income and expenditure. It is only a guide, however, as you will need to take into account known variables such as sales plans and changes in the competitive environment.
2. Create a realistic budget – work out the relationship between variable costs and income and use the organisation's income forecast to estimate variable costs. Estimation provides as accurate a forecast as possible. Estimating each item line-by-line encourages consideration of all costs, potential variables and past experience, and allows for inflation and contingencies. Look at essential and

COMMON MISTAKE

It is a very inaccurate method of budgeting to simply add a percentage to all the previous year's figures.

non-essential expenses and the sources of best value for money. Timescales, priorities and financial resources must be balanced against each other in order to create a realistic budget that contains enough information to monitor income, costs and working capital.

3 Agree the format – agree with users of the budget a format that meets their needs and allows clear communication. The budget categories should allow for responsibilities and authority to be understood and facilitate co-ordination of effort, monitoring, control and feedback.

4 Involve other people – ask people with financial responsibilities within the organisation for estimates of their income and expenditure. Balance their estimates with yours and create an overall budget. If their combined estimates allow you to create a satisfactory overall budget, the job is done. Almost inevitably, there will be either too little income or too much expenditure in their combined estimates. It will be necessary to identify the key or limiting factor, negotiating with the budget holders to identify their needs and most effectively meet organisational objectives. Agreement must include agreeing the responsibilities and accountabilities of all involved. This will encourage acceptance of the budget which will ensure smooth implementation.

ACTIVITY

Create a budget for an area of your work and check it with the person responsible for creating the actual budget.

MONITORING BUDGETS

Having agreed a budget, it is important to monitor actual results against that budget in order to identify **variances** and take any necessary action. There are two areas to monitor:

- Income – compare actual income with the budget. Analyse the reasons for any shortfall, for instance low sales volumes or underperforming products. Look at any over performance; were targets unduly pessimistic? Look at the **phasing** of the budget; were seasonal variations (eg peaks and troughs in sales throughout the year) accurately budgeted for?
- Expenditure – fixed costs should be in line with budget. Variable costs should **fluctuate** in line with income. Analyse any reasons for changes in the relationship between variable costs and income. Look at the phasing of the budget; were suppliers' payment terms accurately accounted for?

Variance

A difference between two or more things

Phasing

Any distinct or characteristic period or stage within a sequence of events

Fluctuate

To change often from high to low levels or from one thing to another

It is important to understand variance when looking at budgets. A variance arises when there is a difference between actual and budget figures. Variances can be:

- Positive/favourable (better than expected) – this might mean that costs were lower than expected in the budget or revenue/profits were higher than expected.
- Adverse/unfavourable (worse than expected) – this might arise because costs were higher than expected or revenue/profits were lower than expected.

Variances may be a matter of concern, even though a budget is just an estimate of what is going to happen. The significance of a variance will depend on:

- whether it is positive or negative – adverse variances (negative) should be of more concern
- whether it was foreseeable
- how big the variance was in money terms and in percentage terms
- the cause of the variance
- whether it is a temporary problem or the result of a long-term trend.

Monitoring the budget allows budget holders to improve efficiency and develop an awareness of the impact of their decisions on other areas and associated activities. Budgets may need to be revised as a result of internal and external factors, such as new product development, industrial relations, inflation, recession, growth and employment, legislative and political factors. Budgets may also need to be revised as a result of errors in their preparation.

SALES AND MARKETING

Assessment criteria

This section covers assessment criteria 5.1, 5.2, 5.3, 5.4 and 5.5

THE PRINCIPLES OF MARKETING

Market segmentation is a central principle of marketing and an organisation's approach to segmentation will directly affect their success.

A market segment is an identifiable group of individuals, families, businesses or organisations that share one or more characteristic or need. Market segments generally respond in a predictable manner to a marketing or promotion offer. Common market segments include:

ACTIVITY

Find out what market segmenting your organisation carries out. How does this affect the products and services offered?

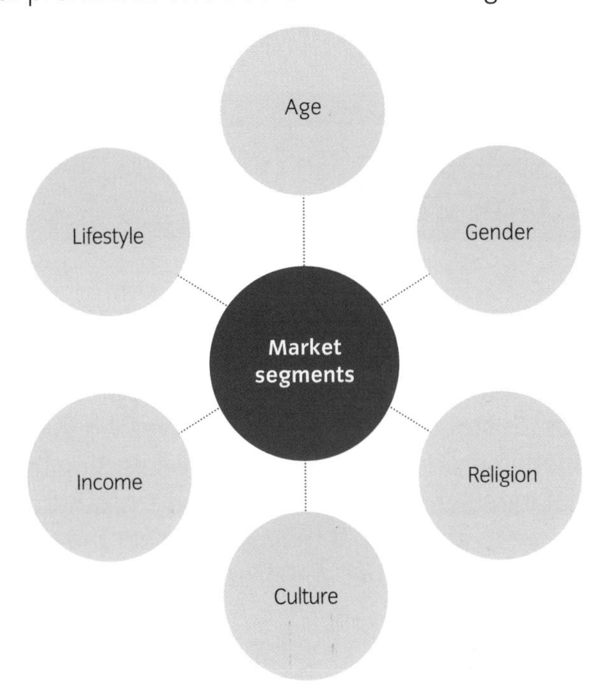

The market segmentation process involves six distinct steps:

1 Define the boundaries of the market. A formal business plan is used to develop a broad definition of the organisation's business, and the offerings of both direct and indirect competitors are used to gain information about the basic needs of consumers in the market.

2 Decide which variables to use in segmenting the market. Organisations use their knowledge of the market to select a few relevant variables in advance. This approach is generally less expensive and will likely provide more useful resources.

3 Collect and analyse data, which involves applying market research tools to identify market segments that are internally the same (ie similar customers), yet are distinctly different from other segments.

4 Develop a detailed profile of each market segment, which involves selecting those variables that are most closely related to consumers' actual buying behaviour.

5 Decide which segment or segments to target. Organisations look for customers with unsatisfied wants and needs that match the organisation and its resources. They consider the size and potential profitability of a market segment and whether the organisation can meet the needs of that segment better than its competitors.

6 Develop a product and marketing plan that will appeal to the selected market segment. This involves identifying the product features that are most important to consumers in the segment, and developing a marketing strategy that will attract their attention.

Customers are often prepared to pay more for a product that meets their needs better than a competing product. Small businesses in particular may find that market segmentation helps them compete with larger firms. Customers segment themselves when choosing between competing products and services by selecting the proposition that meets their needs better than any other. Therefore, organisations have to ensure that their offers meet the needs of customers better than any other and provide better value for money.

CUSTOMER CLASSIFICATIONS

As well as market segments, organisations have to consider customer classifications. The simplest classification is into 'business customers' and 'consumers'. The biggest differences between marketing to business customers and marketing to consumers are the types of goods and services being marketed and the types of people the goods and services are being marketed to.

Marketing to businesses is different than marketing to consumers, although many of the techniques, such as branding, can be transferred successfully. In particular, business-to-business (B2B) markets are more focused on customer relationships.

When marketing directly to consumers:	When marketing to businesses:
• Every customer has equal value and represents a small % of revenue.	• There are a small number of big customers that account for a large % of revenue.
• Sales are made remotely, the manufacturer doesn't meet the customer.	• Sales are made personally, and the manufacturer gets to know the customer
• Products are the same for all customers. The service element is low.	• Products are customised for different customers. Service is highly valued.
• Purchases are made for personal use, so image is important for its own sake.	• Purchases are made for others to use, so image is important only where it adds value to customers.
• The purchaser is normally the user.	• The purchaser is normally a third-party; someone further down the supply chain is the end user.
• Costs are restricted to purchase costs.	• Purchase costs may be a small part of the total costs of use.
• The purchase event is not subject to tender and negotiation.	• The purchase event is conducted professionally and includes tender and negotiation.
• The exchange is a one-off transaction. There is no long-term relationship.	• The exchange is often one of strategic intent, with the potential for long-term value.

For both consumer and B2B markets, the basis of marketing is to know your customers. However, in consumer markets the customer is remote, at arm's length from the seller, and consequently organisations use mass communication and distribution tools. In B2B markets the customer is much closer. The selling organisation has far more knowledge of the customer through personal contacts, although this knowledge is typically ad hoc in nature and may be only partial.

THE MARKETING MIX

An important marketing principle, whether selling to consumers or businesses, is the marketing mix. Often known as 'the 7 Ps', the marketing mix includes:

- People – it's important to find out if there are enough people demanding a product or service.
- Product – it's important to have the right products for the targeted market.
- Price – this is an area where organisations have to be careful and aware of what their target market might actually be willing to pay.
- Promotion – can include several components. How an organisation goes about promotion will depend on its budget, the message they want to communicate and the group of customers they are targeting.
- Place – approximately a fifth of the cost of a product goes on getting it to the customer. 'Place' is concerned with various methods of transporting and storing goods, and then making them available to the customer.
- Process – this refers to the process by which the organisation gets paid and delivers their products. For most digital products this is all done online, while physical products or services might require the use of a distribution company.
- Physical evidence – this relates to how the organisation and its products are presented in the market place. A strong brand image helps to increase sales and retain customers.

Some marketing theories have extended this list to become '9 Ps':

- product
- price
- promotion
- place
- people
- process
- physical evidence
- planning
- presentation.

For a consumer market, the elements of the marketing mix that are of greatest importance to customers are the product and its price. Industrial markets often require a slightly different marketing strategy and mix. In particular, a business may have to focus on a relatively small number of potential buyers while consumer marketing tends to be aimed at the mass market, in some cases with many millions of potential customers.

For B2B markets, although product quality is important, this has to be matched by delivering the product when it is needed, account service and support, and flexibility in the relationship. These supply chain elements may be more important to winning orders than having a perfect product, because supply chain problems create additional costs for the customer.

THE SELLING PROCESS

Every sale, regardless of the product or service involved, follows approximately the same sequence. The characteristics and stages of the sales cycle are:

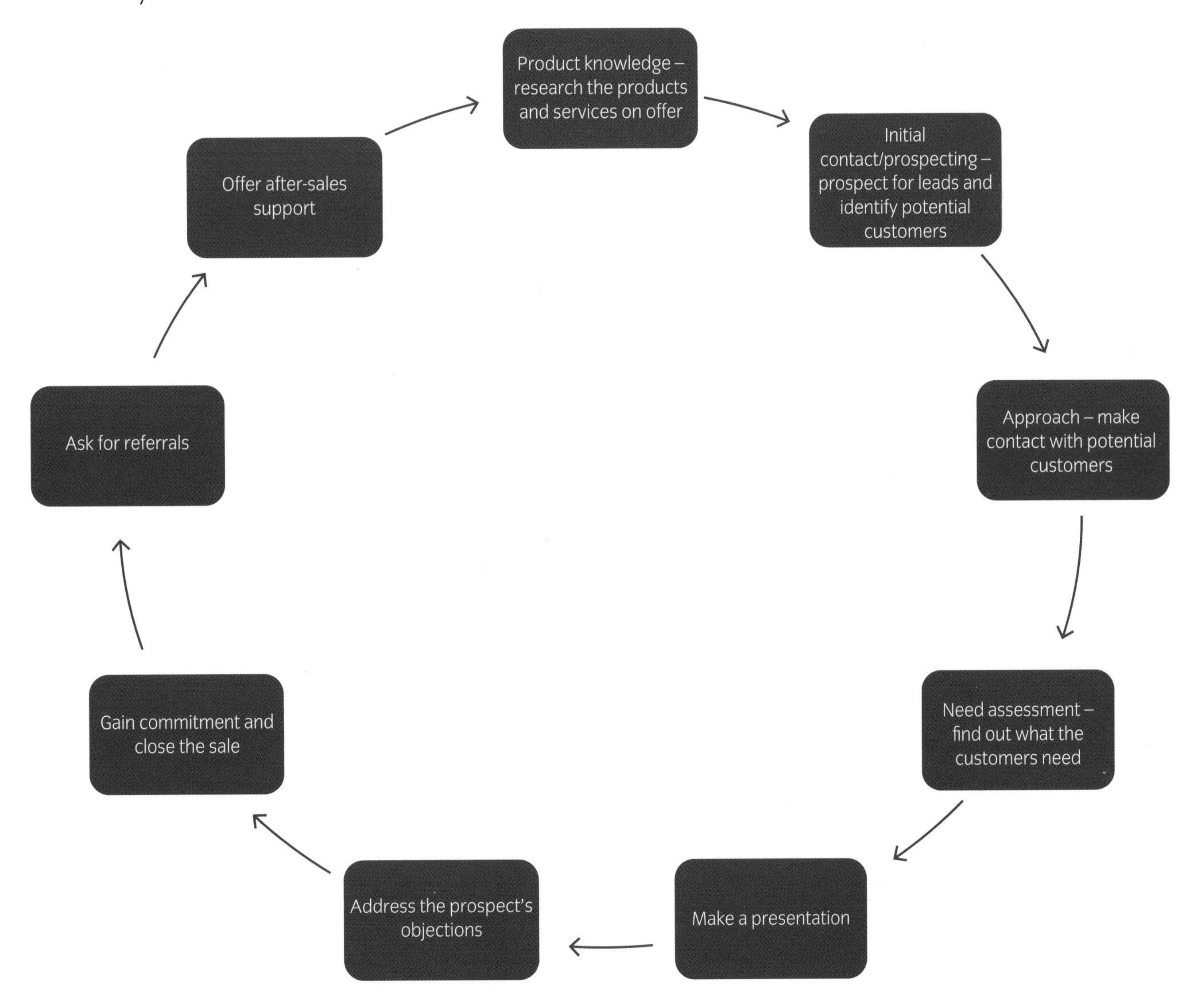

Many salespeople prefer to make their initial contact over the phone, but they may also call in person or send emails or sales letters. They can then 'qualify' the prospect, which means confirming that they are both able and potentially willing to buy the product.

A salesperson may make their initial approach in person

HANDY HINT

Finding leads is the basis of making sales. If there is no one to sell to, there are not going to be many sales.

A little pre-prospecting work will help to come up with leads that are compatible with your products or services. A salesperson who has been selling the same products for a while will probably have an idea of what to look for based on successful sales from the past. Someone new to sales or to the particular product may need to talk with their colleagues. That might include other salespeople, the sales manager and even people in other departments, such as customer service and marketing.

When making a presentation, remind yourself that you have a fantastic product or service that will make a great improvement to your customers' lives or work. This is the core of every sales cycle, and it's where you should spend the most preparation time. Keep in mind that you're not just selling your product, you are also selling yourself. You represent your company, so appearance counts. You're about to give the prospect an enormous gift by telling them about this wonderful product. Then make sure that energy and enthusiasm comes across in your tone of voice.

People are most comfortable dealing with other people who are like them. Jot down a few words or phrases that your prospect uses and work them into your pitch. Try to match their volume, speed and tone of voice as well, without taking it to the point of caricature. Studies show that a person's favourite word is their own name. As soon as the prospect tells you his or her name, write it down and then use it at least three times during the presentation.

Benefits sell because they inspire emotion in the prospect, happy feelings about your product or bad feelings about not having it. Storytelling is very effective so add an anecdote or two about your customers and how your product improved their lives. Offer the prospect something useful regardless of whether or not they buy your product. This can range from a free sample to a no-strings-attached trial period. Giving something valuable to your prospect creates the feeling that they 'owe' you.

If your prospect raises an objection, the fact that they're talking about their concern means that they're giving you a chance to answer it. Someone completely uninterested in buying your product won't bother to object, they'll just sit through your presentation in silence and then send you away.

To resolve your prospect's objections:

- Listen to the objection – give the prospect a chance to explain exactly what's bothering them. Don't tune them out, but listen: you can pick up some really valuable clues from the way a prospect phrases their objection.
- Say it back to the prospect – when you're absolutely sure the prospect has finished speaking, repeat the gist of what they said. This both shows that you were listening and gives them a chance to clarify.

- Explore the reasoning – sometimes the first objections aren't the prospect's real concern. For example, many prospects don't want to admit that they don't have enough money to buy your product, so they'll raise other objections instead. Before you launch into answering an objection, ask a few exploratory questions.
- Answer the objection – once you understand the objection completely, you can answer it. When a customer raises an objection, they're actually expressing a fear. Your task at this point is to relieve their fears. If you have specific examples, such as a story from an existing customer or a few statistics, try presenting these as hard facts make your response stronger.
- Check back with the prospect – take a moment to confirm that you've answered the prospect's objection fully. Usually this is as simple as saying, 'Does that make sense?' or 'Have I answered your concern?'
- Re-direct the conversation – bring the prospect back into the flow of the appointment. If you're in the middle of your presentation when the prospect raises their objection, then once you've answered it quickly summarise what you'd been talking about before you move on. If you've finished your pitch, check if the prospect has any other objections, and then start closing the sale.

Once you've made your presentation and answered your prospect's questions and objections, it's time to ask for the sale. Practise several different closes so that you can match the close to the prospect. Basic closes are fairly simple to implement and will work on a wide range of prospects. If you presented the product well and responded to the prospect's objections, the close follows naturally.

USING MARKET RESEARCH

In order to accurately segment the organisation's potential market, it is important to collect valid and reliable marketing data. Whether an organisation wants to enter the market with a new product, increase the market base of an existing product or give a unique offering to customers, they will carry out market research. This provides the right direction to ensure the customer base is satisfied with the organisation and that the organisation knows which plans and features need to be adopted to retain or expand its customer base.

Market research is a systematic collection of information using questionnaires and other methods designed to collect the required information. The information collected must be useful and collected by a system that can bring the right results. Market research can be connected to existing markets (to help develop marketing strategies) or potential markets (to find a potential product that the market needs). Large organisations have continuous market research activities so that they know what new potential markets can open up.

Market researchers may conduct interviews to collect data

ACTIVITY

List the sources of research used to carry out market research in your organisation. Divide them into primary and secondary sources.

Data may be collected using mail, telephone interviews, the internet and/or shopper interviews. It may be collected using primary or secondary sources, and may produce quantitative or qualitative data. Detailed descriptions of these can be found in Chapter 9 (Unit 332, B&A 61).

Having collected the data, organisations analyse it to find out what actions need to be implemented. If market research shows that the customer is price sensitive, the organisation may lower the price, or bring a lower-priced variant to the market. On the other hand, if brand recognition of the product is low, the organisation may need to invest in advertising and brand-building activities to increase brand recognition and get higher **margins**.

Margin

Net income divided by revenue, or net profit divided by sales

THE VALUE OF A BRAND

A brand is a name, phrase, sign, symbol or design (or a combination of them) intended to identify the goods and services of the organisation and to differentiate them from those of other sellers. Branding is not about getting your target market to choose you over the competition, but it is about getting your prospective customers to see you as the only one that provides a solution to their problem. The organisation's brand lives in the hearts and minds of its customers, clients and prospects. It is the sum total of their experiences and perceptions, some of which can be influenced and some of which cannot.

A good brand will:

- deliver the message clearly
- confirm your credibility
- motivate the buyer
- concrete user loyalty.

To succeed in branding, an organisation must understand the needs and wants of its customers and prospects. They do this by integrating their brand strategies into every point of public contact.

A strong brand is invaluable as the battle for customers intensifies day by day. It's important to spend time investing in researching, defining and building the brand. The brand is the source of a promise to your consumer. It's a basic piece of the organisation's marketing communication and one they wouldn't want to be without. Coherent branding will involve the organisation's logo, the campaign name, the key message, a strong design and recognition.

An organisation's reputation is related to its brand. Its reputation is also intangible and encompasses all areas of the organisation, because every action taken affects it. However, there are key differences. Brand success depends on demand, while reputation success depends on managing expectations, which include the brand but also extend to the whole business. A winning reputation and a winning brand can go hand in hand; a strong brand supports a strong reputation by creating a foundation for the things that people admire in companies. At the same time, relying solely on one's reputation, and favouring it over the brand, is risky. It is a bad idea to rely on accumulated brand strength when other mistakes threaten to damage the organisation's reputation. Reputation and brand are closely related but distinct assets. Each requires careful supervision if their potential is to be fully realised.

ACTIVITY

Make a list of 10 famous brands. How do the organisations use their brand to increase sales of their products?

THE RELATIONSHIP BETWEEN SALES AND MARKETING

Larger organisations that rely heavily on sales and meeting important sales targets often make sales a separate department from marketing, with the result that sales people are managed by people who understand and support sales. The sales department will have a manager to liaise with other parts of the company to ensure smooth co-operation and support of sales. In this environment, companies often see stronger sales results.

However, instead of making sales a separate department, many other businesses attach a sales force to another department. For example, a department that is in charge of a particular line of products may include everyone from managers to designers to salespeople. Making salespeople part of the unit ties them in to the information, the concepts and the team's success, which can drive them to hit targets and objectives. The downside can be that salespeople are then managed by departmental managers who aren't likely to have sales experience, and may or may not support salespeople in the ways that they need.

The role and responsibilities of sales personnel will vary from organisation to organisation, but a typical job description would be:

- Responsible for all sales activities, from lead generation to close, within an assigned territory. Develops and implements agreed marketing plan which will meet both personal and business goals of expanding customer base in the marketing area.
- Works within the sales and support teams for the achievement of customer satisfaction, revenue generation and long-term account goals, in line with company vision and values.
- Demonstrates technical selling skills and product knowledge in all relevant areas to enable the effective presentation of the organisation's products and services.

- Develops annual business plan in conjunction with the sales manager, detailing activities to follow during the year that will focus on meeting or exceeding sales quota.
- Has complete understanding of pricing and proposal models.
- Demonstrates the ability to carry on a business conversation with business owners and decision makers.
- Maximises all opportunities in the process of closing a sale, resulting in the taking of market share from larger competitors.
- Sells consultatively and makes recommendations to prospects and clients about the various solutions the organisation offers.
- Develops a database of qualified leads through referrals, telephone canvassing, face-to-face cold calling on business owners, direct mail, email and networking.
- Assists in implementing the organisation's marketing plans, as needed.
- Responsible for sourcing and developing client relationships and referrals.
- Responsible for identifying and building effective networks to maximise revenue.
- Demonstrates the ability to gather and submit detailed business information.
- Maintains accurate records of all sales and prospecting activities, including sales calls, presentations, closed sales and follow-up activities within their assigned territory.
- Adheres to all policies, procedures and business ethics codes, and ensures that they are communicated and implemented within the team.
- Participates in and contributes to the development of products and services offered to clients and prospects.
- Maintains contact with all clients in the market area to ensure high levels of client satisfaction.
- Demonstrates ability to interact and co-operate with all company employees.
- Builds trust, values others, communicates effectively, drives execution, fosters innovation, focuses on the customer, collaborates with others, solves problems creatively and demonstrates high integrity.
- Maintains professional internal and external relationships that meet company core values.
- Proactively establishes and maintains effective working team relationships with all support departments.

The role and responsibilities of marketing personnel also vary from organisation to organisation, but a typical job description would be:

- Contributes to and develops integrated marketing campaigns.
- Liaises and networks with a range of stakeholders, including customers, colleagues, suppliers and partner organisations.
- Communicates with target audiences and manages customer relationships.
- Sources advertising opportunities and places adverts in the press – local, regional, national and specialist publications – or on the radio, depending on the organisation and the campaign.
- Manages production of marketing materials, including leaflets, posters, flyers, newsletters, e-newsletters and DVDs.
- Writes and proofreads copy.
- Liaises with designers and printers.
- Organises photo shoots.
- Arranges for the effective distribution of marketing materials.
- Maintains and updates customer databases.
- Organises and attends events such as conferences, seminars, receptions and exhibitions.
- Sources and secures sponsorship.
- Conducts market research, such as customer questionnaires and focus groups.
- Contributes to and develops marketing plans and strategies.
- Manages budgets.
- Evaluates marketing campaigns.
- Monitors competitor activity.
- Supports the marketing manager and other colleagues.

The marketing team will develop integrated marketing campaigns

COMMON MISTAKE

In many organisations there is an unseen separation between the sales department and the marketing department.

Large amounts of money might be spent by the organisation on customer surveys to identify the people that it should be targeting in terms of its marketing strategy. However, this information often already exists and is held by the sales team. The data that is held by the sales team is generally more effective than that gathered by the marketing team through traditional methods.

When information is retained about the entire sales process, it is possible for a marketing department to go back and analyse what is working and what is not. Using this overlap between the sales and marketing departments, it is possible to identify whether or not a particular demographic is more likely to purchase a particular product. It is also possible to uncover what marketing strategies have resulted in clients making initial contact with the company. A marketing department can subsequently use this information to establish more productive marketing procedures.

Certain products may have a shorter period of time between the initial client contact and the eventual conversion. It is possible to accidentally overlook certain clients that tend to have a longer-term conversion period. This is an area where information from the sales team can be fed back to marketing, making it possible to identify those customers that have longer conversion periods and potentially complete a sale more quickly.

If the marketing department is left on its own to try and identify clients and tempt them to make contact with the company, it can potentially spend a large amount of money doing this. A large part of a marketing budget is the research that goes into what type of demographic will be interested in that particular product. When this information is already available from a sales team, it can be obtained at no cost.

Integrating the sales and marketing teams allows an organisation to have a much better understanding of its client base and increase its ability to reach out to new clients. There can, however, still be friction between the two functions. Sales may feel that marketing does not deliver enough leads and the leads they do deliver are poor, while marketing may feel that sales does not follow up on the leads delivered to them. To reduce this friction, sales and marketing functions need to agree on:

- The definition of a 'qualified lead' – the clearer both departments are on what leads are the right leads for the sales department, the less friction there will be. Use statistical analysis to determine what are the right leads.
- The number of qualified leads that marketing will deliver to sales – have weekly lead number targets by territory and type of lead so that the sales department can work more smoothly.
- The process that the sales department will use to follow up on the leads – proper follow-up is required to maximise the value of the leads, so agreeing on the follow-up and making sure that it is accomplished is key.
- Marketing should be rewarded for delivering leads that result in sales, not just for producing any leads – they should have a stake in the end result
- The marketing team should think of its task as to help acquire and retain customers – building visibility, generating leads or establishing a brand identity may be part of the process, but it is not all of it.

A marketing department can have difficulty understanding how successful a particular campaign has been. In an organisation where the sales and marketing departments are working collaboratively, it is possible to get quantitative measures about who has been responding to the particular marketing strategies that are in use.

CASE STUDY
CREDIT CRISIS

In 2003 and 2004, Lehman Brothers acquired five mortgage lenders, including one that specialised in loans to borrowers without full documentation. Lehman's revenues surged 56% from 2004 to 2006, a faster rate of growth than other businesses in investment banking or asset management. Lehman reported record profits every year from 2005 to 2007.

In February 2007, their stock reached a record $86.18 per share, giving them a market capitalisation of close to $60 billion. However, by the first quarter of 2007, cracks in the US housing market were already becoming apparent. On 14 March 2007, a day after the stock had its biggest one-day drop in five years on concerns that rising defaults would affect profitability, the firm reported record revenues and profit. Lehman's chief financial officer (CFO) said that he did not foresee problems spreading to the rest of the housing market or hurting the US economy.

As the credit crisis got worse in August 2007, Lehman's stock fell sharply. During that month, the company lost 2,500 jobs, closing offices in three US states. Lehman continued to be a major player in the mortgage market, underwriting more mortgage-backed securities than any other firm, accumulating an $85-billion portfolio, four times its shareholders' equity.

In the fourth quarter of 2007, global equity markets reached new highs and prices for fixed-income assets staged a temporary rebound. However, the firm did not take the opportunity to trim its massive mortgage portfolio. This would turn out to have been its last chance. Further developments led to a 42% plunge in the stock on 11 September.

With only $1 billion left in cash by the end of that week, Lehman was quickly running out of time. Last-ditch efforts over the weekend of 13 September aimed at concluding a takeover of Lehman were unsuccessful. On Monday 15 September, Lehman declared bankruptcy, resulting in the stock plunging 93% from its previous close on 12 September.

UNIT 320 (B&A 59): TEST YOUR KNOWLEDGE

Learning outcome 1: Understand business markets

1. Name the three types of business markets.
2. Name two ways businesses interact with each other.
3. Give two examples of a 'monopsony'.
4. Name three main legal structures that organisations can operate as.

Learning outcome 2: Understand business innovation and growth

1. What is meant by 'innovation'?
2. Describe two models of business innovation.
3. Name UK government programmes that support business innovation.
4. Name the seven steps involved in developing a product or service.
5. What are the four stages of the psychological impact of change?

Learning outcome 3: Understand financial management

1. Why is financial viability important to an organisation?
2. What is the consequence of poor financial management?
3. What is the meaning of 'current assets', 'current ratio' and 'current liabilities'?

Learning outcome 4: Understand business budgeting

1. How are budgets used in a business?
2. What are the four key steps in developing a budget?

Learning outcome 5: Understand sales and marketing

1. Name six common market segments.
2. What are the characteristics and stages of the sales cycle?
3. Explain the difference between primary and secondary research.
4. Why is a brand important to an organisation?
5. What are the benefits of integrating sales and marketing departments?

CHAPTER 5

UNIT 345 (M&L 9) MANAGE PERSONAL AND PROFESSIONAL DEVELOPMENT

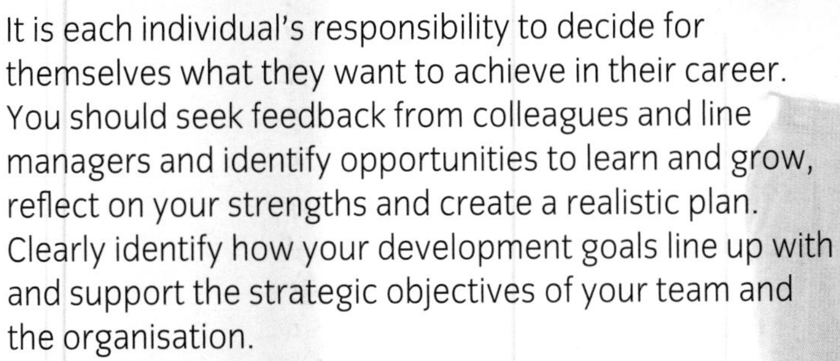

It is each individual's responsibility to decide for themselves what they want to achieve in their career. You should seek feedback from colleagues and line managers and identify opportunities to learn and grow, reflect on your strengths and create a realistic plan. Clearly identify how your development goals line up with and support the strategic objectives of your team and the organisation.

The role of your line manager is to encourage your development and to provide objective and honest feedback on your development plan. They can help you to understand how you can make a contribution to the organisation. The most effective leaders will create development opportunities, remove barriers and hold you accountable for implementing your plan.

In this unit you will cover the following learning outcomes:

1 be able to identify personal and professional development requirements
2 be able to fulfil a personal and professional development plan
3 be able to maintain the relevance of a personal and professional development plan.

Assessment criteria

This section covers assessment criteria 1.1, 1.2, 1.3, 2.1, 2.3 and 2.6

Evolve

To develop gradually, often into something more complex or advanced

IDENTIFYING PERSONAL AND PROFESSIONAL DEVELOPMENT REQUIREMENTS

Most people are ambitious to progress their career as far as they can. Even if you feel you have reached a level of responsibility that you are comfortable to remain at for the immediate future, the demands of your job role will change as the organisation **evolves**, or new processes or procedures are introduced. Identifying your development needs can be difficult.

Career progression will for some people involve getting another job with more or different responsibilities, either within the same organisation or with another employer. For others, career progression may mean taking a sideways job change or even a downward step to gather more or wider experience in order to progress through a career change at a later date. For other people, career progression may involve improving the skills they are already using in their present role. Whichever route you choose to develop your career, it's important to remember that the only person who can make this happen is you.

There are three broad questions to ask when considering your professional development needs:

- What do you want to do next?
- What skills and experience do you have to offer?
- What would you like your next job to look like?

If your organisation offers annual appraisals, take that opportunity to discuss your development needs with your line manager. Discuss the changing requirements of your role as well as your personal development objectives. It is important to consider your development needs before your appraisal meeting as this will enable you to make the most of your discussion.

If you are not given a pre-appraisal form to complete, make notes under these headings in order to prepare yourself:

- The skills, knowledge and behaviour needed to perform your current role well.
- Your level of competence in these skills, knowledge and behaviour.
- Any development you need to reach the required level of competence.

Your role should have a job description and a person specification. The job description will list the things that you are expected to do, while the person specification will identify the skills, experience, knowledge and behaviours that you need to do that job well.

You may find it helpful to talk to your line manager if you feel you want to clarify any of the requirements set out in the person specification.

The annual appraisal meeting is an opportunity to have this discussion, but you can raise the issue of development with your manager at any time.

It's also worth thinking about the skills, knowledge and behaviours that you may need to develop in the future in your current job. You may know, for example, that your role will be changing, that you will be working on different projects or that you are interested in a career change. Trends and developments that influence the need for professional development may include changes in:

- systems
- technology
- the market
- competition
- legislation.

Other sources of information include bodies that your organisation may be a member of, for instance:

- professional bodies such as the Association of Chartered Certified Accountants (ACCA) or the Chartered Institute of Journalists
- professional networks such as the Government Communication Network or the Higher Education Network
- trade associations such as the Society of Archivists or the Federation of Wholesale Distributors.

Any of these will be able to provide information on development activities which are appropriate to your position in your organisation. Information can also be found from:

- your organisation's employee development department
- training organisations
- the internet.

It is important to recognise the new or different skills, knowledge and behaviours you will need. Make a list of the current and likely future skills, knowledge, experience and behaviours that you need and ask yourself how effectively you match against each one. You could consider talking this through with a friend or colleague, or with your line manager. It's important to ask yourself some difficult questions at this stage and to answer honestly:

- Are there areas of your work where developing more confidence would make a real difference to your success in your job?
- Are there knowledge, skills and behaviours that you only need on occasion that would benefit from some development?
- Can you identify areas where you feel confident and believe you perform well that could be an even greater strength for you with some development?

ACTIVITY

Prepare notes for your next performance appraisal.

ACTIVITY

Create a career progression route for yourself within your present organisation. Include realistic timescales for achieving this, along with the development opportunities you will need to achieve it.

One way to identify the skills you need but may not have is to carry out a skills gap analysis. Identify the critical and non-critical skills needed to carry out your job role effectively. Critical skills are those required to complete a task successfully. Non-critical skills are those that enable a task to be completed more quickly or efficiently, or at less cost. If you lack a skill but can still complete the task satisfactorily, the skill is non-critical; if you complete the task but the outcome is unsatisfactory, the missing skill is critical.

By applying skills gap analysis it is possible to find out which skills and knowledge shortfalls you have. It is then possible to concentrate on the necessary skills that require the most attention. Skills gap analysis can be used to produce personal development and training plans, and to support appraisals and pay reviews.

Try to be as detailed and specific as possible about what you need to be able to do differently. This will help you decide how to address your development needs, and to review and measure your success. For example, when it comes to deciding what development you need, identifying that you need to learn how to use the software available on your computer to sort, prioritise and store your emails will be much more helpful than simply identifying that you need to be more organised. It will also help you check how much difference any training you undertake actually makes to your ability to be organised.

HANDY HINT

Keep certificates received and records of courses attended so that you can show them in future job interviews.

It is not a good idea to try to identify your development needs by looking at the training courses available and deciding which of those would be most helpful. It is better to try and identify what the development need is and then to work out ways of meeting that need, which may or may not be a training course.

BENEFITS OF PERSONAL AND PROFESSIONAL DEVELOPMENT

Personal and professional development brings benefits to both you as an individual and the organisation you work for. When evaluating the benefits, however, it is important to consider the costs involved, both financial and personal.

Skills developed in the past that may have become a little unpractised will be polished. It is always good to review these skills because if they are not used constantly they can start to fade away. For example, writing skills that you learnt at school or college by writing essays may not be used in your current role, but revisiting this skill will allow you to maintain and increase it.

Professional development will allow new skills and knowledge to be learnt. This will spread your talents and help you perform tasks that are more highly skilled and demanding. It allows you to build specific knowledge and competencies that are related to your current role and the role you aspire to.

It is important to ensure you are up-to-date with industry trends and developments as this will help you perform your own role and also help the organisation understand their position in the marketplace, which can assist strategic decision making.

Professional development allows you to see fresh viewpoints from outside your organisation and your current role, and to think about new ideas and opportunities. By reflecting on these, you can introduce creative solutions to the organisation. You will learn to use important tools and best practices that can be incorporated into the organisation's strategies and performance. New knowledge creates innovative solutions.

PROFESSIONAL DEVELOPMENT ACTIVITIES

By going on courses, visiting industry events and taking other opportunities for professional development, you will meet new people and **network** with industry experts, leaders and like-minded individuals. Building relationships like this can be extremely useful for finding out about career opportunities, work-related guidance, business opportunities and insider information. This network can come in handy in your current role as well as in your future career. Professional development allows you to consider and appreciate the opportunities available to you. With more skills and advanced knowledge you will begin to appreciate what your career prospects are and where your career path can potentially lead.

Network

To build up or maintain informal relationships, especially with people whose friendship could bring advantages such as job or business opportunities

Sometimes it is a good idea to take a break and refresh your mind. It can be energising and make you feel like new. By taking time out to personally develop, you will be taking a step away from your everyday role to do something different. The energy and sense of fulfilment can be used positively in both your job and personal life.

Most organisations are not **prescriptive** about the types of activity that count as professional development, recognising that you are the best person to assess the value of an activity. However, nothing should be accepted automatically as professional development unless you have actually learnt from it. When considering whether an activity counts, refer back to your professional development plan to see whether it will help your development objectives.

Prescriptive

Establishing or adhering to rules and regulations

Different types of professional development activity include:

- Home-based learning – private study, structured reading on particular themes or topics. The use of audio, video or multimedia resources and other distance-learning material.
- Action-based learning – a systematic, structured approach to solving problems in the workplace.

HANDY HINT

You may come across unexpected opportunities that you had not planned for and these can be considered professional development if you believe that they will improve your competence.

- Preparation of material for courses, technical meetings or publication.
- Supervised research.
- Work-based development – background reading, research or preparation required to tackle a new area of work.
- Conferences, seminars, workshops or other technical and professional events and meetings, including in-house training.
- Courses leading to a qualification.

There are numerous sources of information on professional development. Your organisation's human resources or employee development department and any trade associations, professional networks or professional bodies that you are a member of should be your first point of reference. They will be able to direct you towards any opportunities that are available and help you compare the various sources of information and their validity. Researching the internet will provide information on training organisations that may provide further opportunities.

ACTIVITY

Research the types of professional development activities that are available to you.

When comparing sources of information it is important to look at their relative strengths and weaknesses, and to identify the advantages and disadvantages of each source.

Assessment criteria

This section covers assessment criteria 2.2, 2.4, 2.5 and 3.1

FULFILLING A PERSONAL AND PROFESSIONAL DEVELOPMENT PLAN

A personal and professional development plan will identify your learning objectives, the resources needed to achieve them, the timescales involved and the way that progress will be measured. One way to set out your learning plan is using these headings:

- What – the learning objective.
- Why – the need to be addressed.
- How – the learning activity that will address it.
- When – the timescale for addressing it.
- Measure – how you will know the objective has been achieved.

The learning plan should be agreed with all relevant parties, such as your line manager, the training and development department and the budget holder. The best way to identify which are the most appropriate opportunities for you is to recognise your learning style. The two most common learning styles models are the Fleming VARK learning model, and Honey and Mumford's adaptation of Kolb's experiential model.

In the Fleming VARK model, learners are recognised as being inclined to one of four learning styles, unconsciously preferring that style. The four learning styles are:

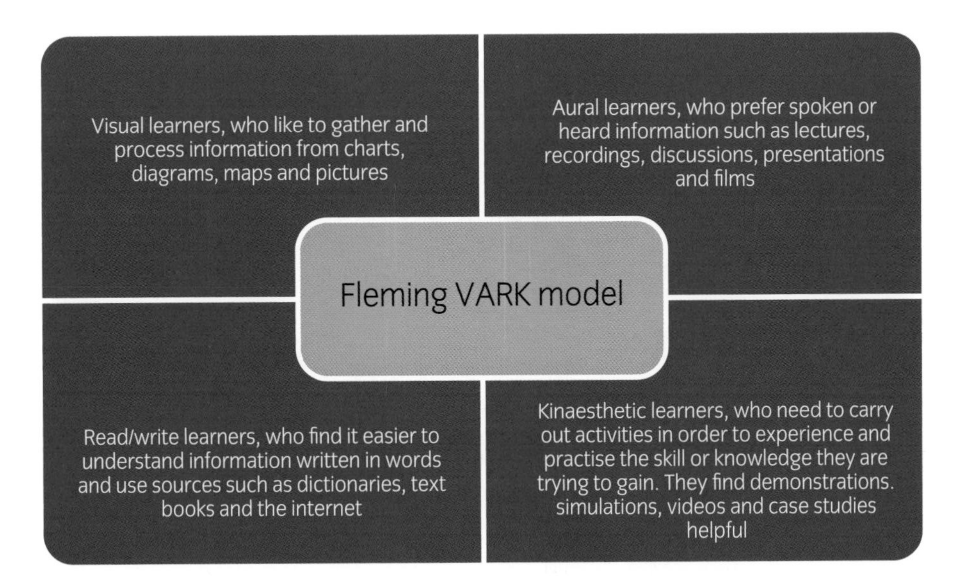

In Kolb's model, learning styles are identified as follows.

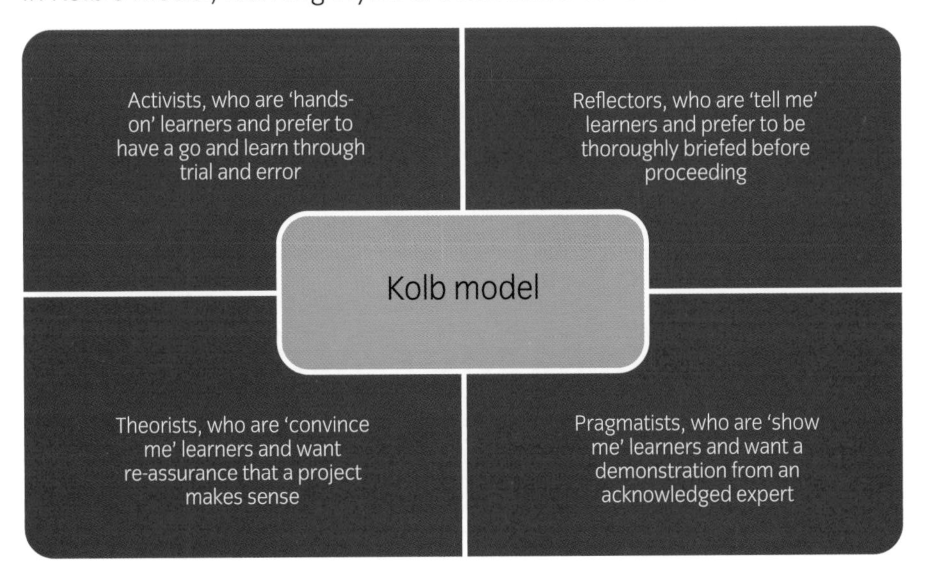

Although each of us has a preferred learning style, in practice a mixture of two, three or even four styles will usually be the most effective.

You should prioritise your learning objectives. If you are unable to complete all of them within the timeframe of the learning plan, identify which would cause the greatest loss or threat to the organisation, the team or yourself if they were not achieved. Some learning will be able to be carried out in stages; this may allow you to more conveniently fit it in around other tasks. Either way, regularly review your progress against the learning objectives and update them.

Learning objectives that involve gaining skills or knowledge of new systems are best scheduled for times when you can access the system, allowing you to practise. If a new system has a fixed date for going live you should, of course, aim to complete the learning activity on or before that date.

HANDY HINTS

- Make sure everybody who needs to know is kept informed of your objectives.
- Out-of-work activities can also be very useful for improving your performance at work.

Individual learning objectives should take account of team objectives

ACTIVITY

- Develop a learning plan for yourself. Agree it with your line manager.
- Keep a work diary recording your learning in order to prepare for your next appraisal.

The learning objectives could have been identified from the self-evaluation carried out for your annual appraisal. Development activities to meet the learning objectives should take into account the overall business needs of the organisation and the objectives of the team that you are part of or leading, as well as your own individual goals.

PUTTING LEARNING INTO PRACTICE

To get started on improving your performance, you need to put some of your learning into practice. If you can use learning plans to identify development opportunities to improve your own performance, and translate those into changes that benefit the organisation, you will be in a position to look at progressing your career. The route this takes will depend entirely on the organisation you are working for.

Career development is about planning your possible career progression route. You need to identify your development opportunities and your future moves. Identify the gaps in your existing skills and experience, and find ways to fill them to achieve your career aims. Development methods may include attending training courses, coaching and mentoring.

COACHING AND MENTORING

Coaching and mentoring are development methods based on discussions to improve the skills, knowledge or work performance of individuals. The two are in many ways identical. Coaching aims to improve performance at work and usually focuses on specific skills and goals, although it may also have an impact on personal attributes such as social interaction or confidence. Coaching usually lasts for a fairly short period.

Coaching is basically a non-directive form of development that concentrates on performance at work, although personal issues may be discussed. Coaching activities have both organisational and individual goals and provide feedback on both strengths and weaknesses. It should be delivered by line managers and others trained in basic coaching skills.

Mentoring is an effective way of helping people progress their careers and is a partnership between two people, normally working in a similar field or sharing similar experiences. A mentor is a guide who can help you to find the right direction and develop solutions to career issues. Mentors rely on having had similar experiences to gain **empathy** and an understanding of the issues. Mentoring provides an opportunity to think about career options and progress.

A mentor helps you to believe in yourself and boost your confidence. They will ask questions and challenge, at the same time as providing guidance and encouragement. Being mentored allows you to explore new ideas and is a chance to look more closely at yourself, your issues and your opportunities. Mentoring is about taking responsibility for your life.

ACTIVITY

Describe an improvement you have made recently in your performance and the impact this has had on the organisation. Explain the benefits to your own job role from the improvement.

Empathy

The ability to understand how someone feels because you can imagine what it is like to be them

MANAGING CHANGE

If you are in a team-leading role and your development activities are going to involve changing systems or processes that involve other people, or affect their work, you must ensure that they are considered. Change can be very difficult for people. They like to know what is expected of them and changes can cause distress. While some people adapt easily to change, others react immediately with scepticism. If planned improvements in your own performance are to work successfully, you will need to manage the change effectively. This will involve planning and communication.

Avoid the temptation to 'prepare' people for change by giving them hints that things are going to change without being able to give proper information. This will only lead to rumours and misinformation which will make it much more difficult to introduce the change. Plan how and when you are going to communicate information to the team so that, wherever possible, all receive the news simultaneously. If this is difficult, try to ensure that team members who receive the information first do not pass it on inaccurately to the others.

Communication of the information should be face to face so that questions can be answered and encouraged. Remember to tell your team why the change is happening, as well as what it is and when it will happen. Explain the benefits to the organisation and to them, rather than the benefits to you, if you need their contribution to make the change work.

ACTIVITY

List the training you have received in the last twelve months. Explain how the training you have received has improved your own work and benefitted your organisation.

Plan how and when you are going to communicate information to the team

People facing change will have more questions after they've talked among themselves

Make yourself available in the days following the announcement of the change. People will think of things they need to discuss after they have had the chance to consider how the change affects them, or have talked among themselves at the coffee machine or after work. If they can't get answers from you, they will become more anxious that the change will not be good for them.

Once the change has been put in place, check regularly that the impact on your colleagues has been as you expected it would be. Remember, you are trying out the improvement at this stage, so gathering information on how it is working will allow you to make adjustments to make the transition more effective.

DEVELOPING YOUR CAREER

Developing your career can also be about how you improve your performance in your existing role. Many organisations now have much flatter structures than they once did, making traditional career paths and progression less common. Sideways moves into new roles within the organisation rather than promotion into more senior roles may not involve greater responsibility, but may give you the opportunity to learn new skills and make your role more challenging. Discuss the possibilities during your appraisal sessions with your line manager so that you can plan your development in conjunction with available career progression routes.

ACTIVITY

Describe the objectives of your current learning plan.

It is important that your personal and professional development plan is executed within the agreed budget and timescale. This will require your personal commitment to completing the agreed actions. One of the most important elements of a thorough personal development plan is a SWOT analysis, which is used to develop personal skills, highlight achievements, confront weaknesses and identify potential barriers. SWOT analysis identifies:

- Strengths – the skills you already possess.
- Weaknesses – the areas for improvement that you have identified.
- Opportunities – the resources or tools you have that can help you add strengths.
- Threats – the possible barriers to meeting your goals.

HANDY HINT

Have some short-term objectives so that you can see you are making progress.

SMART is an acronym used to help determine whether an action plan for personal development is reasonable. Ask yourself if your plan is:

- Specific – the plan is clear, unambiguous, straightforward and understandable.
- Measurable – the plan is related to quantified or qualitative performance measures.
- Achievable – resources are available to meet the goals included in the plan.
- Realistic – the plan is linked to business needs.
- Time-bound – the plan includes a completion date and review dates.

HANDY HINT

Performing self-analysis can point out what needs to be done and put any problems into perspective.

Some objectives will be more difficult to measure than others, for instance if you are looking to improve in areas such as leadership, teamworking or flexibility, or in using your initiative. In these areas, the measure to be used may have to be 'an improvement in feedback'.

Remember to continually review your progress against the objectives in your personal development plan and be prepared to amend the plan in the light of feedback received and your own observations.

HANDY HINT

When creating a personal development plan, it's often helpful to ask a trusted colleague to help you identify other areas of improvement, as well as to determine whether goals are too ambitious.

MAINTAINING THE RELEVANCE OF A PERSONAL AND PROFESSIONAL DEVELOPMENT PLAN

Assessment criteria

This section covers assessment criteria 3.2, 3.3 and 3.4

Evaluating your progress is vital to successfully executing personal development plans. Record keeping can be carried out either using a professional system or by keeping a detailed spreadsheet. Outline any new skills you develop while executing the plan. Keeping a record helps you to measure your progress.

One of the keys to evaluating your own performance is to encourage feedback from others, including your line manager, customers and team members and, having encouraged it, being prepared to accept it even if it is critical. Encouraging feedback is best done by preparing a series of questions for people to answer about your performance, rather than relying on a general query such as 'How do you think I am doing?' to which the most likely response is 'OK'.

You should carefully select the people you seek feedback from; it is no good asking people who:

- do not know your work well enough to give an opinion
- have a vested interest in undermining your confidence
- always look on the bright side of life.

Encourage feedback from others in order to evaluate your own performance

Include your line manager in your feedback panel because you need to know how they view your performance. Asking for and acting on feedback from your line manager can give you an opportunity to correct weaknesses perceived by them that you were unaware of, and to do so before they become an issue. You may have performance shortfalls brought to your attention that have not been recorded during your appraisal. This may be because your line manager didn't feel they needed recording officially but does want to give you the chance to improve on them.

ACTIVITY

Make a list of six or seven questions that you could ask people in order to get constructive feedback on your performance.

Before inviting feedback from others you should have already carried out a self-appraisal, identifying what you think are your strengths and weaknesses, so that you can target the questions at areas where feedback from others will be particularly useful.

Make sure the people you have selected to give you feedback understand that you really do want honest opinions, that this is not an exercise in self-justification. Explain that you are looking to improve your performance and would appreciate their help in doing so.

COMMON MISTAKE

Thinking that feedback from one person is necessarily the truth.

The questions you choose to ask should stem from your self-evaluation and will be different for each individual, but the common thread is that they must be open, specific and not defensive.

When you receive responses to your questions, you shouldn't be drawn into debate or argument. You asked the questions, so you need to listen to the answers. If you don't understand the response then ask for clarification, but if you disagree simply thank them for their input.

When you have read or heard all the responses, you should be able to recognise patterns in them. This will allow you to look at the positive comments, which should reinforce your own views of your strengths. When looking at negative comments, don't try to justify them, even to yourself, or you will not learn from them. If several people have identified a similar issue then it is likely to be a genuine issue, so look at how you can address it.

Other sources of feedback could include organisational performance indicators, customer and employee surveys, or simply informal observations or comments made. Everybody has weaknesses; the object of seeking feedback is to improve your performance by recognising where improvements can be made.

Once all the feedback has been received and considered, go back to your personal and professional development plan and amend it in the light of the feedback.

ACTIVITY

Make a list of people you would ask questions of in order to get constructive feedback on your performance.

CASE STUDY
A DEVELOPMENT PLAN

Kate Ennis has worked for Aspect Property for five years. She knows her job well and consistently receives positive feedback during appraisals. She is keen to get into a management position but does not have the management experience that is required whenever an opportunity arises.

Kate discusses the situation with her manager and they agree a development plan which identifies three stages:

- Research the skills and knowledge needed to work as a manager for Aspect Property. Kate's manager and the company training manager will help her to identify training opportunities and resources that the company can provide. Kate will also look for external resources online and at the public library.
- Gain experience of management by standing in for her manager when he is on holiday or out of the office. Take responsibility for training and mentoring new staff. Look for opportunities to demonstrate leadership outside of work in social or voluntary work.
- Apply for a management position when one becomes available, using the training and experience gained.

Kate attends training courses on team leading and time management, as well as technical courses on property portfolio management and valuation, in order to upgrade her skills and knowledge. She becomes the person in the office that everyone goes to for help and is recognised as the manager's deputy.

She also joins her local amateur dramatics society as a stage manager, as she has always been interested in the theatre, although she has no acting talent.

Twelve months after creating her development plan, Kate's manager is promoted to area manager and Kate is delighted when she is told that she is the obvious choice to replace her.

UNIT 345 (M&L 9): TEST YOUR KNOWLEDGE

Learning outcome 1: Be able to identify personal and professional development requirements

1 Identify a development in your organisation that would influence the need for professional development.

2 Describe your current and future development needs.

3 Explain two benefits of improving performance .

4 Identify two sources of information on professional development.

Learning outcome 2: Be able to fulfil a personal and professional development plan

1 How are types of development actions selected?

2 Describe your current and likely future skills, knowledge and experience needs.

3 What must development actions be consistent with?

4 Why is it important to execute plans as cost effectively and quickly as possible?

5 Explain how learning and development can further your career.

Learning outcome 3: Be able to maintain the relevance of a personal and professional development plan

1 What is 'SMART' an acronym for?

2 Describe two methods of encouraging feedback from others.

3 Describe how to review progress towards objectives.

4 What action should be taken in the light of feedback?

OPTIONAL UNITS

CHAPTER 6

UNIT 302 (B&A 41) CONTRIBUTE TO THE IMPROVEMENT OF BUSINESS PERFORMANCE

It is important for the progress of your career that you are able to contribute to the continuous improvement of business performance in the organisation. This will involve improving your own performance as well as that of your team and the business as a whole. One of the most important skills you will use in this is problem solving. Problems may be minor and able to be solved by making adjustments with little or no assistance, or they may be major with implications for resources or finance.

In this unit you will cover the following learning outcomes:

1 understand the principles of resolving business problems
2 understand improvement techniques and processes
3 be able to solve problems in business
4 be able to contribute to the improvement of activities.

Assessment criteria

This section covers assessment criteria 1.1, 1.2, 1.3, 1.4, 1.5, 3.1, 3.2, 3.3, 3.4, 3.5, 3.6, 3.7 and 3.8

RESOLVING BUSINESS PROBLEMS

The types of problem you may encounter during your career include:

- financial problems
- resource-related problems
- equipment or system failures
- staff-related problems
- unforeseen problems such as bad weather or industrial action.

The nature, scope and scale of a problem are decided by the person with the problem. If the manager of a department needs resources and has a limited budget, he or she has a problem. If another manager does not have a need for the same resources, then a limited budget is not a problem. Because needs are different between managers, they will see an identical situation in different ways. One may see it as a problem but the other may not so, in order to identify a problem, problem solvers must clarify the variance in need.

Problem solving is a common event in business

There are six stages to problem solving:

1. Identify the problem – for example, it may have been pointed out to you that you or your team are not meeting targets or providing services to the standard expected.
2. Define the effects of the problem – if the problem has been pointed out to you, you will probably have been told the effect. If you have identified the problem yourself, you may need to investigate the effects.

3 Find the cause of the problem – you may need to ask other people in order to find out whether the problem has been a result of your failure or theirs.
4 Identify possible solutions – a one-off problem will require a short-term solution. A continuing problem will need a longer-term solution. Once you know the cause of the problem you will be able to identify alternative ways of resolving it. These may include replanning or reprioritising your own work.
5 Choose the best solution – look at the advantages and disadvantages of each solution from the viewpoint of the whole organisation, not just yourself or your team. Select the solution with the most advantages and fewest disadvantages.
6 Plan the way forward – make sure everyone involved agrees that the chosen solution is the best solution. This will help to obtain their commitment when planning the next steps.

To come up with possible solutions to the problem, there is a wide range of techniques available including:

- Analogy – using a solution that previously solved a similar problem.
- Appreciation – extracting the maximum amount of information from a simple fact. Starting with that simple fact, ask the implications of that fact. Keep on asking that question until you have drawn all possible conclusions.
- Brainstorming – suggesting a large number of solutions or ideas and combining and developing them until the best is found.
- Cause and effect analysis – using a diagram-based approach for thinking through all of the possible causes of a problem. There are four steps to using cause and effect analysis; identify the problem, work out the major factors involved, identify possible causes and analyse your diagram.
- 'Divide and conquer' – breaking down a large, complex problem into smaller, solvable problems.
- Failure mode effects analysis – a technique requiring a sequential, disciplined approach to assess systems, products or processes in order to establish the modes of failure and the effects of failure on the system, product or process.
- **Hypothesis** testing – making assumptions about possible solutions to the problem and then trying to prove or disprove the assumptions.
- Lateral thinking – approaching solutions indirectly and creatively, or 'thinking outside the box'.
- Means-ends analysis – choosing an action at each step to move closer to the solution of the problem.
- Morphological analysis – assessing the output and interactions of an entire system.

Hypothesis

A statement that is assumed to be true for the sake of argument

- PEST analysis – this looks at political, economic, social and economic factors that affect the problem.
- Proof – trying to prove that the problem cannot be solved. The point where the proof fails will be the starting point for solving it.
- Reduction – converting the problem into another problem for which solutions already exist.
- Research – employing existing ideas or adapting existing solutions to similar problems.
- Risk analysis – a preventive approach to find the potential risk associated with a product, service, project or process. The aims of risk analysis are to identify the potential risks and decide an appropriate course of action to eliminate or reduce the effects of the risk.
- Root cause analysis – eliminating the cause of the problem.
- Sleeping on it – Don't think about the project or objective for a while. If it's late in the day, get a good night's sleep. You will get renewed energy to work on the problem once your unconscious mind has had time to work on it.
- The 'five whys' – looking at any problem and asking 'why?' and 'what caused this problem?' Very often, the answer to the first 'why?' will prompt another 'why?', and the answer to the second 'why?' will prompt another, and so on.
- Train of thought – gathering facts and data, considering assumptions and risks, before an informed decision is made and appropriate action is taken.
- Trial and error – testing possible solutions until the right one is found. This works best for people who already start with an instinct as to what the solution might be. Managers with less experience may find it more helpful to use a systematic trial-and-error approach. An important aspect of trial and error is that the trial accurately copies the reality.

Another problem-solving method is 'the scientific method'. This is especially useful in testing a theory. It usually includes the following steps:

- gain background information
- formulate a hypothesis or an educated guess to test
- develop a methodology to test that hypothesis or guess
- objectively perform the experiment, complete with control groups, and accurately record observations
- analyse the results to determine whether they support the hypothesis
- draw conclusions.

A different method that can result in creative ideas is 'creative problem solving'. This usually includes the following steps:

- observation or keeping your mind, eyes and ears tuned for seeing possible problems and solutions
- fact finding or gathering data
- problem finding, where a well-formulated problem statement is developed
- idea finding, or the generation of many possible solutions, deferring judgment
- solution finding, or the application of criteria to determine a single solution
- acceptance finding, or finding ways to accommodate and live with the solution.

Solving problems requires knowledge of the decision-making process. A decision is a choice between two or more possibilities: if there is only one option there is no decision to be made. If the decision is between a number of solutions to a problem, it may be that two or more solutions would work better together than any single solution.

The decision-making process involves the following steps:

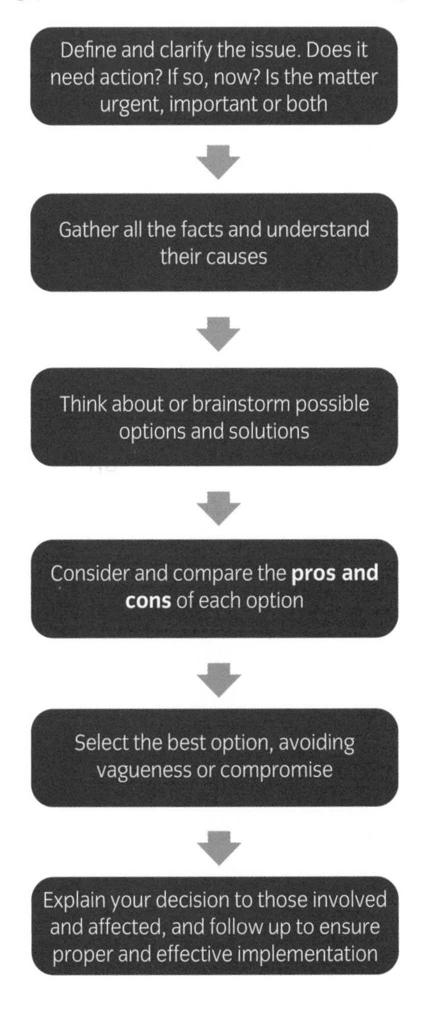

Pros and cons

The arguments for and against something

Another simple process for problem solving is the 'for and against' list. Originally designed as a decision-making technique, it can also be applied to problem solving where issues and implications need to be understood and a decision has to be made. Some decisions are a simple matter of whether to make a change or not, while other decisions involve a number of options and are concerned more with how to do something, involving a number of choices. Use the brainstorming process to identify and develop options for decision making and problem solving.

1 You will need a separate sheet for each identified option.
2 On each sheet, write clearly a summary of the option and then beneath it headings 'for' and 'against'. Many decisions simply involve the choice of whether to go ahead or not, whether to change or not; in these cases you need only have one sheet.
3 Write down as many effects and implications of the particular option that you can think of, placing each in the relevant column.
4 Weight each factor by giving it a score out of five points (5 being extremely significant and 1 being of minor significance).
5 Once you have listed all the points you can think of for the option concerned, compare the total score in the two columns. This will provide an indication as to the overall attractiveness and benefit of that option.
6 Work out the overall score for that option by calculating the difference between the 'pro' and 'con' column totals. The bigger the difference in favour of the 'pros', the more attractive that option is; the bigger the difference in favour of the 'cons', the less attractive that option is.
7 If you have a number of options to consider, repeat the process for all of them.
8 Once all of the options have been considered, compare the points difference between pros and cons for each of them. The solution with the biggest positive difference between pros and cons is the most attractive option.

A third option is to complete a decision matrix analysis, also known as Pugh matrices, decision grids, selection matrices or grids, problem matrices, problem selection matrices, opportunity analysis, solution matrices, criteria rating forms, criteria-based matrices or grid analysis.

A decision matrix can be used:

- when a list of options must be narrowed to one choice
- when the decision must be made on the basis of several criteria
- after the list of options has been reduced to a manageable number by list reduction

- when one improvement opportunity or problem must be selected to work on
- when only one solution or problem-solving approach can be implemented
- when only one new product can be developed.

To complete a decision matrix:

- brainstorm the evaluation criteria appropriate to the situation
- discuss and refine the list of criteria
- identify any criteria that must be included and any that must not be included
- assign a relative weight to each criterion, based on how important that criterion is to the situation, by distributing ten points among the criteria
- draw an L-shaped matrix. Write the criteria and their weights as labels along one edge and the list of options along the other edge
- evaluate each choice against the criteria
- multiply each option's rating by the weight.

You will find that writing things down in this way will help you to see things more clearly and become more objective and detached, which will help you to make clearer decisions. There are usually several right answers when you are faced with a complex decision.

When you've found the best solution you can, get on with it, try to make it work, and it most probably will. Test your decision by asking:

- Does the solution solve the problem?
- Does the solution solve the cause of the problem?
- Has everybody involved agreed to the solution?
- Is the solution practical in terms of cost, time, people and resources?
- Will the solution prevent the problem from re-occurring?
- Have you considered all the disadvantages of the solution?
- Have you considered all the consequences of the solution?

If the answer to all of the above is 'yes', you may have found the best solution. The next stage of the process is to feed back to any stakeholders in the decision to let them know what the decision is. But remember that decisions can be changed by circumstances: today's best solution will not necessarily be the same as tomorrow's.

HANDY HINTS

- Solve the problem that really exists, not the symptoms of a problem, nor the problem you already have a solution for, nor the problem you wish existed, nor the problem someone else thinks exists.
- Be careful not to look for a solution until you understand the problem, and be careful not to select a solution until you have a whole range of choices.

Stakeholders may need to be involved in problem solving

STAKEHOLDERS

A stakeholder is any group or individual that has an interest in, involvement with, dependence on, contribution to, or is affected by the decision. They are people who could lose or gain something because of the decision taken. The question of the needs of each stakeholder, and the effect of the decision on each, has to be considered.

By accepting that stakeholders are a far wider range of people and groups than you might at first think, you effectively expand your appreciation of how important your responsibility really is and how far it extends. Stakeholders can be found in any or all of the following groups, depending on the type of organisation:

- shareholders
- trustees
- guarantors
- investors
- funding bodies
- distribution partners
- marketing partners
- licensers
- licensees
- approving bodies
- regulatory authorities
- endorsers and 'recommenders'

- advisers and consultants
- employees (staff, managers, directors, non-executive directors)
- customers
- suppliers
- the local community
- the general public.

Many of these groups would not conventionally be considered to be stakeholders, but each could have an interest in and be affected by the decisions taken in an organisation that attempt to solve problems.

ORGANISATIONAL AND LEGAL CONSTRAINTS

As well as the need to involve or at least consider stakeholders in the problem-solving process, there is a need to consider any organisational or legal constraints. In law, the people directing an organisation have a responsibility for its:

- policies and protocols
- leadership style and methods
- management structures and practices
- accounting and taxation
- organisational culture and habits
- systems and administration
- strategies and tactics, marketing and advertising
- buying and supply chain management
- manufacturing and distribution
- organisational purposes, aims and priorities and how these are balanced against by-products, effects and consequences
- psychological contract
- decision making and decision-making processes
- quality, safety, sustainability
- staff development, well-being and health
- equality, discrimination, human rights
- risk assessment of activities and decisions
- communications and public relations
- information and communications technology
- technology and innovation
- social and environmental responsibilities
- finance, profit, remuneration
- shareholder relations and returns
- legality, probity, ethics and morality.

Corporate governance

Company management techniques and processes in general, or the way a particular company is managed

Each of these has the potential to go badly wrong so that people, or the organisation itself, suffers in some way. Every decision made within the organisation will feed into this whole concept of **corporate governance**, so every decision must be taken only after careful consideration.

It may be that the solution you have identified is beyond the limit of your authority to implement. This may be because the solution impacts on financial or health, safety and security issues or on the reputation of the organisation with external customers. It may require a deadline to be met that it is not within your power to achieve or may require the help of colleagues that are not within your authority to direct. Some decisions can only be taken by people with specific responsibility, for instance those responsible for strategic planning, operational management or individual roles and responsibilities. Decisions will also be affected by factors such as:

- regulations
- codes of practice
- the organisation's size and structure
- organisational culture.

Making and announcing a decision that is beyond the limits of your authority could have far-reaching implications for your organisation, your colleagues and, of course, for yourself when the impact of the decision is realised.

To evaluate the success of your solutions, subject them to two simple criteria: their impact, and their ease of implementation. Enter your potential solutions into the ease/impact matrix, shown on this page, to see where they fall in the resulting nine-box grid.

The ease/impact grid allows comparison of the impact of each potential solution and the ease of getting that solution into place. Relative positions on the grid help determine the priority of each solution.

Impact	High	1	2	3
	Medium	4	5	6
	Low	7	8	9
		Easy	Moderate	Difficult
		Ease		

The impact of a solution is estimated by projecting its benefits and its **longevity**. The acid test for impact is to evaluate the solution 12 months after its full implementation.

Longevity

Duration

Ease focuses on the in-company politics, the technology required, the difficulty of implementation and the timeframe required for implementation. 'Just do it' solutions rate at the easy end of the spectrum. Solutions with political, technical or cultural barriers rate as difficult. Solutions requiring high capital investment or long lead times also rate as difficult.

In the ease/impact grid:

- Solutions that fall in boxes 1 to 4 are the favoured solutions.
- Solutions that fall in box 5 might get some quick wins but have little impact.
- Solutions that fall in box 6 should be further evaluated to see if they can be combined with other solutions to achieve a stronger impact.
- Solutions that fall in boxes 7 and 8 might need intervention to improve their ease of implementation.
- Solutions that fall in box 9 are not good candidates for adoption.

COMMON MISTAKE

A solution that is technologically brilliant but thoughtless in human terms is not a good solution.

ACTIVITY

Consider a process you are responsible for and complete the following table to see if there is any way it could be improved.

Present method	Challenge	Improvement options	Best option
What is achieved?	Why is it necessary?	What could be done?	What should be done?
How is it done?	Why that way?	How could it be done?	How should it be done?
When is it done?	Why then?	When could it be done?	When should it be done?
Where is it done?	Why there?	Where could it be done?	Where should it be done?
Who does it?	Why them?	Who else could do it?	Who should do it?

Assessment criteria

This section covers assessment criteria 2.1, 2.2, 2.3, 2.4, 4.1, 4.2, 4.3, 4.4 and 4.5

IMPROVEMENT TECHNIQUES AND PROCESSES

If you are to be effective in the organisation, you must first understand how to improve your own performance. The first step is to identify your own training and development needs through:

- Training needs analysis – one method of completing this is to use a template that lists the activities you carry out, the importance of each activity and how confident you feel in carrying them out.
- Appraisals and reviews – these identify your current level of performance, your strengths and weaknesses, your training and development needs, and your potential while rewarding your contribution to the organisation and providing motivation.
- Observation and feedback – while it is nice to hear you have done well, it is probably more useful to be told when you have not done quite as well as you could have done. Feedback may be obtained formally or informally from managers, supervisors, colleagues or customers, but to be useful it must be constructive and explain what you should have done, not just what you should not have done.
- SWOT analysis – 'SWOT' stands for strengths, weaknesses, opportunities and threats. Strengths and weaknesses are internal factors personal to you, while opportunities and threats are external factors. When completing a SWOT analysis:
  - be realistic
  - distinguish between where you are today and where you could be in the future
  - be specific and avoid grey areas
  - keep it short and simple.

A SWOT diagram

In order to benefit fully from a SWOT analysis, it is important to make changes that deal with the identified weaknesses and prepare for the identified threats.

PERSONAL DEVELOPMENT PLANS

Having identified your needs, you can then agree a personal development plan that will list:

- Learning objectives – these will need to be **SMART**.
- Development activities and methods – these should state how the objectives will be achieved and may include in-house training, external training courses, coaching, mentoring, work shadowing, e-learning and performance appraisals.
- Evaluation – how will achievement of the objectives be measured?
- Cost – what budget is available to achieve the objective?
- Time – what is the target time for achievement of the objective?

SMART

A target that is specific, measurable, achievable, realistic and time-bound

Identifying and carrying out development opportunities will help you to improve any weaknesses and gain new skills. This will increase your motivation by enabling you to embrace challenges arising from changes in the workplace and, in the long term, will increase your employability and possibly lead to promotion and an increase in income.

See Chapter 5 (Unit 345, M&L 9) for more about managing personal and professional development.

ORGANISATIONAL CHANGE

In the same way that you need to continuously improve your own performance, organisations need to change in order to grow and, in the private sector, to remain competitive. The need for continuous improvement may be initiated by external forces beyond the control of the organisation, such as alterations in the demographics of the customer base, levels of employment, inflation or technology. Failure to react to these changes will leave the organisation struggling to keep up.

Organisations themselves have a life cycle of creation, expansion, contraction and decline. Successful organisations look for ways to extend the expansion phase and to delay the contraction phase of this cycle. Extending the expansion phase may be accomplished through:

- Mergers – where the organisation joins with another to create a new entity.
- Acquiring new companies – where the organisation buys and absorbs another.
- New ownership – where the organisation itself is taken over.
- Relocation of the organisation to a new site which may be closer to customers, more efficient to operate or create an improved image.

Changes that may initiate the contraction phase include:

- loss of revenue and rising costs
- legislative changes that affect the operation of the organisation
- economic changes that affect the purchasing power of its customers
- political changes, which particularly affect public- and voluntary-sector organisations.

The most effective organisations are constantly improving as a result of innovations initiated from within. These may be the introduction of new ideas or products, such as:

- Creating value from ideas that save money or increase income – an example is supermarkets expanding their range to include clothing and electrical items.
- New ways of satisfying customers in order to increase sales – an example is a furniture store providing a computerised room-design service.
- Improved product design as a result of carrying out a sales review – an example would be a new version of a product replacing a previous version, such as a new, improved version of a mobile phone.

Another way in which organisations can change is by improving their systems or processes that already exist, such as:

- Introducing new organisational structures or strategies which improve efficiency and save money – an example would be re-organising from a centralised structure to a divisional structure.
- Making something in a different way to save time or money – an example would be sewing products by machine rather than by hand.
- Introducing new ways of carrying out routine activities, perhaps through the introduction of new technology, to save time or money – an example would be computerising the accounts function.
- Introducing new approaches to work that improve efficiency – an example would be introducing flexi-time working for employees.

There are two distinct models of continuous improvement techniques used in many large organisations. One is Crosby's 14 steps:

1. **1** Management is committed to quality, and this is clear to all: Clarify where management stands on quality. It is necessary to consistently produce conforming products and services at the optimum price. The device to accomplish this is the use of defect prevention techniques in the operating departments:
    - engineering
    - manufacturing
    - quality control
    - purchasing
    - sales and others.
2. **2** Create quality improvement teams with representatives from all workgroups and functions. These teams run the quality improvement programme. Since every function of an operation contributes to defect levels, every function must participate in the quality improvement effort. The degree of participation is best determined by the particular situation that exists. However, everyone has the opportunity to improve.

3 Measure processes to determine current and potential quality issues. Communicate current and potential non-conformance problems in a manner that permits objective evaluation and corrective action. Basic quality measurement data is obtained from the inspection and test reports, which are broken down by operating areas of the business. By comparing the rejection data with the input data, it is possible to know the rejection rates.
4 Calculate the cost of poor quality: Define the ingredients of the cost of quality (COQ) and explain its use as a management tool.
5 Raise quality awareness of all employees. Provide a method of raising the personal concern felt by all personnel in the company toward the conformance of the product or service and the quality reputation of the company. By the time a company is ready for the quality awareness step, they should have a good idea of the types and expense of the problems being faced. The quality measurement and COQ steps will have revealed them.
6 Take actions to correct quality issues –provide a systematic method of permanently resolving the problems that are identified through previous action steps. Problems that are identified during the acceptance operation or by some other means must be documented and then resolved formally.
7 Monitor progress of quality improvement – establish a zero defects committee. Examine the various activities that must be conducted in preparation for formally launching the zero defects programme. The quality improvement task team should list all the individual action steps that build up to zero Defects day in order to make the most meaningful presentation of the concept and action plan to personnel of the company
8 Train supervisors in quality improvement. Define the type of training supervisors need in order to actively carry out their part of the quality improvement programme. The supervisor, from the chairman down, is the key to achieving improvement goals. The supervisor gives the individual employees their attitudes and work standards, whether in engineering, sales, computer programming, or wherever. Therefore, the supervisor must be given primary consideration when laying out the programme. The departmental representatives on the task team will be able to communicate much of the planning and concepts to the supervisors, but individual classes are essential to make sure that they properly understand and can implement the programme.
9 Hold zero defects days – create an event that will let all employees realise through personal experience, that there has been a change. Zero defects is a revelation to all involved that they are embarking on a new way of corporate life. Working under this discipline requires personal commitments and understanding. Therefore, it is necessary that all members of the company participate in an experience that will make them aware of this change.

10 Encourage employees to create their own quality improvement goals. Turn pledges and commitments into action by encouraging individuals to establish improvement goals for themselves and their groups. About a week after zero defects day, individual supervisors should ask their people what kind of goals they should set for themselves. Try to get two goals from each area. These goals should be specific and measurable.

11 Encourage employee communication with management about obstacles to quality. Give the individual employee a method of communicating to management the situations that make it difficult for the employee to fulfil the pledge to improve. One of the most difficult problems employees face is their inability to communicate problems to management. Sometimes they just put up with problems because they do not consider them important enough to bother the supervisor. Sometimes supervisors don't listen anyway. Suggestion programmes are some help, but in a suggestion programme the worker is required to know the problem and also propose a solution. Error-cause removal (ECR) is set up on the basis that the worker need only recognise the problem. When the worker has stated the problem, the proper department can look into it.

12 Recognise participants' effort. People really don't work for money. They go to work for it, but once the salary has been established, their concern is appreciation. Recognise their contribution publicly.

13 Create quality councils. Bring together the professional quality people for planned communication on a regular basis. It is vital for the professional quality people of an organisation to meet regularly just to share their problems, feelings and experiences with each other.

14 Do it all over again. Quality improvement does not end. If care is not taken, the entire programme will end when goals are reached. It is necessary to construct a new quality improvement team, and to let them begin again and create their own communications.

Crosby defined the four absolutes of quality management:

- Quality is conformance to requirements.
- Quality prevention is preferable to quality inspection.
- Zero defects is the quality performance standard.
- Quality is measured in monetary terms – the price of non-conformance.

According to Crosby, five characteristics of a highly successful organisation are:

- people routinely do things right first time
- change is anticipated and used to advantage
- growth is consistent and profitable

- new products and services appear when needed
- everyone is happy to work there.

The other model frequently used is the Kaizen model. The philosophy behind Kaizen is often credited to Dr W. Edwards Deming. His philosophy of continuous improvement also has 14 steps:

1. Create constancy of purpose toward improvement of product and service, with the aim to become competitive, to stay in business and to provide jobs.
2. Adopt the new philosophy.
3. Eliminate the need for inspection on a mass basis by building quality into the product in the first place.
4. End the practice of awarding business on the basis of price tag. Instead, minimise total cost.
5. Improve constantly and forever the system of production and service to improve quality and productivity and thus constantly decrease costs.
6. Institute training on the job.
7. Institute leadership. The aim of supervision should be to help people and machines and gadgets to do a better job.
8. Drive out fear so that everyone may work effectively for the company.
9. Break down barriers between departments. People in research, design, sales and production must work as a team to foresee problems of production and use of the product or service.
10. Eliminate asking for zero defects and new levels of productivity. Such exhortations only create adversarial relationships as the bulk of the causes of low quality and low productivity belong to the system and thus lie beyond the power of the workforce.
11. Remove barriers that rob the hourly worker of their right to pride of workmanship.
12. Remove barriers that rob people in management and in engineering of their right to pride of workmanship.
13. Institute a vigorous programme of education and self-improvement.
14. Get everyone in the company to work towards accomplishing the transformation – it is everybody's job.

In Western civilisation, Kaizen is often broken down into four steps:

- assess
- plan
- implement
- evaluate.

In Western workplaces, a 'Kaizen blitz' is a concentrated effort to make quick changes that will help achieve a short-term goal.

The purpose and benefits of continually improving the existing ways of working are:

- increased efficiency
- increased profitability
- increased productivity
- greater competitiveness
- better use of resources
- reduced costs
- better response to customer requirements
- increased customer satisfaction
- reduction in waste
- more employee involvement.

COST–BENEFIT ANALYSIS

Before making a major change to the organisation's processes or structure, it is necessary to carry out a cost–benefit analysis. This is a quick and simple technique that you can use for non-critical financial decisions. Cost–benefit analysis was introduced in the 1930s and became popular in the 1950s as a simple way of weighing up a project's costs and benefits, to determine whether to go ahead with a project.

Cost–benefit analysis involves adding up the benefits of a course of action and then comparing these with the costs associated with it. The results are often expressed as a 'payback period': this is the time it takes for the benefits to repay the costs. Many people who use cost–benefit analysis look for payback within a specific period, for example three years.

Cost–benefit analysis can be used when:

- deciding whether to hire new team members
- evaluating a new project or change initiative
- determining the feasibility of a capital purchase.

To carry out a cost–benefit analysis, you must first think of all the costs associated with the projected action and make a list of these. Then do the same for all the benefits. When calculating the costs and benefits, think about the lifetime of the projected change and include all the costs and benefits there are likely to be over time. Make sure that you update the list to include any costs and benefits that you did not initially anticipate.

'Costs' include the cost of physical resources needed as well as the cost of the human effort involved. Costs are often relatively easy to estimate compared with benefits. It is important to include as many related costs as you can, for example any training costs and the cost of any decrease in productivity while people are learning a new system or technology.

Remember to include costs that will continue to be incurred after the change is implemented. There may be a need for additional staff, the team may need ongoing training, or there may be increased overheads.

The next step is less straightforward because it is often very difficult to predict income accurately, especially for new products. Furthermore, along with the financial benefits that you anticipate, there are often **intangible** or 'soft' benefits. For instance, what is the impact on the environment, employee satisfaction, or health and safety? What is the monetary value of that impact? It's important at this point to consult with other stakeholders and decide how you'll value these intangible items.

Intangible

Something non-physical that cannot be seen or touched

Finally, compare the value of your costs against the value of your benefits, and use this analysis to decide your course of action. Determine whether your benefits outweigh your costs. At this stage it's important to consider the payback time, to find out how long it will take for you to reach the breakeven point, which is the point in time at which the benefits have repaid the costs.

REVIEWING EXISTING WAYS OF WORKING

Methods of reviewing existing ways of working should encourage participation from team members and customers. It is important to be aware of signs of resistance to change and identify the reasons for it. Effective communication will reduce the resistance to change.

Where resistance is encountered, it may be active or passive. Active resistance may have valid reasons; find out what they are and deal with them. Sometimes more difficult to deal with is passive resistance, where people don't argue against the change, they ignore it and carry on in the same old way. Resistance arises from three sources:

- Misunderstanding – this can be overcome by communicating the benefits of and reasons for the change.
- Fear – this can be overcome by re-assuring the individual that they will not be adversely affected.
- Distrust – this can be overcome only by time, as the individual's fears are proven unfounded.

COMMON MISTAKE

Reversing a change because it does not immediately work or meets initial resistance.

The way to encourage participation is through communication. Customers can be involved through customer feedback or customer forums, where they are asked to comment on the existing systems and processes from their point of view. Often customers will be able to suggest change that team members would not have thought of as customers see things from an entirely different angle.

Encourage participation through communication

Team members can be involved through employee surveys, team meetings or staff suggestion schemes. The more team members are involved in reviewing systems and processes, the more innovative ideas will be put forward and the more ready to accept changes they will be.

Other benefits of including as many people as possible in the review are that:

- Feedback from team members will help refinement of the idea.
- Team members may have previous experience of operating the proposed system, which will help to introduce it more smoothly.
- The people required to actually carry out the new process will be able to identify where extra resources are needed.
- Team members will understand how the change will benefit the whole organisation through communication with others involved.
- Barriers between teams and between team members can be broken down by sharing ideas – often people will not realise that the way they do things may have an adverse effect on the work of others.

The most important factor in contributing to continuous improvement is attitude. As a supervisor or manager, your attitude must be positive in order to generate a positive attitude in others. Keeping people motivated, enthusiastic and willing to be involved requires a 'can do' attitude. To identify attitudes that are likely to make people positive or negative, look for the following:

- Positive people enjoy the day; negative people wait for something to enjoy.
- Positive people admire and learn from successful people; negative people envy them.
- Positive people enjoy what they have; negative people envy what others have.
- Positive people are self-confident, kind and friendly; negative people feel undervalued and under-rewarded.
- Positive people are compassionate and sociable; negative people are self-focused.
- Positive people are understanding and forgiving; negative people are seeking revenge.
- Positive people are relaxed; negative people are stressed.
- Positive people enjoy what they do; negative people hate their job.
- Positive people create change; negative people fear it.

Overall, positive thinkers will come up with ideas; negative thinkers will come up with reasons why the ideas are not practical, which may be valid but will not in themselves move the situation forward.

IMPLICATIONS OF CHANGE

Change will have positive and negative implications for the organisation, teams and individuals. It is important to understand that some results of change will be positive for some of those involved and negative for others. The individual's attitude will also have an effect on this.

Attitude is the most important factor in continuous improvement

Implications of change may include:

- New work roles – for many this will be seen as a positive, but there will be those who are intimidated by being removed from their comfort zone.
- Promotion – again, many will see this as a positive as it usually involves better pay and conditions, while others will be concerned by added responsibility. They will fear the 'Peter Principle' that states that every employee tends to rise to the level of their incompetence.
- Higher productivity – while this will clearly benefit the organisation, some individuals may see it as working harder for the same returns.
- Retraining – where existing skills are no longer required or no longer up to date, individuals will need to be trained in skills that are current.

- Challenges – positive thinkers welcome challenges as they keep them interested and engaged, while negative thinkers see them as problems.
- Job losses and redundancies – these are almost inevitably negative for the individual, at least initially; their impact on the organisation will depend on the reasons for them. If redundancies are being made due to increased efficiency, the savings will be positive; if they are being made because of a lack of finance, the loss of expertise and capacity will be negative.
- Fear of the unknown – it is natural to be concerned about things that we do not understand. This can be channelled into positive energy by using effective communication.
- Loss of motivation – where change is implemented without communication to obtain the full backing of individuals, they will feel less motivated because they are having changes imposed on them.
- Issues with staff retention – people may feel that, if they are changing what they do and how they do it, they may as well change where they do it.

Changes require detailed planning. Make a plan of what needs to be done to move the organisation from where it is now to where it is going. Fill in the details, listing: the desired outcome; how the plan will be realised; the timescales involved; individual responsibilities; and any training that is required. When the detailed plan is complete, check that it meets the following requirements:

Rationale

The reasoning or principle that underlies or explains something, or a statement setting out this reasoning or principle

- the **rationale** for the change is stated
- resources have been identified and are available
- any need to adapt behaviour has been taken into account
- the individuals responsible have been identified
- a realistic timetable has been set
- effective tracking systems are available
- contingency plans are in place.

Viable

Able to be done or worth doing

If checking reveals that the plan is **viable**, present it in an as to-the-point manner as possible. If the change is agreed, implement the plan, ensuring that communication to everybody involved is maintained throughout the process and that questions are dealt with positively.

DEALING WITH PROBLEMS

Inevitably, problems will arise during the change process. These may arise from a lack of motivation to change among team members, the increased stress levels that individuals may experience or, from an organisational point of view:

- A lack of leadership – the implementation of changes, particularly major changes, must have support from senior levels of the organisation if they are to succeed.
- Difficulty in controlling costs – the cost of any change is almost certain to exceed the estimate; increases in the price of resources and the inescapable disruption will always lead to pressure on the budget. This is why a contingency is so important.
- Introducing new technology – it is a well-known assumption that technology never works, at least not first time and not in the way that you wanted it to. There will always be **teething problems** and the need to employ expertise, either to train existing staff or possibly to replace them.

Teething problems

Problems that you experience in the early stages of an activity

Problems must be dealt with as they occur but can be minimised in advance by good planning and budgeting, effective communication, stress management, and appropriate staff development and training.

Once the change has been in place for some time, it will need to be reviewed and evaluated. The plan will have identified a measurable change that was desired. For instance, a measurable change might have been to reduce by 10% the average length of time taken to recover overdue invoices. It is relatively straightforward to calculate whether such a change has delivered the desired result. But the overall evaluation is not necessarily as simple as that. The evaluation of all changes must consider the impact in relation to finance, customers, the market and employees.

Plans identify measurable change that needs to be evaluated

To take the example above, the reduction in recovery time is clearly effective from a financial point of view. If, however, the effect of pressing customers for payment results in a significant number of them taking their custom elsewhere, then the change will not have been effective. Similarly, if employees are under increased levels of stress to achieve the reduction and this leads to increased absenteeism or increased staff turnover, the change cannot be said to have been effective.

According to Pareto's law, 80% of an organisation's challenges are generated by 20% of its activities. Innovation should address that 20% to avoid introducing a culture of continuous uncontrolled change. A rolling programme of change will allow the effects of one change to be absorbed before another is undertaken. Try not to abandon changes before they have had the chance to **bed in**, as this risks staff beginning to resist change on the grounds that it is never followed through.

Bed in

To give something time to establish itself and fit firmly into place

It is important that the effects of change are monitored. The elements of this are shown in the table.

Element	Description
Defining the measures	It is extremely important to establish clear definitions of your measures before starting the change process. The measures should clarify the objectives of the change and should be agreed upon by key stakeholders
Collecting baseline data	Clearly define a starting point for the change and work backwards to collect 2–3 months' worth of baseline data before making any changes.
Establishing a clear improvement aim or target	This should be realistic yet ambitious, be linked to project objectives, and be clear enough to avoid confusion.
Consistently collect data	The ability to collect measurement data on a regular basis may already exist within the organisation's data systems, but in other cases you may need to manually collect the data.
Charting your progress	Over time you will collect both baseline and post-change data, which should be shared with staff who are affected by the change as well as with others in the organisation.
Asking questions	The most important step in the process is to ask what the information is telling you about change in the organisation.

Another essential for contributing to continuous improvement is resource planning. Many organisations use enterprise resource planning (ERP), a suite of integrated software applications that store and manage data from every stage of their operation, including:

- product planning, cost and development
- manufacturing
- marketing and sales
- inventory management
- dispatch
- payments.

Using common databases, ERP systems track business resources such as cash, raw materials and production capacity, and the status of business commitments such as orders, purchase orders and payroll. The applications share data across the various departments. This facilitates information flow between all business functions and helps manage connections with outside stakeholders.

HANDY HINT

When carrying out resource planning, don't forget to include human resources.

ACTIVITY

Consider a change that has been introduced in your workplace recently. Measure its effectiveness and, where necessary, suggest ways in which its effectiveness could have been improved.

STANDARD OPERATING PROCEDURES

To keep track of changes and the current agreed procedures, many organisations use **standard operating procedures** to describe how tasks should be completed. In order to decide which tasks should be standardised, you may need to spend a week writing down every task carried out to fulfil the daily needs of the business. The first operating procedures to be standardised should be those that an employee will be responsible for performing independently; other more managerial procedures can be added later.

Standard operating procedure

A process that is followed when carrying out an operation or dealing with a situation

The procedures themselves should clearly describe the action to be carried out to complete the task from start to finish. This means that even the most basic act, such as turning on the computer, should be listed. The procedures should allow the operator to follow them step-by-step, to complete the task accurately and meet the standard of performance required without making any independent decisions.

Standard operating procedures have benefits for both the employee and the manager. The manager is able to save time that might be spent explaining procedures, while the employee has clear expectations. Employees are happiest when they fully understand what is required and how to accomplish their daily tasks. Even the most basic instructions can be re-assuring when the employee is in a situation in which a task must be accomplished accurately but quickly, for example when dealing with a long line of customers.

The main benefit of standard operating procedures is the consistency it brings to the functions of the business. Once operational procedures are standardised and followed, several benefits occur:

- Customer perception will be of a well-run, professional company.
- A copy of the company's procedures is usually requested when financing/investment is applied for.
- A copy of a company's procedures is often required in order to obtain insurance.
- Accounts will be accurately maintained, which is not only desirable but required by law.

The standard operating procedures form a basis by which employees can be trained, promoted and disciplined, and through which customer needs are handled, transactions are processed and accounts maintained. It is worth spending the time needed to accurately standardise the procedures required for good company operations.

CASE STUDY
PROPERTY DEVELOPMENT

Aspect Property owns a town-centre building site. This could be sold now for an estimated £1.6 million. Alternatively, the site could be developed with shops and a restaurant at a cost of £1.5 million. The property could then be sold for £4 million, provided that a bypass proposal is rejected by the local council.

The odds of the bypass being rejected are judged at about 75:25 due to environmental objections. If, however, the bypass were to be built, much tourist trade would be lost and the value of the development would only be £2 million.

Aspect Property have a decision to make. There are three possible outcomes to this scenario, each of which can be given a financial value.

Outcome	Probability	Estimated value
1 The site is developed and the bypass is rejected	The development value is £4 million but there is only a 75% chance of this occurring	A 75% chance of receiving £4 million is worth £4 million × 0.75 = £3 million
2 The site is developed and the bypass goes ahead	There is a 25% chance of receiving only £2 million	If the bypass goes ahead it is worth £2 million × 0.25 = £0.5 million
3 The site is sold undeveloped	N/A	Undeveloped, the site is worth £1.6 million

To calculate the possible yield (their return on an investment) of developing the site, the values of outcomes 1 and 2 are combined. The cost of development is then subtracted: £3 million + £0.5 million – £1.5m (the cost of development) = £2 million. This compares to the value of selling the undeveloped site at only £1.6 million. On this basis, depending on its attitude to risk and the likely timescales, Aspect Property is likely to build the shops and restaurant.

UNIT 302 (B&A 41): TEST YOUR KNOWLEDGE

Learning outcome 1: Understand the principles of resolving business problems

1 Explain why it is important not to exceed the limits of your authority in decision making.

2 What is the first stage in the decision-making process?

3 Describe the role of stakeholders in problem solving.

Learning outcome 2: Understand improvement techniques and processes

1 Describe the benefits of continuous improvement.

2 Explain what is meant by 'cost–benefit analysis'.

3 Explain why feedback is important.

Learning outcome 3: Be able to solve problems in business

1 Explain why it is important to obtain approval to implement solutions.

2 Describe different types of business problems that might be encountered.

Learning outcome 4: Be able to contribute to the improvement of activities

1 Explain how to measure the effect of changes.

2 Describe how to justify adopting improvements.

CHAPTER 7

UNIT 308 (B&A 47) MONITOR INFORMATION SYSTEMS

Information systems store data in a way that enables it to be retrieved on demand and used to produce reports for a variety of purposes. The information stored must be relevant, timely and accurate. Information is only relevant if it can be used to make a decision. It is only timely if it is readily available when decisions have to be made. And it must be accurate enough to help the correct decisions to be made.

Information systems must be monitored in order to identify and put right any problems that arise, and to ensure that organisational policies and legal and ethical requirements are met.

In this unit you will cover the following learning outcomes:

1 understand how information systems are used
2 be able to monitor information systems.

Assessment criteria

This section covers assessment criteria 1.1, 1.2, 1.3, 1.4, 1.5, 1.6, 1.7, 1.8, 2.4, 2.5 and 2.6

USING INFORMATION SYSTEMS

CREATING REPORTS

There are many different types of information systems reports. The report created will depend on the intended use and the audience. It is important that the user of the report is asked relevant questions to make sure they obtain the desired results and use the correct format and language.

The business user or subject matter expert will provide you with the requirements for the report. They will advise you what data is needed, how it should be organised and presented, what sub-totals and totals are needed, etc. The data items needed in the report are then placed on the report template and the user asked for feedback. Often, changes to the report will be necessary before the final report's design is completed.

The report can then be created using different software tools. A reports wizard or a query wizard tool can quickly build reports by selecting the report's template, the database and then the relevant data for the report. Creating a template for reports is easy and will save time. The company letterhead, logos and signatures can also be placed on the template and saved onto the computer for future use.

Reports allow the presentation of relevant facts, figures and information for analysis. This helps organisations create business plans and budgets, and make marketing and advertising decisions, as well as purchasing and human resources decisions. It is important to format information in a business report so it can be read quickly and easily. The format and language will depend on the use of the report, as shown in the table.

Type of report	Description
Informational reports	In order to provide information without opinion or suggestions, an informational report is typically the best format. For example, an information report about how many employees work in each department and their job function might include employee names, years of service and salary, and an organisational chart.
Analytical reports	To solve a problem or make a decision, an analytical report might be necessary. These include a narrative of facts as well as data, explanations and conclusions. For example, a quarterly sales analysis might include sales, expenses, and the profit and loss for the period.
Research reports	To make decisions about new products and services, expanding personnel or making redundancies, research reports might be used. Research specialists create a report that provides details about a given topic, including relevant facts and statistics. The report typically offers the conclusions of the researcher as well as alternate options and their potential outcomes, backed up by the appropriate research.

SOLVING PROBLEMS RELATED TO INFORMATION SYSTEMS

Problems with information systems can relate to hardware or software:

- Periodic hardware upgrades can usually be predicted as they often reflect the changing needs of the organisation.
- Upgrading software is an ongoing process using code fixes or 'patches' to reduce errors and address new hardware issues.

However, information systems maintenance often rewards a careful and cautious approach. It has been found that some fixes will also accidentally break other parts of a working system. You must be able to make sound judgements based on the benefits and drawbacks of any planned changes before any action is actually taken.

When investigating problems with information systems it is not always the system that is at fault. Most problems stem from improper implementation, poor training or incorrect procedures. As a result, staff can produce inaccurate or inappropriate data and reports. Fixing information system problems by training or re-training staff can save you time and money while improving your organisation's efficiency.

Some problems will be simple and easily identifiable, enabling a swift solution because they are a common issue. Others will be more complex because they have non-specific symptoms or unknown faults that require a multi-step solution.

The solutions for problems with hardware usually include repairing or replacing the hardware and fixing the communication paths. Problems with software can often be resolved by reconfiguring the software, applying a software patch, re-installing the software or instructing the user in the proper use of the software.

The hardware tools and techniques needed to fix problems include electrical and electronic test instruments, self-test routines, monitoring devices, and tools such as screwdrivers, pliers and a torch. Software tools and techniques include diagnostics such as anti-virus software and error logging programs. You also need to know troubleshooting techniques such as substitution, testing, change, upgrading, re-installing software, elimination, applying bug fixes and generating error codes.

You will need to constantly look for and record feedback from users of the information systems in order to find ways to improve them. Remember, however, that amendments to systems can be expensive and can sometimes create more problems than they solve. It is worthwhile investigating the processes and procedures surrounding the information systems and considering making improvements before looking at the information system itself.

COMMON MISTAKE

Do not ignore problems; instead, fix them as soon as they appear. They will only get worse if left.

HANDY HINT

Shutting down and restarting a system with a problem often does solve the problem, so try it first.

ACTIVITY

Keep a work diary over the period of a month, recording problems experienced with information systems and how they were resolved.

Tools will be needed to fix some hardware problems

VALIDATING THE RELIABILITY OF INFORMATION

Verification is used to ensure that the data entered exactly matches the original source. There are two main methods of verification:

- double entry, which involves entering the data twice and comparing the two copies – this effectively doubles the workload and costs more
- proofreading, which involves checking the data entered against the original document – this is also time consuming and costly.

Validation is an automatic computer check to ensure that the data entered is sensible and reasonable. It does not check the accuracy of data. For example, a secondary school student is likely to be aged between 11 and 16. The computer can be programmed only to accept numbers between 11 and 16. This is a range check. However, this does not guarantee that the number typed in is correct. For example, a student's age might be 14, but if 11 is entered it will be valid but still incorrect.

Validation operations available include:

- data type validation, which is usually carried out on one or more simple data fields – the simplest kind of data type validation checks that the individual characters input are consistent with the expected characters of one or more known data types as defined in a programming language, data storage and retrieval mechanism, or otherwise
- range and constraint validation, which may examine input for consistency within a minimum/maximum range, or consistency with a test for evaluating a sequence of characters
- code and cross-reference validation, which includes tests for data type validation combined with one or more operations to verify that the data is consistent with one or more external rules, requirements or validity constraints
- structured validation, which allows for the combination of various basic data type validation steps, along with more complex processing that may include testing conditional constraints for an entire complex data object or set of process operations within a system.

There are a number of validation types that can be used to check the data that is being entered, as shown in the following table.

Validation type	Method	Example
Check digit	The last one or two digits in a code are used to check the other digits are correct	Bar code readers in supermarkets
Format check	Checks the data is in the right format	A post code is in a set format (LL99 9LL, L99 9LL or LL9L 9LL)
Length check	Checks the data isn't too short or too long	A password that needs to be eight letters long
Lookup table	Looks up acceptable values in a table	There are only twelve possible months of the year
Presence check	Checks that data has been entered into a field	In most databases a key field cannot be left blank
Range check	Checks that a value falls within the specified range	The number of hours of operation in a week must be less than 168 and more than 0
Spell check	Looks up words in a dictionary	When word processing

EVALUATION TECHNIQUES

The information system's success depends on the people who use it. To evaluate the system you will need input from users at all levels. Users often notice flaws and have needs that were unaccounted for in the original design of the system. Gaps may exist between the way the system's designer thinks people work and how they actually work, and these can be revealed through interviews and surveys.

Technical support staff, who are the people who help users with problems, are often the first to find out about defects. When several users experience the same problem, helpdesk and information technology support staff have to figure out if the problem lies with the system or the users. In some cases, system design issues that confuse users and lead to common user errors are a functionality problem because of their widespread effect. Information technology support professionals should track these problems and keep records.

By using observers and server monitoring, you can watch how people use the computer system. It is just as important to understand the aspects of the system that work well and to understand why, as it is to deal with the problems. Studying what works well may lead to solutions for the system problems.

The most important test of an information system is whether it achieves its objectives. It is important to review the original aims and compare them to system outputs. Examine whether efficiencies are created, whether reporting functions work properly and whether intended internal controls are now in place.

THE IMPORTANCE OF CONFIDENTIALITY

There are potentially serious consequences for breaching confidentiality in the use of information systems. The Data Protection Act (DPA) covers personal data that relates to a living individual who can be identified from the data or from the data and other information in the possession of the **data controller**. There are seven principles of information handling outlined in the act. These say that data must be:

Data controller

The person who decides the purpose for which personal data is to be processed

- fairly and lawfully processed
- processed for limited purposes
- adequate, relevant and not excessive
- accurate and up to date
- not kept for longer than is necessary
- processed in line with the rights of the data subject
- not transferred to other countries without adequate protection.

The Information Commissioner's Office (ICO) has extensive powers to impose penalties on organisations that breach the DPA. For example, it can:

- conduct assessments to check organisations are complying with the DPA
- serve information notices requiring organisations to provide the ICO with specified information within a certain time period
- serve enforcement notices and 'stop now' orders where there has been a breach of the act, requiring organisations to take specified steps to ensure they comply with the law
- prosecute those who commit criminal offences under the DPA
- conduct audits to assess whether an organisation's processing of personal data follows good practice.

The Information Commissioner's Office can impose penalties on organisations that breach the DPA

A data controller who persistently breaches the act and has been served with an enforcement notice can be prosecuted for failing to comply with a notice. This offence carries a maximum penalty of a £5,000 fine in a Magistrates' Court, and an unlimited fine in the Crown Court.

To avoid breaching the Data Protection Act, organisations should:

- write a data protection policy that applies specifically to the type of information they hold and the industry sector they work in
- carry out regular audits to ensure all the information held is relevant and timely
- make sure everyone in the organisation is fully aware of the key points of the act
- make sure all the information is password protected and not share passwords unless absolutely necessary
- make sure passwords are changed regularly
- if any data is taken outside the office, ensure it is encrypted and only accessible to relevant employees.

In addition to the legal consequences of breaches of confidentiality, there are business consequences. If the organisation gets a reputation for not keeping information about its customers confidential, or for producing reports containing inaccurate or unsubstantiated information, it may soon have many fewer customers.

ACCURACY OF INFORMATION

As well as ensuring that information held and reported doesn't breach confidentiality, it is also important that reports do not contain inaccurate or unsubstantiated information. The consequences will obviously vary according to the type and content of the report.

When compiling data about an individual, make sure the information is correct. Take particular care if the information could have serious implications for the individual. If, for example, you give an employee a pay increase on the basis of an annual increment and a performance bonus, then there is no excuse for getting the new salary figure wrong in your payroll records.

Where information is provided by individuals about themselves, or by third parties, it may be impractical to check the accuracy. The DPA says that even if you are holding inaccurate personal data you will not be considered to have breached the fourth data protection principle as long as:

- you have accurately recorded information provided by the individual concerned, or by another individual or organisation
- you have taken reasonable steps in the circumstances to ensure the accuracy of the information
- if the individual has challenged the accuracy of the information, this is clear to those accessing it.

What is meant by 'reasonable steps' will depend on the circumstances and, in particular, the nature of the personal data and what it will be used for. The more important it is that the personal data is accurate, the greater the effort you should put into ensuring its accuracy. So if you will be using the data for making decisions that may significantly affect the individual concerned or others, you will need to put more effort into ensuring accuracy. This may mean you have to get independent confirmation that the data is accurate. For example, most employers will only need to check the precise details of job applicants' education, qualifications and work experience if it is essential for that particular role, when they would need to obtain authoritative verification.

If the information source is known to be reliable or is a well-known organisation, it will usually be reasonable to assume that they have given you accurate information. However, in some circumstances you will need to double check, for example if inaccurate information could have serious consequences or if common sense suggests there may be a mistake.

If individuals challenge the accuracy of information held about them, consider whether the information is accurate and, if it is not, delete or correct it. Sometimes the individual may be able to provide convincing documentary evidence that, for example, a date of birth has been recorded incorrectly. In other circumstances, you may need to make some checks yourself.

Where the accuracy of a record has been challenged by the individual it relates to, it is good practice to mark the record as being in dispute. You are not legally obliged to do this; if you are satisfied that a record is correct, you need not flag it as having been challenged. However, in the case of credit reference agency records, it is accepted industry practice that disputed information should be flagged. The advantage of flagging a disputed record is that it avoids you breaching the fourth data protection principle if the information does turn out to be inaccurate. If an individual is not satisfied that you have taken appropriate action to keep their personal data accurate, they may apply to a court for an order that you correct, block, erase or destroy the inaccurate information.

An expression of an opinion about an individual is classed as their personal data. Two people may have very different opinions about the ability or personality of an individual. Personal experiences and preferences, even prejudices, can colour a person's opinions, so it may be impossible to conclude with any confidence which, if either, of two conflicting opinions is accurate. People may only be able to state which of the two they tend to agree with. When recording information about an individual you should record whether it is an opinion and, where appropriate, whose opinion it is. If a court is satisfied that you are holding inaccurate personal data containing an expression of opinion that appears to the court to be based on that inaccurate data, it can order you to delete that data, including the expression of opinion.

MONITORING INFORMATION SYSTEMS

Assessment criteria

This section covers assessment criteria 2.1, 2.2, 2.3 and 2.7

Once an information system is fully implemented and is being used in business operations, maintenance begins. Monitoring is necessary to deal with failures and problems that arise during the operation of a system. Maintenance also includes making modifications to an established system due to changes in the organisation and new initiatives that may require major changes to the business systems.

A monitoring plan must be developed that specifies:

- the objectives of the monitoring – what is to be achieved
- the scope of the monitoring – what is to be covered
- the timescale of the monitoring – when and how often monitoring will take place
- the resources required to carry out the monitoring – time, people and computer capacity needed
- the techniques to be used
- the reporting requirements.

ACTIVITY

Create a monitoring plan for your organisation or department's information systems.

When a new information system has been installed, training and support need to be organised for people who will be required to use it. In a large organisation there may be an IT support department that diagnoses hardware and software faults and solves technical and application problems. They may be able to provide training as well as support to the users of the information systems. If external training resources are needed, these are mainly offered by IT-specialist training companies approved by IT vendors such as Microsoft, Cisco, Oracle and IBM.

Training will be needed when a new information system has been installed

ACTIVITY

Write training notes on using an information system for a new member of staff.

Use of information systems must comply with legal, ethical and organisational requirements. Information management aims to improve the effectiveness of organisations by providing access to relevant information in a timely and cost-effective manner. This carries with it the problem of deciding who needs access to the information, whether the privacy of individuals needs to be protected, and what levels of security need to be in place to ensure not only privacy but also the protection of competitive information.

In the UK, the Data Protection Act established the legal basis for the protection of personal data in computer files and provided citizens with the basis for ensuring that such information was accurate and protected from misuse. In Europe, the European Commission (EC)'s directive on the protection of personal data is intended to harmonise legislation across Europe and to require those states that have not yet produced similar legislation to do so.

The overall aims of the EC are very similar to those of the DPA but grounded in the European Convention for the Protection of Human Rights. The definition of personal data files is wider, covering not only electronic files but also manual files, and a great deal of uncertainty and confusion exists as to its future operation regarding, for example, library catalogues and bibliographic databases that might be regarded as constituting personal data.

In the past, librarians and information managers needed to think of information law almost solely in terms of copyright but the situation is now very different. The information manager should:

- be responsible for identifying any existing information laws that affect the organisation
- be the link between legal services, the human resources and management information systems departments, and the operational units of the organisation to co-ordinate their activities and ensure that information law requirements are being met on a day-to-day basis, regardless of the information technology used
- ensure that information law compliance is integrated into the systems-design methodology of the organisation
- advocate changes in information law when compliance with it prevents the introduction of new information technologies, thereby threatening competitiveness and viability.

Ethics

A system of moral principles governing the appropriate conduct of a person or group

Ethics is required in information systems to overcome the issues outlined in the table.

Issue	Ethical considerations
Privacy	What information about yourself or your associations must you reveal to others, under what conditions and with what safeguards? What things can people keep to themselves and not be forced to reveal to others?
Accuracy	Who is responsible for the authenticity, dependability and accuracy of information? Who is to be held accountable for errors in information and how is the injured party to be **recompensed**?
Property	Who owns information? What are the just and fair prices for its exchange? Who owns the channels, especially the airways, through which information is transmitted? How should access to this scarce resource be allocated?
Accessibility	What information does a person or an organisation have a right or a privilege to obtain, under what conditions and with what safeguards?

Information system ethics evaluate:

- the development of moral values in the information field
- the creation of new power structures in the information field
- the development of ethical conflicts in the information field.

Issues such as the collection of internet users' private data by monitoring web traffic is related to organisational policy as that information can be further used for illegal purposes. These types of privacy issues have to be addressed so that they do not exploit the freedom of the individual.

Computer crime embraces such crimes as **phishing**, credit card fraud, bank robbery, industrial espionage, scams, cyber terrorism, viruses, **spam** etc. All such crimes are computer related and facilitated.

Policing these crimes is turning out to be an uphill battle. The widespread availability of computers and internet connections provides unprecedented opportunities to communicate and learn. Unfortunately, although most people use the internet as a powerful and beneficial tool for communication and education, some individuals exploit the power of the internet for criminal or terrorist purposes.

The term 'cyberethics' refers to a code of safe and responsible behaviour for the internet community. Practising good cyberethics involves understanding the risk of harmful and illegal behaviour online and learning how to protect ourselves, and other internet users, from such behaviour.

Recompense

Compensation for an injury or loss

Phishing

To trick somebody into providing bank or credit card information by sending a fraudulent email pretending to be from a bank or similar institution

Spam

An unsolicited, often commercial, message transmitted through the internet as a mass mailing to a large number of recipients

ACTIVITY

List the legal, ethical and organisational requirements that apply to information systems you use.

CASE STUDY
SUPPORTING USERS

Muttiah Sehwag works in a small office at a college. His main job is to support users of the information system that houses information about students and employees. This includes admissions, applications, grades and transcripts for students as well as payroll data for employees.

To make sure all offices know how to enter the data, he holds training classes for new employees. He also has to double check what people do, even after he has trained them, so he creates reports for the offices to check the data they've compiled. Some of the reports come with the system, others have to be custom designed.

In addition, Muttiah has to keep up with all the updates each year for payroll taxes and forms, and attend weekly meetings to see how they can improve their workload or share ideas with each other.

Muttiah thinks the best part of the job is meeting with people who require his assistance. When a customised report is needed, he meets with the office involved and discusses what they want, what data is available, what data can be added and what format to use. A project of this kind can take days or weeks, but he enjoys them because they are always challenging.

Muttiah thinks the worst part of the job is probably the day-to-day checking to be sure that programs run okay. He knows that some large companies have a computer specialist doing a very small portion of a big job. He thinks this might become monotonous after a time. Working in a smaller company, his job duties are much more varied.

UNIT 308 (B&A 47): TEST YOUR KNOWLEDGE

Learning outcome 1: Understand how information systems are used

1 How does the intended use of a report affect its format and language?

2 How does the audience of a report affect its format and language?

3 Describe the two types of problem in an information system.

4 Explain different ways of resolving problems in an information system.

5 Explain how information can be validated.

6 Describe an evaluation technique for information systems.

7 Describe the consequences of breaches of confidentiality.

8 Describe the consequences of inaccurate information.

Learning outcome 2: Be able to monitor information systems

1 Describe a plan you have developed to monitor an information system.

2 Describe activities you have carried out to monitor an information system.

3 Describe where training and support for users on information systems can be found.

4 Describe the cause of problems with an information system in your organisation.

5 Describe solutions found to the problems identified in Question 4.

6 Explain adaptations that were made as a result of problems in an information system.

7 Describe legal requirements when monitoring an information system.

CHAPTER 8

UNIT 309 (B&A 48) EVALUATE THE PROVISION OF BUSINESS TRAVEL OR ACCOMMODATION

Despite advances in technology, face-to-face communication remains important for building business relationships. Business people know conference calls can never fully replace the personal touch of meetings, and therefore business travel and short- to long-term accommodation are often core requirements. When organising business travel there are two important needs: to minimise the need for further travel, and a comfortable place at the end of a busy day to catch up on emails or prepare for the following day's meetings.

These needs can be met either by arranging the travel and accommodation through travel agents or by making the arrangements in-house using the internet or other means. Evaluating the alternative options of travel and accommodation is an important part of providing a cost-effective service.

In this unit you will cover the following learning outcomes:

1 understand the provision of business travel or accommodation arrangements
2 be able to evaluate the quality of organisational business travel or accommodation arrangements
3 be able to recommend improvements to organisational business travel or accommodation arrangements.

Assessment criteria

This section covers assessment criteria 1.1, 1.2, 1.3 and 1.4

PROVIDING BUSINESS TRAVEL AND ACCOMMODATION ARRANGEMENTS

There are a number of factors to take into account when evaluating the provision of business travel and accommodation. As well as price, the following should be taken into account when selecting from potential suppliers:

- Suitability – will the travel arrangements or accommodation actually meet the requirements of the user?
- Discounts – often there will be deals to be made if bulk orders are placed with a supplier or a deal made for exclusive supply of travel or accommodation for a period.
- Delivery and after-sales service charges – take care that there are no hidden charges that make the purchase price appear lower.
- Reliability and reputation – the maxim 'you get what you pay for' is still often true: a reputable brand is often worth paying extra for.

To ensure that the traveller's needs are fully met, liaise with them to plan the journey and prepare the **itinerary**, taking into account:

Itinerary

A plan for a journey listing different places in the order in which they are to be visited

Climatic

Of or pertaining to the climate and weather conditions

- time and **climatic** differences between their departure point and their destination – remember that departure and arrival times will be shown in local time
- time and budget available – the cheapest form of transport is not necessarily the most cost effective.

The precise steps to take when planning an itinerary will depend on the type of trip planned but, as an example, for a business trip involving meetings with clients, the steps might be:

- Schedule the itinerary at least a month in advance so that you can get reasonable rates/quotes and access to the exact arrangements that you need.
- Call the business contacts to schedule any meetings before you start setting travel plans. (This step may have already been taken by the traveller themselves, but you will need this information.)
- Book the transport required for the trip. Depending on the destination, schedule arrival for one to two days before the first business meeting, if possible, to allow time for the traveller to rest and go over their plans for the trip.
- Arrange a rental car or book a car to pick up the traveller at the airport, if needed.
- Book a hotel and contact the hotel ahead of time to book meeting rooms, if needed. Check that the hotel has an internet connection, wake-up service and any other details needed for a successful and pleasant business trip.

Transport options available will vary depending on location

- If there is more than one traveller of the same sex, ask them if they would consider sharing a hotel room to save money.
- Create a written itinerary based on the plans made. List all of your important appointments, including the dates, times and locations, in their order of occurrence.
- Use an online map program or website, such as www.mapquest.com which allows you to set up a series of stops within one search, and print directions to guide the traveller through the trip.
- Check the weather forecast in that location for the dates of the trip ahead of time, so the traveller can pack accordingly.
- Confirm all meetings and trip arrangements a few days before the trip. Print off the written business itinerary and directions, and give them to the traveller to pack in their case along with their laptop.

A table or spreadsheet like the example below may help to make sure that the itinerary prepared gives the traveller all the information they need in a convenient format. Summarise the 'five Ws' (who, what, where, when and why) for each entry on the itinerary so that every detail is clear.

HANDY HINT

About 17% of business people share rooms with co-workers, according to a 2010 study.

Date	Depart from	Depart time	Destination	Arrival time	Destination address	Tel. number	Travel time	Comments

Depending on the destination there may be a choice between travelling by road, rail and/or air. The decision should take into account the overall cost, the cost of the traveller's time and the traveller's personal preferences.

ACTIVITY

Select a destination abroad that interests you and plan a journey and itinerary for a visit.

Road travel can be a tiring way to travel

ROAD TRAVEL

When considering road travel, take into account:

- the number of travellers and the number of vehicles they would need
- availability of parking at the destination
- overall time required
- the effect of the length of the journey on the driver.

Railways can allow people to carry on working while they travel

RAIL TRAVEL

When considering rail travel, take into account:

- the convenience of the departure railway station
- the convenience of the destination railway station
- travelling time
- number of changes
- the reliability of the train service
- whether luggage and equipment can be easily transported.

Air travel is sometimes the only way to reach meetings abroad

AIR TRAVEL

When considering air travel, take into account:

- the convenience of the departure airport
- the convenience of the destination airport
- the reliability of the air service
- additional time for check-in and luggage retrieval.

TRAVEL REQUIREMENTS

Travellers going abroad will need information on requirements for:

- Passports – everybody travelling abroad must hold a valid passport. In many cases the passport must be valid for six months beyond the expected return date, so it is important to check this.
- Advance Passenger Information System (API or APIS) – this means the traveller's passport/identity card details and in some instances contact information are provided to the authorities before travelling.
- Visas – many countries require visitors to have a visa permitting entry for a specific purpose, such as a holiday, study, business etc. Failure to supply the correct **visa** can result in the visitor being refused entry to the country.
- Health certificates – some countries require visitors to have certificates showing that they have been vaccinated against certain

Visa

An official endorsement in a passport authorising the bearer to enter or leave, and travel in or through, a specific country or region diseases. As this requirement changes regularly, it is important to check the government website (www.gov.uk) for the latest information.

- Luggage restrictions – some airlines restrict the weight and number of bags that can be carried, either in the hold of the aircraft or in the cabin.
- E-tickets and boarding passes – some airlines do not provide conventional tickets or boarding passes but require passengers to print these off themselves before travel.
- Travel insurance – medical travel insurance provides medical coverage during the trip. Travellers should check their own health insurance policy to see what cover they have already. Many people find that their own policies restrict cover to a limited geographic area, and outside that area cover emergencies only. Insurance plans differ in their requirements for cover. Many medical insurance plans have a **pre-existing** condition period. In this case, the traveller will not be covered for an illness or injury for which they are already seeking treatment if they were advised to see a doctor for the condition, had symptoms or were taking medication for the condition within a defined length of time. Medical evacuation travel insurance plans evacuate ill or injured people to a nearby medical facility and back to their home. Requirements are generally that the injury or illness is sudden and unexpected.
- Driving licences – travellers who intend to drive during their journey must have a valid driving licence. Check that a UK driving licence is valid in the destination country.
- Car insurance – valid insurance will be needed if driving abroad. This can be purchased as part of a car-hire package but this isn't always the most economical method so check with your organisation's insurance company, if you have one, or the individual's insurer may be able to help. There are other legal requirements for driving abroad which differ from country to country – even within Europe, as shown in the table – so again, check these before the journey.
- Credit cards and foreign currency – the traveller abroad will have day-to-day expenses that they will need to meet either by charging a credit card or by using the currency of the country they are in. Many organisations have credit cards that they authorise certain of their staff to use, but these and the individual's credit cards will often have **punitive** charges or interest rates for transactions carried out abroad, so it is important to check these before the visit takes place. Foreign currency can be bought from a wide range of financial institutions, travel agents and **bureaux de change**, but the rates offered vary, often considerably and even from minute to minute, so again it is important to take care to get the best possible rate. When the traveller returns, they may have some foreign currency left over. A decision will have to be made on whether to

Pre-existing

Something that already existed

Punitive

Causing great difficulty or hardship

Bureau de change

An office, often found in a bank, that allows consumers to exchange one currency for another. The bureau de change charges a commission for the currency exchange service

	Austria	Belgium	France	Germany	Italy	Netherlands	Switzerland	Spain
GB sticker displayed	C	C	C	C	C	C	C	C
Headlight beam converter	C	C	C	C	C	C	C	C
Warning triangle carried	C	C	R	R	C	R	C	C
High visibility jacket carried	C	C				C		C
First-aid box	C	R		R				
On-the-spot fines	Yes	Yes	Yes	Yes	Yes	Yes	Yes	Yes

C = compulsory R = recommended

Sterling

The currency in pounds and pence used in the United Kingdom

Consulate

The office of a government official living in a foreign city to promote the commercial interests of the official's own state and protect its citizens

change this back into **sterling**, which will be at a less favourable rate than when it was bought, or to keep it in a safe place for the next person visiting a country where it can be used.

After confirming the itinerary with the traveller, then accommodation, travel tickets and car hire can be booked. Useful sources of information when planning business travel include **consulates**, timetables, hotel guides, maps and directories. Arrangements might be made through travel agents or via the internet. Travel tickets can be purchased via the internet and paid for using a company credit card or purchased through a travel agent who will invoice the company. Look for the most cost-effective tickets as major discounts can be achieved by booking as far in advance as possible.

Some organisations have arrangements with hotel groups that provide reduced room rates. Where these exist they should be used. In other situations, use the internet or a travel agent. It is important that reservations are confirmed before the traveller departs to avoid difficulties on arrival. Remember to take into account any organisational policy on standard of travel and accommodation to be used. When selecting potential suppliers and comparing quotations, consider financial restrictions, the available budget, organisational policies and equality of opportunity.

ACTIVITY

For the journey you planned in the previous activity, check the need for travel documentation and the best way to cover day-to-day expenses.

Some organisations have hotel deals that provide reduced rates

COMMON MISTAKE

It is often cheaper to book travel and accommodation not through a travel agency but online.

Whether travel and accommodation is booked online or through a third party, the following information will be required:

- Details of the people travelling – not just the number of people but, if they are travelling abroad, their names as they appear on their passport, their passport number, the country of issue and their date of birth.
- Where they are travelling from and to – remember that they may not be travelling directly from their starting point to their finishing point.
- Their required arrival and departure and times.
- The class of travel and accommodation required – air travel may be first class, business class, club class or economy; rail travel may be first class or standard class; accommodation may be anything from a guest house to a five-star hotel.
- Their documentation requirements – they may need train tickets, air tickets, hotel reservations, visas, car hire information or directions.
- Special requirements. They may have mobility issues, special dietary requirements or need access to facilities such as wireless connectivity or an interpreter.

HANDY HINT

Whether purchasing by comparing quotations or by choosing from a range of websites, it is not necessarily the most efficient use of the organisation's resources to simply buy the lowest-priced option if this compromises another aspect of the trip.

If you are using a travel business to organise flights, they must comply with the Civil Aviation Authority (CAA)'s Air Traffic Organiser's Licence (ATOL) regulations. ATOL is a financial protection scheme managed by the CAA. All UK-based travel companies selling air holiday flights are required by law to hold a licence called an ATOL which is given after the company has met the CAA's requirements. The scheme is designed to protect consumers in the event of the travel business going out of business. An ATOL holder provides guarantees to customers that their money is financially protected in the event of the seller or supplier's failure. Each ATOL holder has a unique ATOL number that can be checked on the ATOL website.

SECURITY AND CONFIDENTIALITY

One of the major risks connected with travel is the danger of confidential information being compromised. Documents may be mislaid or overseen by fellow travellers, or conversations overheard. Remind colleagues who are travelling to follow the rules below to keep their confidential information safe when out of the office or on the road:

- Know their environment – information they may be carrying is highly confidential. They should never work on this type of information while travelling. Using travel time as work time is fine as long as the information isn't confidential. If the work is confidential, it needs to be completed in a confidential area and not in a crowded public space.
- Remember that voices travel and people have eyes – if you can see or hear someone then they can see and hear you. When you have a laptop screen up, the people behind you and to the sides have visual access to that screen as well. When something needs to be immediately addressed, find the most secluded area available to make the call or get out a needed document. Select the area with the lowest likelihood that a confidential call will be overheard or document seen. Let the person on the other end of the phone or text message know that you are in a public space with limited ability to discuss the topic.
- Keep documents secure – in today's electronic age, where documents tend to be in an electronic format, it is important to keep devices secure. Think of the damage someone could cause if a Blackberry, Android, iPhone or laptop ended up in the wrong hands and wasn't locked. Set devices to lock themselves if they are not used for five minutes.

Safeguarding material while travelling is easy; it just requires some common sense and an organisational culture that recognises that travel time is not necessarily the best time to carry out work.

EVALUATING THE QUALITY OF TRAVEL OR ACCOMMODATION ARRANGEMENTS AND RECOMMENDING IMPROVEMENTS

Assessment criteria

This section covers assessment criteria 2.1, 2.2, 2.3, 2.4, 3.1, 3.2 and 3.3

After each journey, your organisation should keep records of the travel and accommodation details in order to:

- account for costs incurred and paid for directly by the organisation
- meet expense claims from the traveller for costs incurred and paid for by them
- use the information for future reference if a similar journey needs to be planned.

When selecting a travel or accommodation supplier, you will need criteria to enable you to compare potential providers. There are eight common supplier-selection criteria:

These criteria can be summarised as follows:

- Cost – the total cost of dealing with the supplier.
- Quality and safety – the level of sophistication of the supplier's quality system.
- Delivery – the supplier's ability to meet current and potential requirements within the desired delivery schedule.
- Service – the previous experience and past performance of the supplier with the product/service to be purchased.

Suppliers should be evaluated against criteria such as service

- Social responsibility – the supplier's record on issues of sustainability, inclusivity etc.
- Convenience and simplicity – the technical support available and the supplier's willingness to participate in developing and optimising design.
- Risk – the supplier's financial stability, the possibility they might fail to meet their commitments and the results of any failure.
- Agility – the supplier's ability to react to future changes in requirements.

Some criteria should be treated as unbreakable rules in the supplier selection process. To determine whether the constraint is necessary or simply an important criterion, ask questions such as:

- If you had to choose between having the best quality for all items by using two suppliers and having the best quality for only half the items by using one supplier, would you still insist on using one supplier?
- If you could save 34% by accepting a seven-week lead time instead of six weeks, would you choose to save the money or would you still insist on the six-week lead time?

The fewer constraints, the more flexibility you have in your decision making. After determining the constraints and criteria, agree a hierarchy, an order of attributes from the most important to the least important, with constraints coming before criteria. In most cases, potential providers' offerings will differ and there will be trade offs involving the criteria: you may get a better price from one supplier (cost) but that supplier insists on contract terms less favourable to you (risk). Creating a hierarchy in advance will help you remain focused on what's most important to make a balanced decision.

Having selected a supplier, monitoring their performance is critical. Your organisation may have a supplier-performance rating programme in place that is used to monitor the performance of suppliers in other areas of the organisation's activities. The supplier performance rating programme should consider:

- which suppliers will be rated
- who will participate in the rating process
- what performance measures will be used
- how performance data will be collected
- how performance data will be used.

HANDY HINT

Performance rating must be used to reward exceptional performance as well as to correct inadequate performance.

The benefits and limitations of existing arrangements for organising business travel and accommodation must be evaluated and, where necessary, alternative providers identified using the same criteria as were used to identify the original supplier.

To compare the existing arrangements with potential changes and improvements, a costed plan must be produced that sets out:

- the different options
- the benefits of the different options
- the limitations of the different options
- the implications of the different options.

ACTIVITY

Create a costed plan to recommend improvements to organisational business travel and accommodation arrangements.

Outsourcing the provision of business travel and accommodation by getting a third-party to arrange this may help the organisation save money. There are other advantages to outsourcing:

- Focus on core activities – in periods of growth, the back-office activities of an organisation may start to use human and financial resources at the expense of the core activities of the organisation. Outsourcing those activities will allow refocusing on the business activities that are important to the organisation, without sacrificing quality or service in the back office.
- Cost and efficiency savings – if the organisation's travel and accommodation needs are complicated but the size of the organisation prevents you from performing it at a consistent and reasonable cost, outsourcing may be the answer.
- Operational control – departments that have become uncontrolled and poorly managed areas are prime areas for outsourcing.
- Staff flexibility – if the organisation's travel and accommodation needs are seasonal or cyclical, bringing in additional resources will be a costly exercise, whereas outsourcing removes this consideration.
- Continuity and risk management – if staff trained to organise travel and accommodation leave, it will add uncertainty and inconsistency to the operation. Outsourcing provides a level of continuity.

The choice of suppliers of travel and accommodation should be based on their reputation, quality and reliability. An ethical problem can occur when staff are already acquainted with suppliers as such a relationship poses a conflict of interest. Ethical policies should require the staff to disclose any personal relationships with suppliers and to not take any gifts or bribes in return for contracts.

CASE STUDY
BUSINESS TRAVELLER

The world of the frequent flyer on expenses, travelling the world on business, looks glamorous to those who don't have to do it. While there's no denying that it's nice to have the perks, many business travellers would rather stay at home and see their families once in a while.

One former business traveller, Brian, has sworn to hang up his carry-on case for ever. Once you get past a certain point in his company's hierarchy, travel from the UK to foreign locations becomes inevitable. At first most of the trips were to Europe. Brian found himself on the road in Europe, with a boot full of computers, on average for two weeks in every month.

'Fortunately I can speak French and German and the language was always English in meetings or presentations,' he says. 'At first it was glamorous and friends were envious, particularly when I was one of the first people to get a mobile phone installed in my company car.

'But after a while I was always missing out on birthday parties and other social events because I was always travelling, never in the country at the right time. Having to spend a weekend on your own in a foreign city, because there was no point in coming back, was quite dull.'

When the travel to the United States started, it was fun at first, particularly since products and clothes were good quality and very cheap, so it was fun shopping for gadgets and things. But, not being high enough up in the hierarchy to be able to travel in business class or first class, the flights themselves were not that comfortable. Brian is well over six feet tall, so flying economy class is no joke.

One year Brian had four trips to the US and another to Thailand for work, and then a holiday in South America and another to a friend's wedding in Australia. In the end he told his wife that he wouldn't be going on any more long-haul flights.

UNIT 309 (B&A 48): TEST YOUR KNOWLEDGE

Learning outcome 1: Understand the provision of business travel or accommodation arrangements

1 List the evaluation criteria for selecting suppliers of travel and accommodation.

2 What are the different standards of travel and accommodation that may be needed?

3 What does the acronym 'ATOL' stand for?

Learning outcome 2: Be able to evaluate the quality of organisational business travel or accommodation arrangements

1 Why is it important to identify instances of exceptional and inadequate performance?

2 Name two different ways that travel and accommodation arrangements could be made.

Learning outcome 3: Be able to recommend improvements to organisational business travel or accommodation requirements

1 What are the eight common supplier-selection criteria?

2 What should be set out in a plan to recommend improvements to travel and accommodation arrangements?

3 Why is a previous relationship with a potential supplier an ethical issue?

CHAPTER 9

UNIT 322 (B&A 61) ANALYSE AND PRESENT BUSINESS DATA

Analysing and presenting business data is an important area of working within the business environment. Research may produce large amounts of information but that information will be of no use in informing decision making until it has been analysed so that trends can be identified. The information also needs to be evaluated for relevance (being directly connected to the matter under consideration), validity (the soundness of the information) and reliability (its accuracy) so that the results are not skewed and can be checked for freedom from bias.

Providing decision makers with data that can be relied upon and which is presented in a readily understood, user-friendly format, without distorting the information in order to support a conclusion that has already been made, is critical to enabling the correct decisions to be made.

In this unit you will cover the following learning outcomes:

1. understand the analysis and presentation of business data
2. be able to analyse quantitative and qualitative business data
3. be able to present the analysis of business data.

Assessment criteria

This section covers assessment criteria 1.1, 1.2, 1.3, 1.4, 1.5, 2.1, 2.2, 2.3, 2.4, 2.5, 2.6 and 2.7

Parameters

Limits

ANALYSING DATA

Before researching data, it is important to agree the **parameters** of the analysis required. Too much information can be as unhelpful as too little. When you are asked to research information, the person making the request will have an objective in mind and a deadline for receiving the information. It is important that you understand what these are. It would not be helpful, for example, to supply a list of team members for every World Cup match played by England three weeks after being asked to find out who played in goal in the 1966 final if the answer was needed the next day.

It is also necessary to clarify any ethical issues surrounding the analysis. In designing and carrying out research, it is important to consider any potential harm that could be caused and to think of how that harm might be avoided. Individuals whose data is involved in the research should be given detailed information wherever possible to allow them to give informed consent.

One way of avoiding potential harm in the development of research is by communicating openly with everyone involved. You are then likely to uncover possible problems and can take steps to ensure that they are made harmless. Issues and pitfalls that arise can be dealt with immediately and any doubts that any stakeholder has can be dealt with. As the research develops, it will become increasingly difficult to deal with such issues and problems.

Tenet

A principle, belief or doctrine that is generally held to be true

A second basic **tenet** of research ethics is integrity. The reader of the research must be able to trust that the researcher actually carried out the research as they say they did.

Methods of researching data can be categorised according to the sources used and the type of research carried out. The sources used can be divided into primary research and secondary research.

PRIMARY RESEARCH

Primary research involves the collection of new first-hand information or resources. For instance, interviewing people is a primary research method, as is looking at original documents from their period being researched. For example, in a market research context primary research might gather information using market surveys, telephone interviews, questionnaires and/or focus group interviews.

Primary research uses the closest information to the subject, information that has not been altered by previous researchers adding their own views or interpretation. This information is more reliable but takes longer to gather as primary sources are more difficult to find. Examples of relevant primary sources include:

- original research studies
- technical reports
- original documents
- newspaper articles
- first-person accounts
- case studies
- official documents.

SECONDARY RESEARCH

Secondary research involves processing data that has already been collected by previous researchers. This information may be found in reports, press articles and previous market research projects. This type of research is less expensive compared with primary research as it does not require new research methods. However, its main disadvantage is that the information gathered may be old and obsolete, and therefore that the results of analysis may be inaccurate.

Secondary research uses information which has already been interpreted or analysed by others, without access to their primary source. This allows access to a wider field of research which can be cross-referenced to give more detailed analysis, but brings into the information other researchers' analysis and opinions, which may distort the accuracy of the information and/or introduce **bias**.

Bias

The distortion of a set of statistical results either by a variable not considered in the calculation or by the variable itself

Secondary research may include:

- statistics already researched and analysed by other organisations, such as the Office for UK National Statistics , the UK Statistics Authority and local councils
- information contained in print, such as books, magazines, journals, pamphlets and the internet.

Secondary research can save time but it is important to check how reliable the source of the information is. It is important that data sources used are relevant. Remember that print sources may not be up to date and that anyone can publish on the internet without any guarantee that the information is accurate or truthful.

Examples of relevant secondary sources include:

- review articles or analyses of research studies
- reviews or critiques
- analyses of original documents or archival material.

QUANTITATIVE AND QUALITATIVE RESEARCH

Whether the sources of research are primary, secondary or a combination of the two, the type of research may be quantitative or qualitative.

Quantitative research uses a scientific approach where information gathered is usually easy to measure and able to be analysed mathematically. It generates numerical data or at least data that can be converted into numbers. Examples include the national census and opinion polls.

Quantitative research often uses questionnaires to gather data from a large number of sources. Questions are usually closed, giving the option to choose 'yes' or 'no' or from a limited number of options. An advantage of questionnaires is that large volumes of data can be gathered relatively quickly. A disadvantage is that questions must be carefully phrased or people may select an answer at random, distorting the results.

Another method of quantitative research is experiment. For instance, testing of a new diabetes drug could be carried out by giving one group of participants the new drug and another group a **placebo**. Testing the blood sugar levels of both groups would give a numerical result which could indicate the effect of the drug. An advantage of experimentation is that an **hypothesis** can be tested and strong evidence in support or in contradiction can be found. A disadvantage is that only one variable can be tested.

Placebo

Something prescribed for a patient that contains no medicine but is given for the positive psychological effect it may have because the patient believes that he or she is receiving treatment

Hypothesis

A statement that is assumed to be true for the sake of argument

Qualitative research is more concerned with opinions and feelings and does not necessarily produce numerical information that can be analysed. It is used to explore the beliefs, experiences, attitudes, behaviours and interactions of people. Techniques used include focus groups, observation and in-depth interviews.

Focus groups can provide qualitative research

Observation involves studying the behaviour of participants, often while they are carrying out their natural activities. The researcher may tell the participants exactly what they are looking for or they may observe covertly, where the participants are aware of the researcher's presence but unaware that they are being observed. An advantage is the ability to observe participants in their natural surroundings, while the disadvantages include the limited sample that may be observed and the fact that participants act unnaturally because they are aware they are being observed.

In-depth interviews collect detailed information from a small number of participants, whereas focus groups collect more generalised information from a larger number. In-depth interviews have the advantage of giving the interviewer greater control over the direction the conversation takes, but the disadvantages of an inability to generalise from the views expressed and the fact that the person being interviewed may be influenced into giving the answers they think are expected or required.

INFORMATION EXTRACTION

Information extraction (or information retrieval) is used to extract using pre-defined criteria relevant details from computer systems that hold large volumes of data. This makes it possible to identify data relevant to an enquiry without having to search manually through all of the data.

Information extraction is more refined than a simple search process, as the software involved can scan data sources and, through a process known as natural language processing, find relevant data by identifying not only specific words or phrases but also their context and meaning.

Data sources that can be searched using information extraction include hard copy documents that can be scanned into the computer, spreadsheets, word processed documents and databases. The software program is given parameters within which to search the data sources for information, which it then prioritises and extracts.

DATA CHECKING AND ORGANISATION

Having collected the data, you need to evaluate it to check that the information available matches the information required and that it is complete and accurate. There are various reasons why data may need to be cleaned in order to prepare results which are accurate and free from bias. There may be:

- Incomplete information – if surveys for instance, are used as a source of information, they may not have been completed fully by the respondents. This may affect the statistical analysis of the answers as some questions will have a greater number of responses than others. It may be necessary to exclude some questions from the results entirely for this reason.

- Data entry errors – all information held in an electronic system depends on the quality of the input – 'garbage in = garbage out' (GIGO).
- Questionable entry – inconsistencies in the data may be due to data entry errors (mistakes), or deliberate input or provision of incorrect information (manipulation).

HANDY HINT

Don't believe everything a computer tells you unless you are sure of the source of the data.

The data presented must also be accurate and free from bias. This is particularly difficult to achieve from qualitative research as, by its very nature, it contains people's feelings and opinions. But there are ways to help eliminate bias from qualitative research:

- Understand the limitations of the sample group – if the topic excludes certain age groups or occupations, for instance, or the sample group is too small, then bias can occur.
- Ensure that the participants do not have reason to provide information that proves or disproves a hypothesis – research into the viability of providing a cycle path should include the views of motorists, pedestrians and cyclists, for instance.
- Make sure that participants have ample time to complete any questionnaires – hurried opinions will not necessarily be accurate.
- Be aware of the fact that people will sometimes give opinions that they think are 'the right thing to say' rather than the truth – anonymous questionnaires are more likely to produce accurate results than face-to-face interviews.
- Questionnaires can create bias through the questions they ask, prompting respondents to give the answers that the researcher is hoping to get rather than honest answers.

An interview taking place

Data must be organised if useful information is to be extracted from it. Data can be collected in a variety of forms, including measurements, survey responses and observations. While this collection of data will be useful, it can also be overpowering. In order for the meaning of the data to be understood, the data must be structured. For instance, the responses to a survey must be collated so that the responses to specific questions can be seen. Trends will emerge from organising the data and it is these trends that need to be highlighted when reporting the data.

HANDY HINTS

- Be wary of research findings – some researchers will hide results that do not support their own view and exaggerate those that do.
- It is extremely easy to manipulate data to support desired conclusions. Look at the data and think critically about the conclusions drawn.

DATA ANALYSIS

Once you are satisfied that any bias has been eliminated, the data can be analysed and the results presented. (Presentation is covered in the next section of this book.) There are two methods of analysis: descriptive and inferential.

Descriptive data analysis uses the results to provide a summary of the information, for instance what percentage of customers like a particular product. If you are calculating averages from the collected data, remember that there are different ways of reporting averages. Mean, median, and mode are the three most common.

- The 'mean' is the average obtained from adding up all the numbers and then dividing by the number of numbers.
- The 'median' is the middle value in the list of numbers. To find the median, your numbers have to be listed in numerical order.
- The 'mode' is the value that occurs most often. If no number is repeated, then there is no mode for the list.

You may also want to report on the 'range'. This is just the difference between the largest and smallest values.

The most common methods of analysing numerical data are visual representations such as charts, graphs and tables. These allow the reader to glean interesting information in a clear and understandable way. Examples are shown in the table below.

 Bar charts	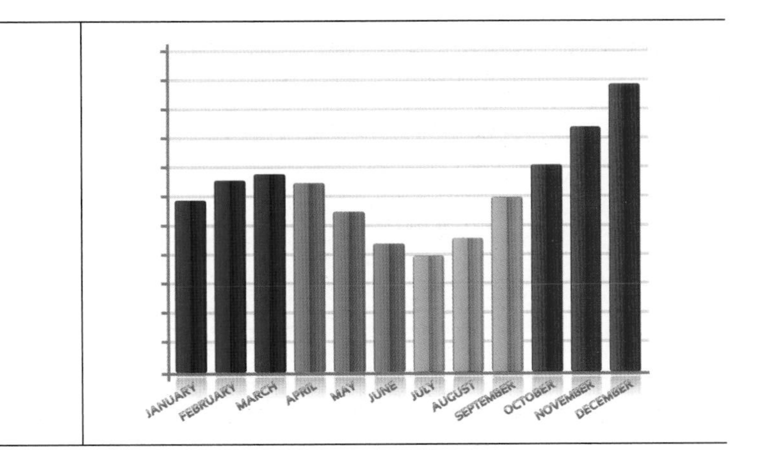

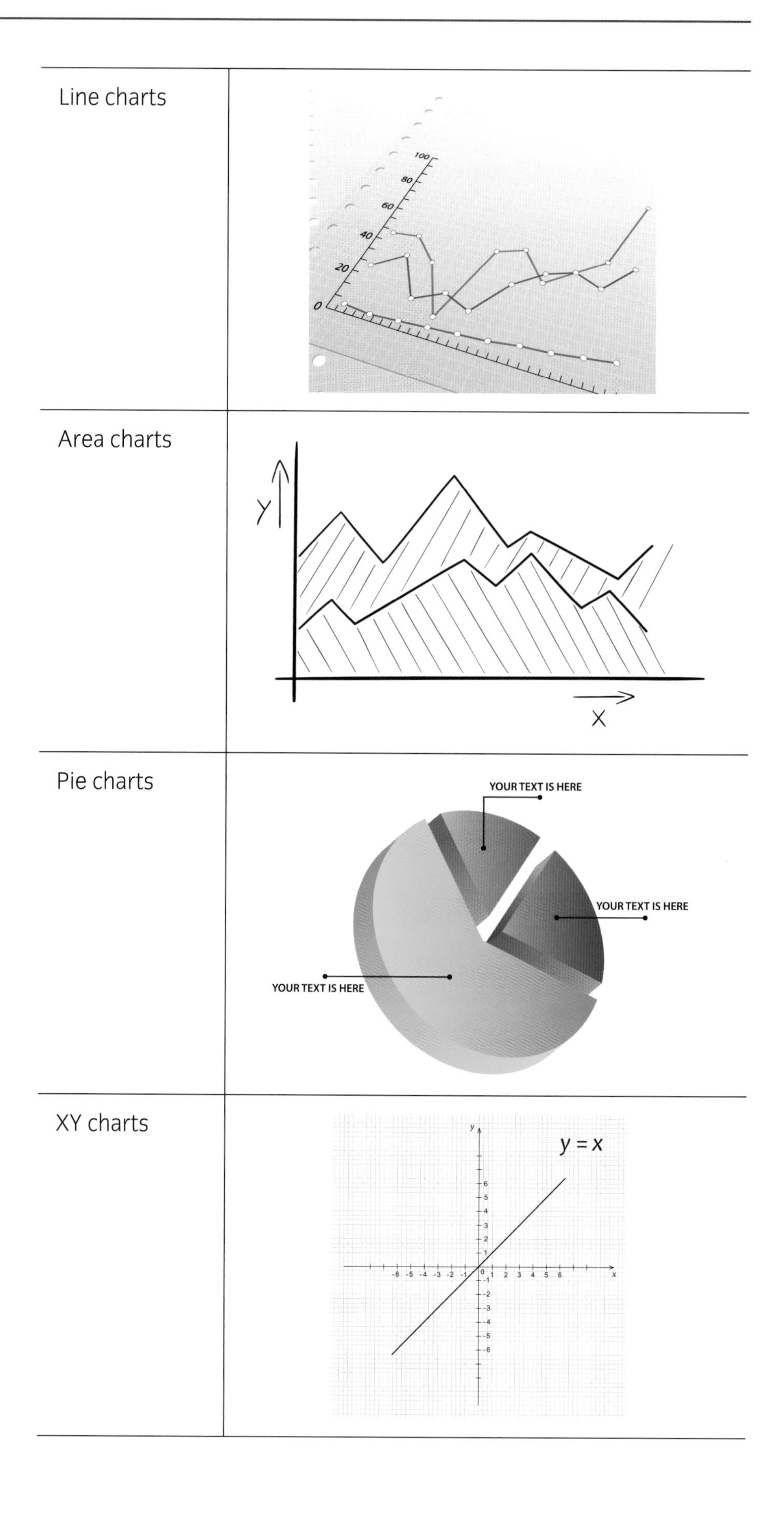
Line charts
100
80
60
40
20
0
Area charts
Y
X
Pie charts
YOUR TEXT IS HERE
YOUR TEXT IS HERE
YOUR TEXT IS HERE
XY charts
y = x
y
x

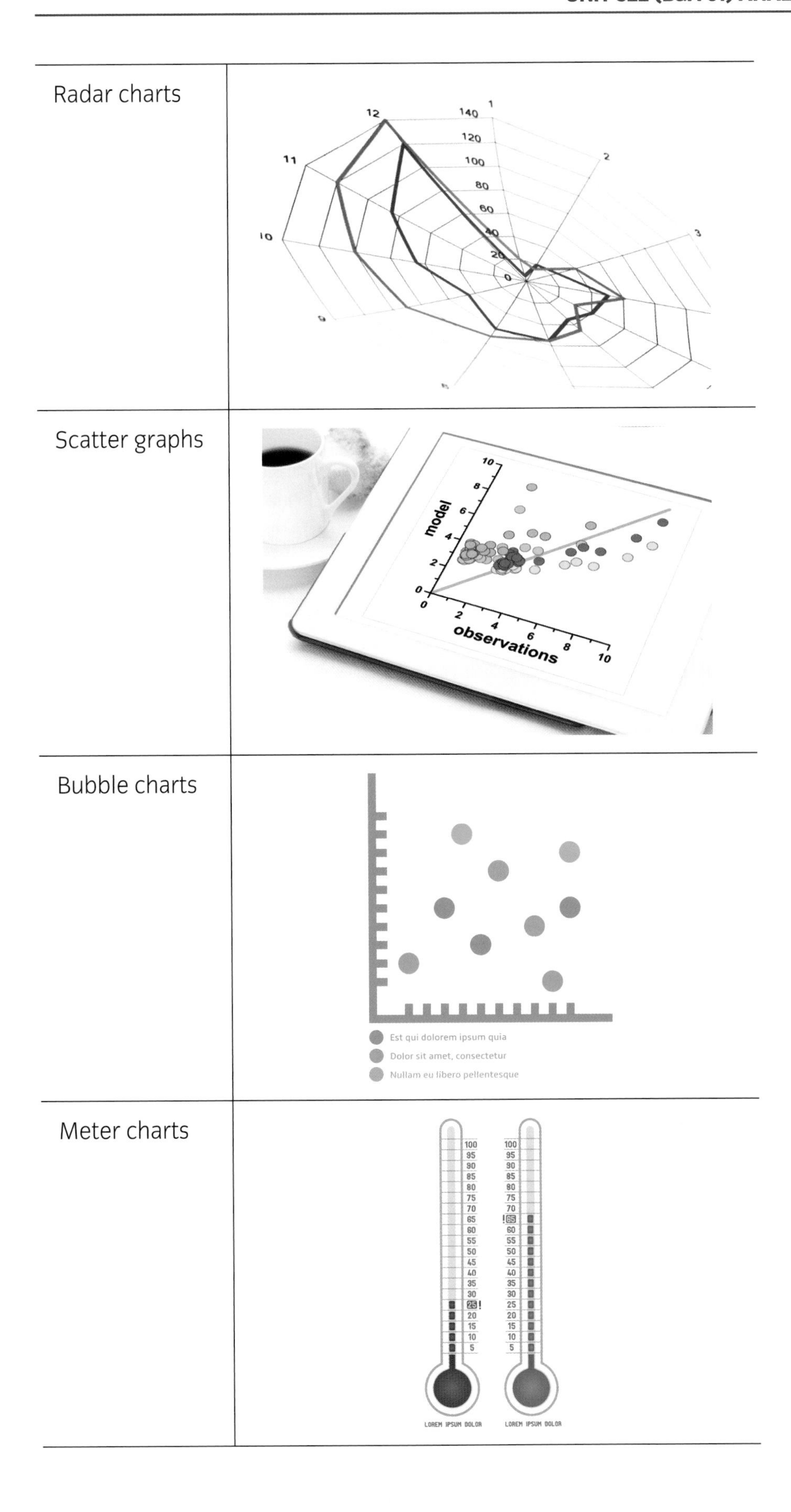
Radar charts
Scatter graphs
model
observations
Bubble charts
Est qui dolorem ipsum quia
Dolor sit amet, consectetur
Nullam eu libero pellentesque
Meter charts
LOREM IPSUM DOLOR
LOREM IPSUM DOLOR

ACTIVITY

Your line manager is planning a trip to Ankara in Turkey, Cairo in Egypt, Faisalabad in Pakistan, and Manila in the Philippines. You have been asked to research information on currency, visas required and inoculations required for each country to be visited. Present the information in a suitable format.

Line/bar charts	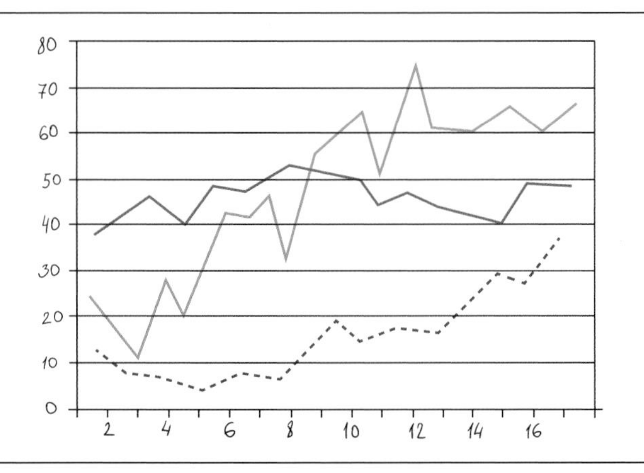

ACTIVITY

Ask your line manager to nominate a topic for data analysis that will be useful to your organisation. Carry out the analysis and present your findings.

Inferential data analysis allows information obtained from a small group to be used to make judgements about a larger group. Information can also be used to compare different groups or to forecast future events based on the past results. This kind of analysis offers more insight than descriptive data analysis.

There are many different analytical techniques available. The important considerations are that the analysis should be:

- logical
- systematic
- methodical
- reasoned.

One popular analytical technique is key driver analysis, sometimes known as an importance-performance analysis. This is a study of the relationships among many factors to identify the most important ones. A key driver analysis can be used in many applications. One of the most common is in the area of customer satisfaction and loyalty.

A key driver analysis can help you understand what your customers feel is important to them having a good experience with your organisation. By doing an analysis of their answers and comparing their satisfaction level answer to their rating of each performance metric you can derive which factors have the greatest impact on the customer's perceived level of satisfaction. You can then plot this data in a scatter diagram called a key driver chart or an importance performance map.

A key driver chart plots the results of a key driver analysis in a graphical format that can be quickly read and easily understood. Each metric is plotted on the graph by its importance to the customers' satisfaction (on the x-axis) and your performance in that area on the y-axis.

This generates four quadrants. The most important is the lower right quadrant. The items plotted here have high importance to your customers, but your performance in those areas is low. These are the areas where your action will have the biggest impact and generate the greatest improvement in customer satisfaction for the effort expended.

Another technique is correspondence analysis. This has several features that distinguish it from other techniques of data analysis. An important feature of correspondence analysis is the **multivariate** treatment of the data through simultaneous consideration of multiple categorical variables. The multivariate nature of correspondence analysis can reveal relationships that would not be detected in a series of pairwise comparisons of variables. Another important feature is the graphical display of row and column points in **biplots**, which can help in detecting structural relationships among the variable categories and objects (ie cases). Finally, correspondence analysis has highly flexible data requirements. The only strict data requirement is a rectangular data matrix with non-negative entries. Correspondence analysis is most effective if the following conditions are satisfied:

Multivariate

Involving several statistical variables relating to or used to describe a statistical distribution that involves a number of random but often related variables

Biplot

A type of exploratory graph used in statistics, a generalisation of the simple two-variable scatterplot. A biplot allows information on both samples and variables of a data matrix to be displayed graphically

- The data matrix is large enough, so that visual inspection or simple statistical analysis cannot reveal its structure.
- The variables are **homogeneous**, so that it makes sense to calculate the statistical distances between the rows or columns.
- The data matrix is 'amorphous', ie its structure is either unknown or poorly understood.

Homogeneous

Having a common property throughout

A distinct advantage of correspondence analysis over other methods yielding joint graphical displays is that it produces two dual displays whose row and column geometries have similar interpretations, facilitating analysis and detection of relationships. In other multivariate approaches to graphical data representation, this duality is not present.

A third technique is decision tree algorithms. Decision trees are powerful and popular tools for classification and prediction. The attractiveness of decision trees is that they represent rules. Rules can readily be expressed so that humans can understand them or even directly used in a database access language like **SQL** so that records falling into a particular category may be retrieved.

SQL

Structured Query Language is a special-purpose programming language designed for managing data held in a relational database management system

There are a variety of algorithms for building decision trees that share the desirable quality of interpretability. A well-known algorithm frequently used over the years is C4.5 (or improved, but commercial version C5.0).

A decision tree is a classifier in the form of a tree structure where each **node** is either:

Node

The place on a plant stem where a leaf is attached

- a leaf node – indicates the value of the target attribute (class) of examples, or
- a decision node – specifies some test to be carried out on a single attribute-value, with one branch and sub-tree for each possible outcome of the test.

A fourth technique is factor analysis. Factor analysis is a statistical method used to describe variability among observed, connected variables in terms of a potentially lower number of unobserved variables called factors. For example, it is possible that variations in four observed variables mainly reflect the variations in two unobserved variables. Factor analysis searches for such joint variations in response to unobserved latent variables. The observed variables are modelled as linear combinations of the potential factors, plus 'error' terms. The information gained about the interdependencies between observed variables can be used later to reduce the set of variables in a dataset. Computationally this technique is equivalent to low rank approximation of the matrix of observed variables. Factor analysis originated in psychometrics, and is used in behavioural sciences, social sciences, marketing, product management, operations research, and other applied sciences that deal with large quantities of data.

After analysing the data, you will be in a position to draw conclusions and present the information.

Assessment criteria

This section covers assessment criteria 1.6, 1.7, 3.1, 3.2 and 3.3

PRESENTING DATA

Whatever methods of collecting data you have used, you will need to present your findings. It is important that this is done in a way that meets the aims and objectives that were originally agreed, in the agreed format and to the agreed timescale.

If you are analysing data for someone else to use to support or oppose a decision, you will need to get their feedback on the type of analysis they require and the format in which they want the information presented. They may require a slideshow presentation to a group, a verbal presentation at a meeting or a formal report, for instance. If a formal report is required, there is a recognised structure that is used to make the information easy to find and understandable. This structure is shown in the table below.

Title page	Report title, your name, date
Executive summary	Overview, methods of analysis, findings, recommendations
Contents	Numbered sections and page numbers
Introduction	Terms of reference, structure
Body	The main contents of the report, divided by headings and sub-headings

Conclusions	The inferences that can be drawn from the data
Recommendations	Recommendations for actions based on the conclusions
Bibliography	List of sources used during research
Appendix	Supporting detail

The report should acknowledge the limitations of the analysis carried out. Analysis can be limited because quantitative research may collect a narrow and sometimes artificial dataset and provide only numerical descriptions. Quantitative research is often carried out in an unnatural, artificial environment so that a level of control can be applied to the exercise. This level of control might not normally be in place in the real world, producing 'laboratory' results rather than 'real world' results.

Other potential limitations are that pre-set answers do not necessarily reflect how people really feel about a subject and might just be the closest match, and that the development of standard questions by researchers can lead to 'structural' bias where the data actually reflects the view of the researcher instead of the subject.

A limitation to qualitative research is that it may seem to be less than valid in its approach, methods or conclusions. Qualitative research often depends on the individual judgement of the researcher and is heavily dependent on the researcher's own interpretation. This can allow the researcher's own opinions to prejudice the information presented or the conclusion drawn.

A significant limitation of qualitative research is that it is difficult to **extrapolate** findings to more broad populations, or to draw general or far-reaching conclusions from the findings.

Extrapolate

To say what is likely to happen or be true by using information that you already have

Qualitative research is specific to one setting so it is difficult to make broad recommendations based on the outcome of the research. Because qualitative research provides in-depth answers about just one very specifically defined individual or group, it does not provide assurance that the findings can transfer across individuals or groups. It also presents issues involving reliability and the ability to reproduce the study with consistent results.

All of these limitations need to be acknowledged when presenting the information, particularly if recommendations are being made.

When the report is complete, it is important that it is checked for spelling, grammar and punctuation as well as correctness. Remember that spell checking facilities on your computer will only find some errors – it cannot tell whether you meant to say 'your' or 'you're', for instance. Check that it is set to English (UK) rather than English (US) or it will insist on changing words like 'behaviour' to 'behavior'. Present the report using the correct house style, if your organisation uses one.

You should also reference the sources of the data used. Write down the details of your sources as you research. When using information from books, you should record:

- the author's or editor's name (or names if more than one person)
- the year the book was published
- the title of the book
- the name of the publisher.

For articles you should record:

- the author's name (or names)
- the year in which the journal was published
- the title of the article
- the title of the journal
- the page number(s) of the article in the journal
- the volume and issue numbers.

For electronic resources, you should record:

- the date you accessed the source
- the type of electronic resource (eg email, discussion forum or internet page).

ACTIVITY

Look at the way your organisation sources its supplies; these may be raw materials, products for re-sale or consumables such as stationery or utilities. Gather information on alternative sources and write a reasoned recommendation either to change supplier or to keep the present arrangement.

CASE STUDY
CONVENIENCE-STORE CUSTOMERS

A successful line of convenience stores realised that they seemed to be visited by many more men than women. They informally kept track of the proportions of men to women who came into one store and found that this confirmed their suspicions. The information was passed along to other stores and they found the same trend. A decision was made to study this phenomenon and to try to understand why it was taking place and whether anything could be done about it.

Twenty female customers were paid to come in to discuss their use of convenience stores. The major qualitative findings included the following:

- Women viewed convenience stores to be primarily designed for men, with little or no consideration for women.
- Convenience stores were believed to be the dirtiest that could be found in a city and that perception permeated everything that women felt about convenience stores.
- Convenience stores were the 'kind of place for a man to buy cheap beer and cigarettes, but not the kind of place I want to go'.

The company then decided to conduct 250 telephone interviews with female respondents. The major results from the quantitative phase indicated that:

- Over 76% of all female convenience store customers were women under 30 years old, without children, while women with children and with higher incomes were five times less likely to shop there.
- Of the women who didn't currently use the stores, 64% indicated that if the company updated their colour scheme, cleaned up the stores and updated their health and feminine products, then they would be willing to try them again.

The research gave the management team a very good understanding of where they currently stood with regard to female customers and why.

UNIT 322 (B&A 61): TEST YOUR KNOWLEDGE

Learning outcome 1: Understand the analysis and presentation of business data

1 Give two examples of:
   - Primary research
   - Secondary research.

2 Explain the differences between qualitative and quantitative research.

3 Explain why it is necessary to evaluate the reliability of data.

4 What IT tools can be used to carry out research?

5 What type of samples should not be used to make judgements?

6 Why must care be taken when generalising research findings?

Learning outcome 2: Be able to analyse quantitative and qualitative business data

1 What is meant by the 'parameters of analysis'?

2 How should data be organised?

3 Name two techniques for qualitative research.

Learning outcome 3: Be able to present the analysis of business data

1 Give two examples of formats for presenting analyses.

2 What should be recorded about the sources of data?

CHAPTER 10

UNIT 204 (B&A 16) STORE AND RETRIEVE INFORMATION

In recent years, there has been a theory that it is possible to operate a paperless office. The development of the computer was expected to reduce the need for hard copies of documents to nil. What has happened in practice is that producing documents has become so much easier and their number has greatly increased. We are all guilty of printing off an email so that we can consider our response. We then send a reply email to the original sender, who prints off both our reply and their original email! This is environmentally unfriendly, as well as being an expensive waste of resources such as paper and ink. Storing and retrieving information has never been more important.

In this unit you will cover the following learning outcomes:

1. understand information storage and retrieval
2. be able to gather and store information
3. be able to retrieve information.

Assessment criteria

This section covers assessment criteria 1.1, 1.2, 1.3, 1.4, 2.1, 2.2, 2.3 and 2.4

STORING INFORMATION

If you cannot find information on which the completion of a task depends, the task will be delayed with possible serious consequences. The purpose of storing information is to be able to retrieve it when it is needed. An effective information storage and retrieval system enables you to find complete, accurate and up-to-date information so that you can make decisions based on all the available information. Storing information is much more than simply keeping papers or saving electronic files. If there is no system for retrieving the information when it is required, the information is likely to be lost or difficult to find. This will inevitably lead to problems such as a waste of time and money and, possibly eventually, a loss of business.

Many organisations are moving towards a more general use of electronic information systems rather than the more traditional paper-based ones. To decide which is more appropriate in a given situation, you need to ask:

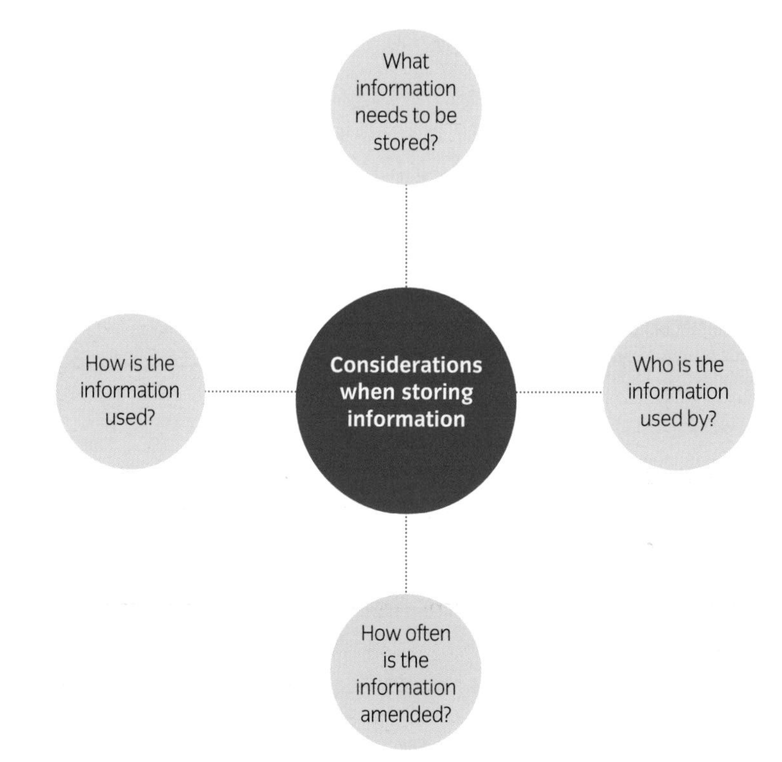

- What information needs to be stored? If the information is recorded currently on paper, it may be best to store it as paper. If the information is electronic, there is no point in printing it simply to store it as paper.
- Who is the information used by? If the people needing access to the information are situated in different locations, electronic records may be accessible to all of them via a shared server, whereas paper documents would have to be copied for each of them.

- How often is the information amended? Information which needs regular updating, such as customer names and addresses, may be best stored electronically as it is easier to amend than paper records which may need completely recreating to record the change.
- How is the information used? Some information, such as legal records including deeds, wills, contracts etc, may depend for its validity on signatures and witnesses' signatures. While these documents could be scanned into an electronic filing system, the original will need to be retained in case of any future dispute.

LEGAL AND ORGANISATIONAL REQUIREMENTS

A recurring issue with the storage of information is the length of time for which it must be retained. The Data Protection Act says that personal information should not be kept for longer than is necessary, but this is not particularly helpful. There are a number of factors involved in deciding when records may be deleted including:

- legal requirements
- the cost of storage
- the need to refer to the information
- any historical value the information may have.

The last three of these factors will be decided at the organisation's **discretion**. Many documents that are available for academic research and public interest have only survived because an organisation has decided to retain their records far beyond the point at which they have a need to refer to them or a legal requirement to keep them. If organisations such as Cadbury, Lever Bros and the BBC hadn't kept **archives** of material from their early days, we would not have access to so much information today.

Discretion

The power to make decisions sensitively on the basis of one's knowledge and the ability to keep sensitive information secret

Archive

A collection of documents or computer records, kept for future reference

Outside of the organisation's authority are the legal requirements for retaining records. These apply to accounting records, personnel records, health and safety records, medical records, wills, military records, criminal records, academic records, contracts, etc. You need to know what the legal periods are for retention of any records that you are responsible for, as deleting information before the due date is a serious matter, possibly leading to criminal prosecution for the organisation.

Some examples of the type of records that are kept by most organisations and their retention periods are shown in the following table.

Record type	Retention period
Income tax and salary records	6 years plus current year
Unsuccessful job applications	6 months after notification
Sickness and statutory maternity pay records	3 years after the end of the tax year
Purchase ledger, invoices and petty cash records	6 years from the end of financial year
Banking records	6 years from the end of financial year
VAT records	6 years
Employer's liability insurance certificate	40 years
Health and safety records	3 years; permanently for records relating to hazardous substances

Archiving records involves deciding which files are no longer required to be kept within the active storage system and organising their storage or destruction, depending on retention requirements.

Archiving files regularly:

- speeds up locating files by reducing the number of files in the active filing system
- makes disposal more efficient by reducing the backlog
- reduces the space required for current filing.

Many organisations will use an outside company to manage their archives. This is preferable to an in-house system where records are simply dumped in storerooms, which can lead to:

- vast backlogs of records no-one knows about, some of which may be important
- poor storage conditions
- increased storage requirements.

Some information will need to be kept secure and access to it controlled. This may be because the information is confidential or because it is **commercially sensitive**. The legal requirement to keep information confidential is covered by the Data Protection Act. This act covers personal data which relates to a living individual who can be identified from the data or from the data and other information in the possession of the **data controller**. There are eight principles of information handling outlined in the act. These say that data must:

Commercially sensitive

Information that an organisation would not like to be in the public domain as it may give an advantage to a competitor

Data controller

The person who decides the purpose for which personal data is to be processed

- be fairly and lawfully processed
- be processed for limited purposes
- be adequate, relevant and not excessive
- be accurate and up to date
- not be kept for longer than is necessary
- be processed in line with the rights of the data subject
- be secure
- not be transferred to other countries without adequate protection.

The data subject is the individual about whom data is held. Data subjects have rights which include being allowed to:

- know if data is held about them
- request a copy and description of the data
- inspect the data and have it changed if it is inaccurate
- seek compensation if the data is inaccurate
- know the purpose for which the data is being processed
- know who will have access to the data
- seek compensation if unauthorised access has been permitted
- prevent the processing of data likely to cause damage or distress
- ensure decisions against them are not made only on the basis of automatic processing.

Information must be stored in accordance with the Data Protection Act

Data subjects have to pay an administration fee to the data protection commissioner to prevent the processing of data or to correct or delete it.

As well as the legal requirement to protect personal information, there will be organisational requirements to keep information confidential. This may be because there is a duty of trust to your clients or customers or because the information would be useful to competitors.

One of the principles of the Data Protection Act that causes organisations some difficulty is the requirement that information must be accurate and up to date. The Information Commissioner's Office (ICO) provides some useful information on this which can be applied to all stored information.

The ICO says that the Data Protection Act does not define the word 'accurate', but it does say that personal data is inaccurate if it is incorrect or misleading as to any matter of fact. It will usually be obvious whether information is accurate or not. For example, if an individual has moved house from Chester to Wilmslow, a record showing that he currently lives in Chester is obviously inaccurate. However, a record showing that he once lived in Chester remains accurate, even though he no longer lives there. You must always be clear about what a record is intended to show.

There is often confusion about whether it is appropriate to keep records of things that happened which should not have happened. Individuals understandably don't want their records to be tarnished by, for example, a penalty or other charge that was later cancelled or refunded. However, the organisation may legitimately wish its records to accurately reflect what actually happened – in this example, that a charge was imposed, and later cancelled or refunded. Keeping a record of a mistake and its correction might also be in the individual's interests.

It is acceptable to keep records of events that happened in error, provided those records are not misleading about the facts. You may need to add a note to a record to clarify that a mistake happened. This depends on what the information is used for. If the information is used for a purpose that relies on it remaining current, it should be kept up to date. For example, your employee payroll records should be updated when there is a pay rise. Similarly, records should be updated for customers' changes of address so that goods are delivered to the correct location. In other circumstances, it will be equally obvious when information does not need to be updated.

Also, where information is held only for statistical, historical or other research reasons, updating the information might even defeat the purpose of holding it. Where you use your own resources to compile personal data about an individual, then you must make sure the information is correct. You should take particular care if the information could have serious implications for the individual. If, for example, you give an employee a pay increase on the basis of an annual increment and a performance bonus, then there is no excuse for getting the new salary figure wrong in your payroll records. It may be impractical to check the accuracy of personal data someone else provides. In recognition of this, the act says that even if you are holding inaccurate personal data, you will not be considered to have breached the fourth data protection principle as long as:

- you have accurately recorded information provided by the individual concerned, or by another individual or organisation
- you have taken reasonable steps in the circumstances to ensure the accuracy of the information
- it is made clear to the individuals accessing the data if the individual has challenged the accuracy of the information.

The definition of taking reasonable steps will depend on the circumstances and, in particular, the nature of the personal data and what it will be used for. The more important it is that the personal data is accurate, the greater the effort you should put into ensuring its accuracy. So if you will be using the data in making decisions that may significantly affect the individual concerned or others, you will need to put more effort into ensuring accuracy. This may mean you have to get independent confirmation that the data is accurate. For example, most employers will only need to check the precise details of job applicants' education, qualifications and work experience if it is essential for that particular role, when they would need to obtain authoritative verification. If your information source is someone you know to be reliable, or is a well-known organisation, it will usually be reasonable to assume that they have given you accurate information. However, in some circumstances you will need to double check – for example if inaccurate information could have serious consequences, or if common sense suggests there may be a mistake.

Some information may also be subject to the Freedom of Information Act (2000) that makes information in relation to certain organisations accessible to members of the public.

As well as your legal responsibilities, if you have access to information systems you must act **ethically** when using the technology. The law considers some computer activities illegal. Accessing, using or destroying hardware, software or the information contained in information systems can be a form of theft. It is also illegal to use an information system to release unauthorised information. The theft of copyrighted material is also illegal. You must not use computer networks for piracy or to obtain protected information.

Ethical

Consistent with agreed principles of correct moral conduct

Information systems have transformed the way organisations such as banks and hospitals keep records and organise their customers' or patients' personal information. On the other hand, information storage brings risks to the privacy of the individuals with personal information filed in the system. Sometimes databases are broken into and people's personal information such as names, addresses and national insurance numbers are stolen. Identity thieves use stolen personal information to steal from their victims' bank accounts or take out credit cards or loans in the victims' names.

Hospitals use information systems to store patients' personal information

Some employers closely monitor their employees' computer use, sometimes going as far as logging websites or looking at email. Other employees think computer monitoring is an unethical form of privacy invasion. Privacy is one of the chief concerns when it comes to ethics in information technology, especially in a work environment. Computer users expect privacy when it comes to their passwords, personal information and emails, while employers want to determine if the employee's time is being used inappropriately. Many organisations have installed programs to track the websites that employees visit. While this may seem unethical to some computer users, the fact that the organisation owns the computers means it has rights regarding what can be done with them. If you don't want your employer to know which sites you visit, limit personal use to your home computer.

INFORMATION STORAGE SYSTEMS

There are different information systems available with different features to meet the organisation's business needs. Three main information systems are:

- transaction processing systems
- management information systems
- decision support systems.

Transaction processing systems (TPSes) process business transactions. Transactions can be any activity, for example, in a hotel reservation system, booking, cancelling, etc are all transactions. Any query made is a transaction. Some transactions are common to almost all organisations, such as employees' holiday entitlement, purchase ledger systems, etc. TPSes provide high speed and accurate processing of record keeping of basic operational processes including calculation, storage and retrieval.

Management information systems (MISes) help in problem-solving and making decisions. They use the results of transaction processing and other information. They handle queries as quickly as they arrive. An important element of an MIS is the database. A database is a collection of interrelated data that can be processed through application programs and is available to many users.

Decision support systems assist management to make long-term decisions. They handle unstructured or semi-structured decisions. Some decisions have to be made infrequently or even only once, so a decision support system must be very flexible. The user should be able to produce customised reports by giving particular data and format specific to particular situations.

Features of different information systems are summarised in the following table.

Information systems and their features

Transaction processing system (TPS)	Substitutes computer-based processing for manual procedures. Deals with well-structured processes. Includes record-keeping applications.
Management information system (MIS)	Provides input to be used in the decision process. Deals with supporting well-structured decision situations. Typical information requirements can be anticipated.
Decision support system	Provides information to make judgements about particular situations. Supports decision-makers in situations that are not well structured.

Once the decision has been taken whether to use paper-based or electronic information systems, you need to choose between the various different filing methods. There may be organisational policies or procedures already in place which will determine which are used.

Paper-based information can be stored in either vertical or lateral filing cabinets

FILING METHODS

ALPHABETICAL

Alphabetic filing systems group information together using the letters A–Z. Any type of information can be filed alphabetically and can be readily retrieved as long as certain rules are agreed and adhered to. If the information is to be filed under a person's name, it is usual to file it by reference to the surname followed by the forename. For instance if filing records for Ann Johnson, Anne Johnson and Amy Johnson, the sequence would be:

- Johnson, Amy
- Johnson, Ann
- Johnson, Anne.

Titles such as Mr, Mrs, Miss, Dr, Prof or Sir are ignored for this purpose. If, for instance, Amy Johnson were a doctor, her entry would be Johnson, Dr Amy, but she would still be filed before Johnson, Ann.

Alphabetical sequence needs to be strictly followed, so that records for McDougal, MacManus and Manning would be filed in the sequence:

- MacManus
- Manning
- McDougal.

Surnames that include 'St' as an abbreviation of 'Saint' should be filed as if the 'Saint' were spelt in full. Records for St John, Saint, Sampson and Sabberton would be filed in the sequence:

- Sabberton
- Saint
- St John
- Sampson.

Company names are filed under the full company name, so Amy Johnson Ltd, Amy Johnson Hairdressers and Amy Johnson & Co would be filed in the sequence:

- Amy Johnson & Co
- Amy Johnson Hairdressers
- Amy Johnson Ltd.

Company names that consist solely of initials such as BBC, AA or RAC are filed at the beginning of the section for their first letter. Records for BBC, Barber & Co, BT and Burrows Ltd would be filed in the sequence:

- BBC
- BT
- Barber & Co
- Burrows Ltd.

COMMON MISTAKE

Filing names such as McTavish as if they were spelt MacTavish.

The definite article ('the') is ignored when filing. For example The Bathroom Company is filed under 'B'.

The advantage of alphabetical storage of information is that, as long as the rules are agreed and understood by everyone involved, there is no difficulty in locating information. There is no need for any form of **cross-referencing**. The disadvantage is that names are not unique, so there may be two or more Michael Johnsons in the system. To retrieve the information on a particular Michael Johnson you would need to refer to another piece of information such as a middle name, date of birth or address.

Cross-referencing

A reference from one part of a file to another part containing related information

NUMERICAL

Numerical filing is used for any information where the most important reference to it is its number. For example, invoices and purchase orders. The important thing to remember when creating a numerical filing system is that there must be sufficient digits in the system if electronic information systems are to be used. A computer will read numbers from left to right as if the digits were individual letters, so 111 will be read as starting with 1 while 27 will be read as starting with 2 and therefore stored after 111. To avoid this problem, if the numbers 000111 and 000027 are used, the computer will get it in the right order.

The advantage of a numerical system is that every number is unique and you can store and retrieve an infinite number of documents without ever duplicating their file name. The disadvantage is that if you don't know the number of the file you are looking for, there is no easy way to find it without a cross-referencing system.

ALPHA-NUMERICAL

Alpha-numerical filing is used where the file name consists of letters and numbers. The postal codes used in the United Kingdom are known as postcodes. An example is the postcode. A typical UK postcode may read as MK41 8LA. MK refers to the postcode area, as the letters at the beginning are based on letters from a city, town or district in the area. There are 120 postcode areas in the UK. MK41 refers to the district within the area. There are 2,900 districts within the country. The 8 in the second set of characters refers to the postcode sector. There are about 9,000 of these sectors. The final two characters are the postcode unit and define a group of about 15 properties within the sector, which could be a street, part of a street, or even an individual large user. It is estimated that there are 1.6 million postcode units in the UK to cover 24 million delivery points. Some special delivery points such as Buckingham Palace and the House of Commons have postcodes that may **differentiate** them from surrounding areas because of the large volume of mail that these sites receive from around the world.

Differentiate

To establish a difference between two things or among several things

GEOGRAPHICAL

Geographical filing is used where the information needs to be grouped with reference to its location within a country or region. For instance information will be divided into countries, sub-divided by region or county and then by town or city. So an address in Churchtown, Southport, Lancashire, England would be filed under:

- England
- Lancashire
- Southport
- Churchtown.

Information can be filed geographically

Within each division or sub-division information will be stored alphabetically.

The advantage of a geographical filing system is that information can be retrieved more easily covering a geographic area rather than having to extract specific information from an alphabetic system that covers the whole world or the whole country.

SUBJECT

Filing by subject is used where access to the information is needed by reference to its subject. Probably the most common example of filing by subject is the system used in reference libraries, where all the books about plumbing will be stored on one shelf and all the books about fishing will be on another. Similarly, information stored electronically may be stored in folders by subject.

The advantage of filing by subject is that all the information is in one place. If you want information on plumbing, you don't need to know the names of the authors to find it. The disadvantage is that a single piece of information may refer to more than one subject. The question then arises whether to make copies of the information to place in each subject file or to create a cross-referencing system.

CHRONOLOGICAL

Chronological filing simply means storing information in date order. It is mostly used within one of the other systems. For instance, correspondence with Amy Johnson will be placed in her file chronologically, with the most recent on top. This allows a record of events to be built up over a period of time in sequence. Often, people will reply to emails by using the 'reply' option which results in a sequence of e-mails each replying to the previous one. This creates a form of chronological information storage.

It is important, when creating electronic records, that dates are entered as YYYY/MM/DD if the record is to be stored chronologically, although we use DD/MM/YYYY when we date a letter, for example. A computer will store 15/04/1971 before 25/12/1963, but will store 1963/12/25 before 1971/04/15.

The advantages of chronological filing are that information can be retrieved in chronological order, allowing you to see how one piece of information influences another and where information is to be deleted after a given period of time, it is much easier to recognise which information should be destroyed. The disadvantage is that a purely chronological filing system would make it very difficult to trace a particular piece of information if you didn't know the date it originated.

Electronic information systems will carry out these functions automatically; manual systems will require the skill and knowledge to handle these categories. To help electronic information systems to **classify** information, it is important to name electronic files in a consistent and coherent way. A number of file-naming **conventions** have been established to facilitate this. These include:

- making names short and clear
- avoiding repetition
- using capital letters to delimit words

ACTIVITIES

- Make a list of the types of information that is stored in your organisation. Place the list in a table showing electronic and paper-based information and the sources of the information.
- Sort the following into alphabetical order:
  - Maroon 5
  - Lianne La Havas
  - The View
  - Adele
  - Linkin Park
  - Lana Del Rey
  - Train
  - Jessie J
  - J-Z & Kanye West
  - Noel Gallagher's High Flying Birds
  - One Direction
  - Florence + The Machine
  - Beady Eye
  - Green Day.

Classify

To assign things or people to categories

Conventions

The customary way in which things are done within a group or organisation

- using at least two digits when including numbers; 09 will appear before 10, but 9 will appear after it
- when using dates in file names, always stating the date yyyymmdd as this maintains a chronological order
- when using names, putting the surname first
- avoid words like 'draft', 'letter' or 'memo' at the start of file names.

Where large numbers of files are involved, they are often grouped into folders and directories to enable them to be retrieved more easily.

HANDY HINT

Don't fill file drawers too full as tightly packed files will slow down storage and retrieval as well as causing a potential safety hazard if they do not close completely.

RETRIEVING INFORMATION

Assessment criteria

This section covers assessment criteria 1.5, 3.1 and 3.2

When retrieving information it is important to confirm exactly what information is involved as retrieving incorrect information can cause serious problems for the person you are providing the information to. For example, if someone is working on a contract with a customer whose name is Albert Smith and you provide them with information on Alfred Smith, this could create confusion and a possible loss of business. It is important, therefore, when asked to retrieve information, that you check the accuracy of the information carefully. If asked for a file on 'Albert Smith' you should check a separate piece of information such as the address or date of birth so that you can confirm that you have retrieved the correct file.

SEARCHING DATABASES

Information can be retrieved from a database using search functions. As you become more experienced in using different databases you will find this easier. It is important to take care when typing terms into the search box. If you enter too many terms, you may retrieve no references or very few references because the database is trying to find references that contain all the words entered. If you type too few words, you may retrieve too many references. If you don't enter terms commonly used to describe the subject you are searching for, you may retrieve irrelevant references.

Some databases search the full text of the references that they contain. Other databases only search a brief description, or summary, of the references. If you are searching a full-text database, you will be able to search on very specific terms. If you are searching a database that only has summaries of the references, you may have to use fewer terms and less specific terms.

Connectors, sometimes called Boolean operators, are used to combine search terms. There are three connectors:

- 'AND' placed between words means both words must appear in each reference. This will narrow your search. For example, 'audio AND video' will retrieve all references which contain both 'audio' and 'video'.
- 'OR' placed between words means that either word or all words may appear in each reference. This will broaden your search. For example, 'audio OR video' will retrieve all references with 'audio' or 'video' as well as references which contain both 'audio' and 'video'.
- 'NOT' placed between words means that the second word must not appear in any reference. This will narrow your search. For example, 'audio NOT video' will retrieve all references with 'audio' except references which include 'video'. Take care when you use this connector as you may exclude useful references.

If you use more than one type of connector in a search statement, eg AND as well as OR, you need to use parentheses to keep the groups of terms together. This procedure is sometimes called nesting. For example '(women OR woman OR female) AND (smoking OR tobacco)'. This is a technique for experienced searchers. The less sophisticated alternative is to do several searches with different combinations of the search terms.

Truncation, or the use of wildcards, involves abbreviating words to retrieve all the alternative terms. For example, using the term 'comput*' will retrieve 'computer', 'computers', 'computate' and 'computation'. Some databases also provide internal truncation to facilitate searching on alternative spellings. For example, 'p?ediatric' will retrieve 'paediatric' and 'pediatric'. Wildcards vary from database to database. Some databases will automatically include plurals or variant spellings in the search. Familiarise yourself with each database's requirements by consulting the help screens or searching tips.

Some databases will assume that a string of words should be searched for as a phrase and will only retrieve references in which the words occur side by side or in very close proximity. This works well if you have entered the phrase 'information technology', but it will be a problem if you have entered 'depression teenagers' instead of 'depression in teenagers'. In some databases, there will be a separate search box for phrase searching.

Many databases will give you the option to limit your results. For example, you may be able to specify that you want to retrieve only articles with full text, or articles from peer-reviewed journals. Or you may be able to limit your results to articles published in certain years or in a particular journal. Field searching is another way of limiting your results. The references on the database are normally split up into fields, such as author, title, journal title or subject descriptor. If the database has an advanced search option, you will probably be able to restrict your search to a particular field. If your search terms appear in the title or subject descriptors of the reference, the reference is likely to be more relevant. Field searching can also be used to distinguish between, for example, Dickens as an author and Dickens as a subject. You may also be able to search electronically by reference number or by storage end date.

Some databases keep a record of all the searches that you have done during the current session. Use this search history to retrieve an earlier search. You can also use it to combine two or more searches that you have already done, using the normal Boolean operators (AND, OR, NOT).

SUPPLYING INFORMATION TO A THIRD PARTY

Having collected the information, you will need to organise it in order to meet the requirements of the person who asked for it in the first place. The way in which you do this will depend on the purpose the information is to be put to. It is also necessary to check when asked to retrieve information what format the information is required in and the timescales involved. Your information system will be capable of providing a whole range of information on any requested subject, but it will not be cost effective to produce a wide-ranging report if all that is required is the subject's contact details. For example, if you are asked for the purchase orders raised to a supplier in the last 12 months, it is more likely that what is wanted is a list containing information such as dates, values, etc than a pile of actual purchase orders. While checking this, you can also enquire whether the information should be supplied electronically or printed off. Similarly, if the information is required for an important meeting the following day, it will not be helpful to produce an in-depth dossier that will take three days to collate.

You need to be able to search through large volumes of information to find what you need

In many organisations, there is a system of signing out files so that you will always know where they are. This is extremely useful if someone else requests the file, as you will be able to direct them to the person who currently has it. It also allows you to trace the file should it not be returned when finished with.

DEALING WITH PROBLEMS

The worst problem that could possibly occur with the storage of information would be if it were permanently lost or destroyed. For this reason, most organisations will have some form of back-up system. This may involve keeping the most important information from paper documents on an electronic record so that, if the paper records are destroyed, the information can be recreated. Electronic records are usually backed up onto **peripheral** storage media such as external hard drives, pen drives or CD-ROMs which are either removed from the premises or stored in fire-proof cabinets. It is likely that CD-ROMs will be phased out in the near future as technology progresses.

Peripheral

Externally related or connected, for example, a device linked to a computer to provide communication (as input and output) or auxiliary functions (such as additional storage)

Filing needs to be done frequently so that records are up to date, otherwise you may not be able to find the information you need.

Day-to-day problems that you may experience with electronic information systems include a system crash. This is where a computer or a program ceases to function properly. The computer may freeze, so that there is no reaction to input from the keyboard or mouse. Depending on the type of program you are working on, you may be able to close down your computer and start it again to solve the problem or you may have to call for technical support. When inputting new data or editing existing data, frequent saving of the information should be carried out to prevent any loss through a system crash.

HANDY HINT

Make sure there is a security system that protects confidential files, whether paper or electronic.

Other problems with electronic information systems include accidental deletion of records or infection with a computer virus. You may be able to recreate deleted records if you still have the source information. Where source information is not available or a virus is detected you may require a restore by your technical support.

Computer viruses are a risk when storing information electronically

ACTIVITIES

- Create a form which can be used in your organisation by people requesting information. The form should be sufficiently detailed to ensure that the correct information is retrieved.
- Keep a work diary recording when you have stored and retrieved information.

Paper records are really only subject to two types of problem. They may be damaged by mishandling, fire or flood or they can be lost through misfiling or poor description. Misfiling is a potential nightmare as it is very difficult to guess where the file might have been put by mistake. The only advice we can give is to use educated guesswork. The file might be one letter away from where it should be, under 'N' instead of 'M' or it could be filed under the forename instead of the surname. The person responsible for filing it away may remember that they filed it under a different system.

CASE STUDY
ARCHIVING INFORMATION

Janice was appointed Office Manager at a company providing financial services. They had amassed a large volume of highly confidential files. It was vital that the files be secure and accessible over the long term to support the company's day-to-day operations, and for use in the event of customer default. The files were also needed to respond to regular internal and external audits requiring occasional retrieval and delivery of up to 300 files at short notice.

The company had for several years been using the services of a storage company. Whilst resolving a storage problem, archiving remained time-consuming and retrieval was becoming increasingly difficult. The list of archived files was often found to be inaccurate, the storage company would deliver boxes rather than just the required files and a request for a single file required delivery of up to 10 boxes for the company to search.

Janice designed a solution which involved identifying errors in the existing boxes, such as absence of department or destroy dates, or inadequate contents description; collection of boxes from the storage company; and destruction of obsolete records. In future, the system enabled the company to have access to all files via a tracking system. The company's files were now securely stored, precisely tracked and available upon demand.

Accuracy of file-tracking was greatly improved, and labour costs and overall cost of archiving were reduced.

UNIT 204 (B&A 16): TEST YOUR KNOWLEDGE

Learning outcome 1: Understand information storage and retrieval

1 For how long must unsuccessful job applications be retained?

2 Give two reasons why files should be retained in archives using the same system as is used in the live filing system.

3 Complete the table showing what types of confidential information may be found in each type of record.

Types of record	Types of confidential information
Human Resource records	
Accounts records	
Telephone directories	
Register Office records	
Medical records	
Search engine information	

4 True or false?

a It is an offence under the Data Protection Act to transfer information on an individual to a country outside of the European Union.

b The employer's liability insurance certificate must be retained for 40 years.

5 State the most effective way of storing each of the following, explaining your reasons:

a Purchase invoice

b National insurance numbers

c Vehicle registrations.

Learning outcome 2: Be able to gather and store information

1 Explain how confidential information is disposed of when it is no longer required.

2 List the legislation which affects the storing and retention of information in your organisation.

3 List the types of confidential information dealt with in your organisation and how it is stored.

Learning outcome 3: Be able to retrieve information

1 List the information which is stored in your organisation showing the length of time it must be retained.

2 Explain how information is archived in your organisation.

CHAPTER 11

UNIT 227 (B&A 39) EMPLOYEE RIGHTS AND RESPONSIBILITIES

An employee has both rights and responsibilities in the workplace. An employer may not refuse an employee time off for legitimate reasons, but the employee must notify the employer immediately when requesting leave. Employers may not discriminate or harass employees, and employees may not discriminate or harass other employees. Employees have the right to be paid for any work they have carried out, but the employee must be honest when reporting the number of hours he has worked. The privacy of employees must be respected by an employer, unless the employer has justifiable reasoning for conducting a search.

In this unit you will cover the following learning outcomes:

1 understand the role of organisations and industries
2 understand employers' expectations and employees' rights and obligations.

Assessment criteria

This section covers assessment criteria 1.1, 1.2, 1.3, 1.4, 1.5 and 1.6

YOUR ROLE IN AN ORGANISATION AND INDUSTRY

Sector

A component of an integrated system such as an economy or a society

Working in business administration, your occupation is not limited to one **sector**, but can be practised in all sectors across the economy. Business requires constant monitoring and informed decision-making in order to work at its best. Both the day-to-day operations and projects aimed at improving the business depend on the efforts of people with strong organisational skills. Business administrators are responsible for making sure that the details are taken care of.

It is important that you know:

- the type of organisation you work for, including the number of staff employed and the type of market in which they operate
- how your organisation is structured
- the way your organisation carries out different functions such as finance, operations, personnel, marketing and health and safety
- the different ways in which these tasks may be split between different people, departments and/or sites
- the changes that have taken place over recent years which have affected working practices and the way in which your organisation operates, and the impact that these changes have had on your organisation and the way in which your job role is carried out
- where to find out about the training and development opportunities within your organisation
- any issues of public concern that affect your organisation or industry.

The actual requirements of an individual job role are decided by the job holder's place within the organisation. However, there are several key functions that are found in most organisations. These include:

Planning	Involves a range of activities and may involve working out the sequence of steps for the development of a new product, or creating or updating critical software.
Budgeting	This means prioritising the financial needs of the company based upon the amount of money available. Invoices and salaries must be paid, supplies must be ordered and it is the job of the business administrator to make sure that every aspect of the business is funded while staying within appropriate financial boundaries.
Human resources	Part of most business administration careers. Every organisation needs the right mix of people in order to function, and it is often the responsibility of a business administrator to handle filling positions, providing training where necessary and even handling discipline and termination when needed.
Sales	Where a business administrator might lead a team of salespeople, co-ordinating sales routes to grow an existing customer base.

Business administrators can be found in the public sector as well, where they may be involved in the financial or personnel operations of local government, schools or other public organisations. Business administrators are found wherever a large number of details must be co-ordinated in order to ensure that the efforts of a group of people result in the most effective possible outcome. The organisational skills required in business administration are used to ensure that every aspect of the business has the people and supplies needed to accomplish their assigned tasks.

The directing of employees, issuing instructions and information so that everyone knows their role in the process and what is expected of them, can be the most challenging and rewarding part of a business administration job. No matter what product or service the organisation offers, quality control is necessary to detect and fix any problems or defects. Business administration jobs frequently include roles responsible for setting up quality control measures to ensure that the client or customer has their expectations met.

Because of the central role that the business administrator plays, they are most often found where business operations are happening. Whether the business is located in a factory, an office building or a construction site, business administrators will be found onsite, monitoring supply levels, equipment operation, the efficiency and well-being of employees and many other factors necessary to success. Being located near the core operations allows the business administrator to know what progress is being made and to respond quickly to any problems that arise.

In response to rising costs of travel and increasing traffic in major cities, many businesses now offer the option of **telecommuting**. Using internet-based communication tools, planning, organising, budgeting and other administrative tasks can be performed from

Telecommuting

Working from home on a computer linked to the workplace via a modem

Many businesses now offer the option of telecommuting

COMMON MISTAKE

People think working from home is easier than going to the office – it can often be more stressful, with interruptions and temptations distracting you from getting the work done.

ACTIVITY

Consider whether there are any parts of your role that you could do from home. What advantages and disadvantages would there be?

nearly any location. Companies are discovering that full-time or part-time telecommuting can in many cases increase employee productivity and job satisfaction by reducing the stress associated with travelling. As roads and trains become more crowded and the cost of commuting increases, businesses may find that telecommuting is an effective option.

CAREER PATHWAYS

Career pathways in business administration will depend on the organisation and the industry you work in. As an example, people working in the public sector have several careers paths to choose from:

- The foreign service – people in foreign policy public administration jobs serve in embassies, consulates and other diplomatic missions. They analyse political and economic events and help UK citizens abroad.
- The security services – people working as administrators in national security help maintain a strong national defence by programming computers, updating and maintaining processes, etc.
- Planning – people working in planning departments help to develop plans that involve growth and renewal of urban, suburban and rural communities. Planners promote the best use of resources for residential, commercial, institutional and recreational purposes.
- Public administration jobs are also found in government agencies and public corporations, which have strict standards for the management of public resources. Public management careers require budgeting skills, personnel management, procurement and knowledge of regulations and policies.
- Public administration jobs in regulation and auditing suit people who possess technical knowledge about financial, public utility and transportation industries, the environment and/or technology. Their work includes conducting physical inspections, audits and investigations.
- Taxation – careers along the revenue and taxation pathway suit people who enjoy ensuring that governments receive revenues by collecting taxes, conducting audits, monitoring taxes payable and collecting overdue tax.

Another area where there are opportunities to follow a career pathway in business administration is in the healthcare industry. Healthcare administration career paths follow three levels:

- entry level positions
- middle management positions
- executive level positions.

Your first healthcare administration job will depend on your level of education and experience. People often start out in junior positions in larger organisations, but may obtain higher-level positions in some smaller organisations. People typically enter a career in healthcare administration by one of two paths: either they have just completed a degree and have little or no on-the-job experience or they began working in a related field and have sufficient career experience to move into a healthcare administration position.

Entry-level healthcare administration jobs include assistant administrative positions such as operating assistants, marketing assistants, insurance company representatives and accounting technicians. Graduates may obtain jobs as managers and supervisors in smaller organisations such as clinics and public health agencies.

Healthcare administration jobs at middle management level include department managers, case managers, marketing directors and contract negotiators. Positions at this level include chief financial officers, chief operating officers and chief executive officers. Healthcare administration executives often work 60 or more hours per week.

HANDY HINT

It may take as long as 10 years for healthcare administration managers to become senior level managers and executives.

INFORMATION AND ADVICE

When considering your career options, you will need to know who to go to for information and advice in your organisation. This may be your line manager or the human resources department, who can give advice on a range of topics related to:

- employment and personnel issues
- training
- additional learning support (ALS).

Additional learning support provides employees with the additional resources to access their learning. ALS requirements would normally be highlighted during the recruitment process and, following an initial assessment, would generally be discussed during induction.

Factors that may require ALS include:

- Asperger's and Autistic Spectrum Disorders (ASD)
- attention deficit hyper-activity disorder (ADHD)
- dyslexia, dyspraxia or dyscalculia
- hearing or visual impairments
- mental health problems
- physical difficulties
- missed schooling or interrupted education.

Types of ALS include:

- needs assessments
- access to and/or the loan of specialist equipment and/or software
- information provided on a computer or through different printed formats, such as large print.

There are also external sources of information and advice and it is important that you know where to locate information outside your organisation. This can be obtained from a range of sources, including:

- Citizens Advice Bureau
- trade unions
- 'Access to Work' contact centres.

CODES OF PRACTICE AND PRINCIPLES OF CONDUCT

Organisations are regulated by legislation but in addition, many industries have specific codes of practice which can have an impact on the way they carry on business. A code of practice is a set of professional standards or written guidelines agreed on by members of a particular profession or written guidelines issued by an official body or a professional association to its members to help them comply with its ethical standards.

Codes of practice are normally considered when:

- government regulations are unlikely to occur or are inappropriate
- legislation exists and the objective is to assist in ensuring compliance
- there is need for, and commitment to, the development of controls to improve industry standards
- the objective is to provide customer-focused benefits beyond the minimum standards.

In some industries, principles of conduct are agreed which serve as models of **exemplary** conduct for organisations. In order to support the basic objectives of high levels of competence, performance and ethical conduct, all organisations are expected to understand and adhere to these principles of conduct.

Exemplary

So good or admirable that others would do well to copy it

An example of a set of principles of conduct is:

- In all professional, business or **fiduciary** relationships, an organisation shall act with honour and integrity in dealings with the public, employees, clients and other professionals.

Fiduciary

Adjective describing a legal or ethical relationship of trust between two or more parties

- An organisation shall continually strive to maintain and improve the knowledge, skills and competence needed for effective performance in their profession.
- An organisation shall apply care, skill, prudence and diligence.
- An organisation shall avoid any activity or conduct which constitutes a dishonest, deceitful, fraudulent or knowingly illegal act.
- An organisation shall maintain knowledge of and comply with the enforcement of laws, regulations and codes that foster the highest level of competence, performance and ethical conduct.
- An organisation shall respect confidential relationships that may arise in business or professional activities.

ISSUES OF PUBLIC CONCERN

Industries have become more concerned in recent years with demonstrating that they have practices in place to deal with issues of public concern that have faced different industries and different organisations.

Worries about corporate tax payments have replaced **remuneration** as the top public concern about business behaviour. According to a survey for the Institute of Business Ethics, 37% cited 'tax avoidance' as the main concern businesses needed to address, pushing remuneration out of top place. The ability of employees to speak out about company wrongdoing was rated the third most significant concern, at 22%, with business attitudes to the environment and human rights coming in at 16% and 15% respectively.

Remuneration

The paying or rewarding of somebody for their work or input

The survey also shows an increase in the proportion that think business as a whole is behaving ethically, as well as showing that people aged 55 and above are more likely to think that business is not behaving ethically than younger people. Tax is now clearly an issue of public concern and has risen very rapidly up the scale. The findings follow controversy over low tax bills paid by **multinationals** such as Amazon, Google and Starbucks, and a series of high-profile hearings by the Public Accounts Committee.

Multinational

A large company that operates or has investments in several different countries

REPRESENTATIVE BODIES

Within any industry there is a range of representative bodies that promote the views of a group of people with common interests. Representative bodies collect the views of their members and act as their voice in discussions with other groups on issues that affect them all. Representation occurs both within organisations and across sectors and industries, and can occur at both local and national levels.

It is important that you are aware of:

- any trade unions relevant to your occupation/industry and what membership can do for you
- any professional bodies relevant to your occupation/industry and what membership can do for you
- any regulatory bodies relevant to your industry and occupation, for example, the Chartered Institute of Legal Executives
- the name and role of the standard-setting organisation relevant to your occupation.

ACTIVITY

Find out which representative bodies operate in your organisation.

EMPLOYEES' RIGHTS AND OBLIGATIONS

Assessment criteria

This section covers assessment criteria 2.1, 2.2, 2.3 and 2.4

Statutory

Covered by a permanent established rule or law, especially one involved in the running of a company or other organisation, and subject to the penalty laid down by that statute

Your rights at work will depend on your **statutory** rights and your contract of employment. Your contract of employment cannot take away rights you have by law. So if, for example, you have a contract which states you are only entitled to two weeks' paid holiday per year when, by law, all full-time employees are entitled to 28 days' paid holiday per year, this part of your contract does not apply.

If your contract gives you greater rights than you have under law, for example, your contract gives you six weeks' paid holiday per year, then your contract applies. There are special rules about the employment of children and young people.

Statutory rights are legal rights based on laws passed by Parliament. Nearly all workers, however many hours per week they work, have certain legal rights. Some workers are not entitled to some statutory rights. They are:

- Anyone who is not an employee, for example an agency or freelance worker. However, most workers are entitled to certain rights such as the national minimum wage, limits on working time and other health and safety rights, the right not to be discriminated against and paid holiday.
- Employees who normally work outside the UK.
- Members of the police service. However, members of the police service are covered by discrimination law.

- Members of the armed forces. However, members of the armed forces are covered by discrimination law.
- Merchant seamen and share fishermen.
- Some workers in the transport industry are not entitled to paid holidays or limits on their working hours by law and have to rely on their contract.
- Trainee doctors are not entitled to paid holidays and have to rely on their employment contract. They are also limited to working a 58-hour week, rather than 48 hours.

Unless you are in the group of workers who are excluded, you will have the following statutory rights:

- A written statement of terms of employment within two months of starting work.
- An itemised payslip.
- To be paid at least the national minimum wage.
- Not to have illegal deductions made from pay.
- Paid holiday – full-time employees are entitled to at least 28 days a year.
- Paid time off to look for work if being made redundant. This applies once you have worked for two years for an employer.
- Time off for study or training for 16-17 year-olds.
- Paid time off for antenatal care.
- Paid maternity leave.
- Paid paternity leave.
- To ask for flexible working to care for children or adult dependants.
- Paid adoption leave.
- Unpaid parental leave for both men and women (if you have worked for the employer for one year) and the right to reasonable time off to look after dependants in an emergency.
- To work a maximum 48-hour working week.
- Weekly and daily rest breaks. There are special rules for night workers.
- Not to be discriminated against.
- To carry on working until you are at least 65.
- Notice of dismissal, provided you have worked for your employer for at least one calendar month.
- Written reasons for dismissal from your employer.
- To claim compensation if unfairly dismissed.

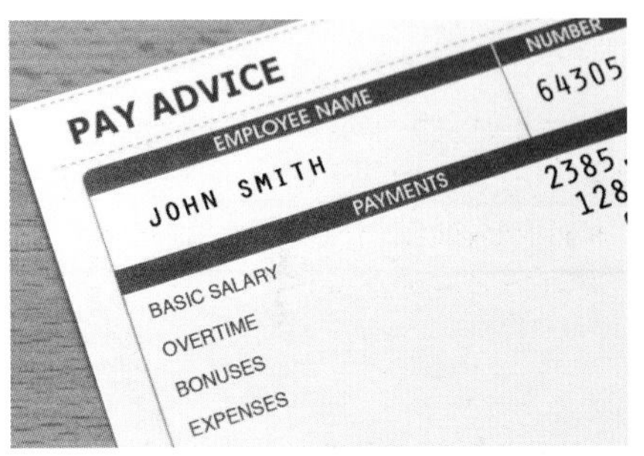

Employees have statutory rights, such as receiving an itemised payslip

- To claim redundancy pay if made redundant. In most cases you will have to have worked for two years to be able to claim redundancy pay.
- Not to suffer detriment or dismissal for 'blowing the whistle' on a matter of public concern (malpractice) at the workplace.
- The right of a part-time worker to the same contractual rights (pro rata) as a comparable full-time worker.
- The right of a fixed-term employee to the same contractual rights as a comparable permanent employee.

HANDY HINT

You may have additional rights which may be set out in your contract of employment.

Note that sometimes an employee might only gain a right when you have been employed by your employer for a certain length of time as indicated in the list above where this is the case.

Your contract of employment is the agreement made between you and the employer. This could be in the form of a written agreement or what has been agreed verbally between you. It will also include 'custom and practice' agreements. These are how things are usually done in the workplace, for example if the employer always gives the employees a day's holiday in August. Even though this is not mentioned in the written contract this will form part of the contract of employment as it is the usual practice.

ACTIVITY

List any 'custom and practice' issues that you have in your workplace.

If the written contract says one thing, but in practice all the employees have been doing something else with the employer's knowledge and agreement, the 'custom and practice' would form the contract rather than the written statement.

A trade union may have negotiated an agreement with an employer about conditions at work. The negotiated agreement will often form part of a contract of employment, particularly if the conditions negotiated are more favourable than the previous ones.

All employees, regardless of the number of hours they work per week, are entitled to receive a written statement from their employer, within two months of starting work. The statement describes the main terms of the contract of employment.

The statement must give the following details:

- job title
- wages
- hours of work
- holiday entitlement
- sick pay
- pension schemes
- notice
- grievance, dismissal and disciplinary procedure.

EMPLOYER'S EXPECTATIONS

While employees enjoy all the rights described above, they also have responsibilities to meet their employer's expectations in respect of their personal presentation, punctuality and behaviour. Employers will require employees to exhibit a range of personal attributes and behaviours including:

- Personal appearance – your clothes, hair, hands, nails, shoes, etc need to be clean and tidy and suitable for your job role.
- Positive attitude – you need to adopt a 'can do' approach to work.
- Approachability – customers and your colleagues need to feel that you are easy to talk to.
- Honesty – you may have access to stock and cash that belongs to the company. They will need to be able to trust you with it. Customers will also need to be able to believe information that you give them.
- Professional attitude – customers will look on you as the expert in the products and services you are providing. You shouldn't let any outside influences prevent you from doing your job to the best of your ability.
- Courtesy – customers and colleagues will expect to be treated with politeness.
- Helpful attitude – always try to be helpful to both customers and colleagues wherever possible.

You should also try to be punctual. If you aim to arrive at work 10 minutes before your start time, you will have a cushion against unexpected delays. If you arrive early, you can prepare yourself for the day's work, and be ready to start on time.

From time to time you may need to be absent from work

From time to time you may need to be absent from work. It is important that you inform your employer as soon as you realise you will not be at work when you should be. There will be a rule telling you who you have to inform and by what time; you may have to phone your supervisor before 10am, for instance.

When you return to work you may have an interview with your supervisor or someone from the human resources department. These can help identify short-term absence problems at an early stage. They also provide managers with an opportunity to talk to you about any issues which might be causing the absence.

The important thing is to remember that if you are not at work, someone else will have to do your work for you. If you are not happy when other people leave you to do their work, it is not fair if you take time off unnecessarily and leave your work to them.

Disciplinary procedures may be used to make it clear that inexcusable absence will not be accepted and that absence policies will be applied. The main causes of sickness absence are:

- minor illness including colds, flu, stomach upsets and headaches
- bone or muscle injuries
- back pain
- stress
- recurring medical conditions
- home or family responsibilities
- mental ill health, for example clinical depression and anxiety.

REGULATIONS

There are regulations to protect you from being unfairly treated. These include:

- The Employment Relations Act which covers among other things:
  - the recognition of trade unions
  - maternity/paternity leave and time off for dependants
  - the right to be accompanied at disciplinary and grievance hearings.
- The Employment Equality (Age) Regulations which make it illegal to treat an employee less favourably because of their age in:
  - recruitment
  - promotion
  - terms and conditions
  - redundancy and dismissal.
- The Employment Rights Act which includes sections on:
  - fair dismissal
  - complaints to a tribunal
  - reasonable notice
  - written contracts
  - rights to time off
  - flexible working
  - redundancy payments
  - compensation for lost earnings
  - time off for public duties, antenatal care and training
  - dismissals related to health and safety
  - protection against detriment caused by disclosing information.

- Working Time Regulations which impose an obligation on employers to ensure that employees:
  - work an average of no more than 48 hours per week calculated over a 17-week period including working lunches, job-related travel and time spent on business abroad
  - have an 11-hour continuous rest period between working days
  - have a continuous 24-hour period off work each week
  - have a break of 20 minutes if the day is more than six hours long.
- The Employment Act which includes sections on:
  - paternity leave and pay
  - maternity leave and pay
  - adoption leave and pay
  - dispute resolution.

Protection from unlawful discrimination is provided by the Equality Act in relation to the following protected characteristics:

- age
- disability
- gender reassignment
- marriage and civil partnership
- pregnancy and maternity
- race
- religion and belief
- sex
- sexual orientation.

The following pieces of legislation have been absorbed into the Equality Act:

- the Equal Pay Act which makes it illegal to offer different pay and conditions to men and women who perform the same type of work. This is defined as work of equal value in terms of effort and skills
- the Race Relations Act which makes it illegal to treat employees differently because of their race, colour, nationality or ethnic origins
- the Sex Discrimination Act which makes it illegal to treat employees differently because of their gender
- the Disability Discrimination Act which makes it illegal to discriminate against disabled people in the areas of:
  - employment
  - access to goods, facilities and services
  - management, buying or renting land or property.

SOURCES OF INFORMATION

If you want any more information on your employment rights and responsibilities, you can try your line manager, your human resources department, your union representative, the intranet or external sources such as the Health and Safety Executive, the Department of Business, Innovation and Skills, professional associations such as the Chartered Institute of Personnel and Development (CIPD), the Trades Union Congress (TUC), the Advisory, Conciliation and Arbitration Service (ACAS), your trade union, the Citizens Advice Bureau, the internet, the public library or government agencies.

CASE STUDY
EMPLOYEE PROTECTION

Linda joined dental clinic Aspect Dentistry in June 2012, on a maternity leave contract. The 25 year-old had previously worked for the firm for 18 months before she left to have her daughter, Rachel, in 2009. She returned to work as a receptionist in 2012 and covered four morning shifts a week. Her contract was further extended by five weeks. Then Linda, who lives in Nantwich with her husband, Paul, a self-employed builder, told her boss that she was expecting her second child.

Linda told the practice manager her good news in February 2013, and the practice manager told the owner of the business. Everyone was happy for her. Then they took her aside at the beginning of March 2013 and said, 'we have no more work that we can give to you'. The owner said there were no hours available and that was that. The practice was really busy at the time, so Linda thought that it didn't add up. She took it further to her solicitor and he said it wasn't right.

Her employment was terminated and she left the business at the end of March, but she started legal proceedings and following a two-day employment tribunal held in Nantwich in December, a judge ruled in favour of Linda and she was awarded more than £7,000.

Her daughter, Sheila, was born on 6 August 2013.

UNIT 227 (B&A 39): TEST YOUR KNOWLEDGE

Learning outcome 1: Understand the role of an organisations and industries

1 Explain the role of your organisation.
2 Describe a career pathway that you could follow.
3 State two sources of information and advice on training.
4 Explain what is meant by a code of practice.
5 List two issues of public concern that affect your organisation.
6 Describe the role of trade unions.

Learning outcome 2: Understand employers' expectations and employees' rights and obligations

1 State two statutory rights that you have in a workplace.
2 Explain what you must do if you are going to be absent from work.
3 List two pieces of legislation that protect the rights of the employees.
4 List two external places you can obtain advice on your rights.

SUGGESTED ANSWERS TO TEST YOUR KNOWLEDGE QUESTIONS

CHAPTER 1 UNIT 301 (B&A 40)

Communicate in a business environment

Learning outcome 1
Understand business communication models, systems and processes

1 Communication needs of internal stakeholders include:
- knowing what business the organisation is in
- knowing who the customers are
- knowing specific details about products or services
- knowing where forms are located
- Knowing who to see when there is a problem.

2 Internal communication occurs within an organisation, for example between managers in different sections, or from directors to shareholders.

3 Informal communication could result in rumours that can cause messages to be mistrusted or convey inaccurate information.

4 An organisation uses different methods in its communications plan because it has a number of different objectives and requires information to be passed to different stakeholder groups.

5 It is important for organisations to evaluate their communications to ensure that the communication is reaching the correct audience and having the correct impact.

Learning outcome 2
Be able to communicate in writing in business

1 Barriers to communication are those things that affect the smooth and effective flow of information from the sender to the intended receiver or receivers.

2 Types of barriers to communication include:
- physical barriers
- experiential barriers
- psychological barriers.

3 'Structure' refers to the layout of the communication.
4 'Style and tone' refer to the way the communication is written.
5 'Content' refers to what the communication is about.

Learning outcome 3
Be able to communicate verbally in business

1 Appropriate language is important to help ensure that the message is correctly understood.
2 Two positive examples of body language are:
   - smiling
   - an open posture.
3 It is important to check that a recipient understands a verbal message in order to avoid misunderstanding.
4 It is important to respond to verbal messages in an appropriate way in order to meet organisational policies and standards.

CHAPTER 2 UNIT 318 (B&A 57)

Principles of business communication and information

Learning outcome 1
Understand negotiation in a business environment

1 Negotiation is important to achieve a deal that is beneficial to the organisation.
2 A 'win/win situation' is one where both sides achieve acceptable terms.
3 The counter tactic is to specify a timeframe at the beginning of the negotiations.

Learning outcome 2
Understand how to develop and deliver presentations

1 Two types of presentation are:
   - informative
   - persuasive.
2 Types of visual aid that might be used in a presentation include:
   - flipcharts
   - whiteboards
   - slideshows.
3 Three to five slides should be used to develop each theme.

4 Reasons not to start a presentation with a joke include:
- that jokes are difficult to deliver
- that jokes can sometimes accidentally offend people.

5 Feedback can be collected after a presentation using an evaluation sheet.

Learning outcome 3
Understand how to create bespoke business documents

1 'Bespoke documents' are those that have been personalised for use by the organisation, a department within the organisation or an individual.

2 Serif fonts have 'flicks' at the edge of each letter, whereas sans serif fonts don't.

3 The principles of the Data Protection Act are that data must be:
- fairly and lawfully processed
- processed for limited purposes
- adequate, relevant and not excessive
- accurate and up to date
- not kept for longer than is necessary
- processed in line with the rights of the data subject
- not transferred to other countries without adequate protection.

4 The first finished version of a document will be numbered 1.0.

5 Spell-check must be set to English (UK) so that words such as 'colour' and 'organisation' are spelt correctly.

Learning outcome 4
Understand information systems in a business environment

1 Methodologies developed for information systems include:
- the waterfall model
- rapid application development (RAD)
- joint application development (JAD)
- the fountain model
- the spiral model
- build and fix
- synchronise and stabilise.

2 Decision support systems help management to make long-term decisions.

3 The four principles that ensure security of information are:
- confidentiality
- integrity
- availability
- back-up.

4 Sampling methods used to monitor information systems include:
- random sampling
- systematic sampling
- cluster sampling
- haphazard sampling
- judgemental sampling.

CHAPTER 3 UNIT 319 (B&A 58)

Principles of administration

Learning outcome 1
Understand how to manage an office facility

1 Legal requirements relating to the management of an office facility include:
- contract law
- environmental law
- the Data Protection Act
- distance selling regulations
- copyright law.

2 Typical services provided by an office facility include:
- record keeping
- accounting
- personnel
- payroll processing
- discipline and grievance records.

3 Office resources that have to be managed include office furniture, office equipment and stationery.

4 Workflow management is important because it is a way of overseeing the process of passing information, documents and tasks from one employee in an organisation to another.

5 Welfare facilities are important to allow staff to work to the best of their ability.

Learning outcome 2
Understand health and safety in a business environment

1 The Display Screen Equipment Regulations.

2 An employee's responsibilities are to:
- work in a safe and sensible way
- use equipment safely and correctly
- report potential risks
- help identify training needs.

3 The answer to this question will be personal to the learner.

Learning outcome 3
Understand how to take minutes of meetings

1 Verbatim minutes would be taken in parliamentary and courtroom proceedings.

2 At some meetings there is a legal requirement under the Freedom of Information Act to make a record. At board meetings there may be a requirement under the Companies Act.

3 It is important that minutes are accurate as they are a record of events, discussions and decisions taken at a meeting. Inaccuracy can lead to disputes or incorrect decisions. It is important they are grammatical because poor grammar can lead to confusion or misunderstanding.

4 See the glossary provided within the chapter for possible answers.

5 Notes would record the discussion so that minutes can give a precise account. Notes should leave a line between each line to allow further comments to be added in if necessary.

Learning outcome 4
Understand how to chair, lead and manage meetings

1 Formal meetings include:
- shareholder meetings
- board meetings
- management meetings
- team meetings
- committee meetings.

2 The role of the chairperson is to:
- agree the items to be included on the agenda
- start the meeting on time
- clarify roles and responsibilities
- establish ground rules and guidelines

- participate as an attendee
- follow agenda items in sequence, inform the minute taker of any departures from the agreed agenda, and keep the meeting focused on the agenda items
- retain the power to stop what's happening and change the format
- encourage accountability
- summarise key decisions and actions
- record recommendations and allocate responsibilities for specific tasks
- make the most of the experience of those people present, asking questions to draw out people's experience
- allow time to hear experts' points of view but allocate time with clear directions
- for important issues when time is limited set up a sub-committee to collect facts, review the situation and prepare recommendations to be considered at the next meeting
- summarise specific points, decisions or courses of action agreed for each specific agenda item before moving on to the next item
- provide specific guidance to the minute taker on what to record for a particular agenda item where lengthy discussion has occurred or a complex issue has been discussed
- close the meeting on time
- take time to review the minutes when they are drafted.

3 It is important to work in partnership with the chairperson so that the meeting is as effective as possible.

4 If you require clarification you should address your request directly to the chairperson.

Learning outcome 5
Understand how to supervise an administrative team

1 Targets are important to allow management to measure achievement.

2 Delegation retains responsibility, abdication doesn't.

3 The answer to this question will be personal to the learner.

4 The answer to this question will be personal to the learner.

Learning outcome 6
Understand how to organise events

1 Types of layout include:
- theatre-style layout
- classroom layout
- cabaret layout
- horseshoe layout
- boardroom layout
- banquet layout.

2 The answer to this question will be personal to the learner.

3 A contingency plan covers any incidents that might occur and how to react to them, helping ensure the event runs smoothly.

4 Resources required may include:
- accommodation
- catering
- equipment
- car parking.

5 The event organiser agrees a brief and a budget for events with the client.

CHAPTER 4 UNIT 320 (B&A 59)

Principles of business

Learning outcome 1
Understand business markets

1 The three types of business markets are:
- the free market
- the command market
- the mixed market.

2 Businesses interact with each other as customers and as competitors.

3 Two examples of a 'monopsony' are:
- major employers in a small town, such as a car plant, a major supermarket or the head office of a bank
- nursing homes as employers of care assistants.

4 Three main legal structures organisations can operate as are:
- sole trader
- limited company
- partnership.

Learning outcome 2
Understand business innovation and growth

1 An innovation is a product, service or idea that is perceived by customers as new.

2 Business innovation models include:

- The phase gate model – this modifies the linear model by recognising that there are feedback loops and time variations between steps, and establishes readiness criteria for moving between major phases of innovation development. Phase gate approaches are often represented by a funnel approach.
- The connect and develop model – developed by Proctor and Gamble in the 1980s, this model addresses the increasing cost of keeping all research and development within the company, representing an example of open innovation. In this model, parts of research and development come from outside the company as a result of networking and partnerships.

3 UK government programmes to support business innovation include:

- The Small Business Research Initiative
- Forward Commitment Procurement
- Joint public–private procurement compacts
- EU innovation procurement projects
- UK Innovation Investment Fund.

4 The seven steps involved in developing a product or service from being an idea to being a product or service which will contribute to the organisation's growth are:

- idea generation
- screening
- concept development and testing
- business analysis
- product and marketing mix development
- market testing
- commercialisation.

5 The four stages of the psychological impact of change are:

- shock and resistance
- confusion
- integration
- acceptance.

Learning outcome 3
Understand financial management

1 Financial viability is important to an organisation because without it the organisation would cease to operate.

2 The consequence of poor financial management is bankruptcy.

3 The meanings are:
- Current assets – cash and anything that is expected to be converted into cash within 12 months of the balance sheet date.
- Current ratio – the relationship between current assets and current liabilities, indicating the liquidity of a business, ie its ability to meet its short-term obligations.
- Current liabilities – money owed by the business that is generally due for payment within 12 months of the balance sheet date, for instance creditors, bank overdraft and taxes.

Learning outcome 4
Understand business budgeting

1 Budgets provide a framework for responsibility and control by considering growth areas, competitors, cash flow and profit.

2 The four key steps in developing a budget are:
- using historical information
- creating a realistic budget
- agreeing the format
- involving other people.

Learning outcome 5
Understand sales and marketing

1 Common market segments include:
- age
- gender
- religion
- culture
- income
- lifestyle.

2 The characteristics and stages of the sales cycle are:
- product knowledge – research the products and services on offer
- initial contact/prospecting – prospect for leads and identify potential customers
- approach – make contact with potential customers

- need assessment – find out what the customers need
- make a presentation
- address the prospect's objections
- gain commitment and close the sale
- ask for referrals
- offer after-sales support.

3 Primary research is the use of first-hand data and/or resources. Secondary research involves comments written about a primary source, including interpretations, discussions or studies by other researchers.

4 A brand is important to an organisation because a good brand will:
- deliver the message clearly
- confirm your credibility
- motivate the buyer
- concrete user loyalty.

5 Integrating the functions of sales and marketing allows an organisation to have a much better understanding of its client base and increase its ability to reach out to new clients.

CHAPTER 5 UNIT 345 (M&L 9)

Manage personal and professional development

Learning outcome 1
Be able to identify personal and professional development requirements

1 The answer to this question will be personal to the learner.

2 The answer to this question will be personal to the learner.

3 Benefits of improving performance are:
- it allows new skills and knowledge to be learnt
- it allows you to perform more highly skilled and demanding tasks
- it allows you to build specific knowledge and competencies that are related to your current role and the role you aspire to.

4 Sources of information on professional developments include:
- human resources departments
- professional networks
- professional bodies.

Learning outcome 2
Be able to fulfil a personal and professional development plan

1 Types of development action are selected by identifying which would cause the greatest loss or threat to the organisation, the team or yourself if they were not achieved.

2 The answer to this question will be personal to the learner.

3 Development actions must be consistent with business needs and personal objectives.

4 Plans should be executed as cost-effectively and quickly as possible to meet the agreed budget and timescales.

5 Learning and development can further your career by enabling you to benefit from opportunities for advancement that you might not otherwise be able to.

Learning outcome 3
Be able to maintain the relevance of a personal and professional development plan

1 'SMART' is an acronym for specific, measurable, achievable, realistic and time-bound.

2 Feedback can be encouraged by preparing a series of questions for people to answer about your performance and by carefully selecting the people you seek feedback from.

3 Progress can be reviewed using a professional system or by filling in a detailed spreadsheet.

4 The plan should be amended in the light of feedback received.

CHAPTER 6 UNIT 302 (B&A 41)

Contribute to the improvement of business performance

Learning outcome 1
Understand the principles of resolving business problems

1 It is important not to exceed the limits of your authority in decision making because if you do so there is a risk that you will have to undo the decision if instructed to by someone with greater authority, or you may commit the organisation to a course of action that is not in its best interests.

2 The first stage of the decision-making process is to define and clarify the issue.

3 Stakeholders must be involved or at least considered in the problem-solving process because in law the people directing organisations have a responsibility to all the stakeholders in the organisation.

Learning outcome 2
Understand improvement techniques and processes

1 The benefits of continuous improvement include an increase in efficiency, profitability, customer satisfaction, employee involvement and productivity, greater competitiveness, better use of resources, reduced waste and costs, and better responses to customer requirements.

2 Cost–benefit analysis involves adding up the benefits of a course of action and then comparing these with the costs associated with it. The results are often expressed as a payback period; this is the time it takes for the benefits to repay the costs.

3 Feedback is important because, while it is nice to hear that you have done well, it is probably more useful to be told when you have not done as well as you might have done. Feedback may be obtained formally or informally from managers, supervisors, colleagues or customers, but it must be constructive and explain what you should have done, not just what you should not have done.

Learning outcome 3
Be able to solve problems in business

1 It is important to obtain approval to implement solutions because the solution may impact on financial, health, safety and security issues, on the reputation of the organisation with external customers, may require a deadline to be met that it is not in your power to achieve, or may require the help of colleagues who are not within your authority to direct. Some decisions can only be taken by people with specific responsibility, for instance those responsible for strategic planning, operational management or individual roles and responsibilities.

2 Different types of business problems that may be encountered include financial problems, resource-related problems, equipment or system failures, staff-related problems, and unforeseen problems such as bad weather or industrial action.

Learning outcome 4
Be able to contribute to the improvement of activities

1 The effect of change can be measured by defining the measure, collecting baseline data, establishing a clear aim, collecting data consistently, charting progress and asking questions.

2 Adopting improvements can be justified by carrying out detailed planning to ensure that the identified change will be of benefit to the organisation and carrying out a cost–benefit analysis to demonstrate what the benefits will be.

CHAPTER 7 UNIT 308 (B&A 47)

Monitor information systems

Learning outcome 1
Understand how information systems are used

1 The format and language will depend on the use of the report. It may be:
   - an informational report
   - an analytical report
   - a research report.

2 The user of the report will advise what data is needed, how it will be organised and presented, what sub-totals and totals are needed etc.

3 Problems with information systems may relate to hardware or software.

4 Some problems will be simple and easily identifiable, enabling a swift solution because they are a common issue. Others will be more complex because they have non-specific symptoms or unknown faults, requiring a multi-step solution.

5 Validation operations available include:
   - data type validation
   - range and constraint validation
   - code and cross-reference validation
   - structured validation.

6 An evaluation technique for an information system is to seek input from users at all levels.

7 A breach of confidentiality carries a maximum penalty of a £5,000 fine in a Magistrates' Court and an unlimited fine in a Crown Court.

8 If the organisation gets a reputation for not keeping information about its customers confidential, or for producing reports containing inaccurate or unsubstantiated information, it may soon have many fewer customers.

Learning outcome 2
Be able to monitor information systems

1 The answer to this question will be personal to the learner.

2 The answer to this question will be personal to the learner.

3 In a large organisation there may be an IT support department that may be able to provide training as well as support. If external training resources are needed, these are mainly offered by IT-

specialist training companies approved by IT vendors such as Microsoft, Cisco, Oracle and IBM.

4 The answer to this question will be personal to the learner.
5 The answer to this question will be personal to the learner.
6 The answer to this question will be personal to the learner.
7 The legal requirements when monitoring an information system include compliance with the Data Protection Act and the European Commission's directive on the protection of personal data.

CHAPTER 8 UNIT 309 (B&A 48)

Evaluate the provision of business travel or accommodation

Learning outcome 1
Understand the provision of business travel or accommodation arrangements

1 The evaluation criteria are:
   - price
   - suitability
   - discounts
   - delivery and after-sales service charges
   - reliability and reputation.

2 The different standards are:
   - air travel may be first class, business class, club class or economy
   - rail travel may be first class or standard class
   - accommodation may be anything from a guest house to a five-star hotel.

3 'ATOL' stands for Air Traffic Organiser's Licence.

Learning outcome 2
Be able to evaluate the quality of organisational business travel or accommodation arrangements

1 It is important to identify instances of exceptional and inadequate performance to help inform future decisions.
2 Travel and accommodation arrangements could be made online or through a travel agency.

Learning outcome 3
Be able to recommend improvements to organisational business travel or accommodation requirements

1 The eight common supplier-selection criteria are:
- cost
- quality and safety
- delivery
- service
- social responsibility
- convenience and simplicity
- risk
- agility.

2 A plan to recommend improvements to travel and accommodation arrangements should include:
- different options
- the benefits of the different options
- the limitations of the different options
- the implications of the different options.

3 A previous relationship with a potential supplier is an ethical issue because it poses a potential conflict of interest.

CHAPTER 9 UNIT 322 (B&A 61)

Analyse and present business data

Learning outcome 1
Understand the analysis and presentation of business data

1 Examples of primary research include market surveys, telephone interviews, questionnaires and focus group interviews. Examples of secondary research include reports, press articles and previous market research projects.

2 Quantitative research uses a scientific approach where information gathered is usually easy to measure and able to be analysed mathematically. It generates numerical data or, at least, data that can be converted into numbers. Examples include the national census and opinion polls. Quantitative research often uses questionnaires to gather data from a large number of sources. Questions are usually closed, giving the option to choose 'yes' or 'no' or from a limited number of options.

3 It is necessary to evaluate the reliability of data so that results can be checked for accuracy and freedom from bias.

4 IT tools that can be used include hard copy documents scanned into the computer, spreadsheets, word-processing programs and databases.

5 Limited or unrepresentative samples should not be used to make judgements.

6 Care must be taken when generalising research findings in order to not extrapolate results from qualitative research which was focused on a particular group or situation.

Learning outcome 2
Be able to analyse quantitative and qualitative business data

1 The parameters of analysis are the limits of the information that is to be included.

2 Data should be organised in a way that will enable it to be easily analysed.

3 Techniques for qualitative research include focus groups, observation and in-depth interviews.

Learning outcome 3
Be able to present the analysis of business data

1 Formats for presenting analyses include bar charts, line charts, area charts, pie charts, XY charts, radar charts, scatter graphs, bubble charts, meter charts and line/bar charts.

2 When referencing sources of information from books, you should record:

- the author's or editor's name (or names)
- the year the book was published
- the title of the book
- the name of the publisher.

For articles you should record:

- the author's name (or names)
- the year in which the journal was published
- the title of the article
- the title of the journal
- the page number(s) of the article in the journal
- the volume and issue numbers.

For electronic resources, you should record:

- the date you accessed the source
- the type of electronic resource (email, discussion forum, www page etc).

CHAPTER 10 UNIT 204 (B&A 16)

Store and retrieve information

Learning outcome 1
Understand information storage and retrieval

1 Unsuccessful job applications must be retained for six months after notification.

2 Files should be retained in archives using the same system as live files because this makes them easier to find and easier to archive.

3

Types of record	Types of confidential information
Human Resource records	Staff names, addresses, national insurance numbers, salaries, disciplinary information
Accounts records	Customer financial information, discounts, terms and conditions, overdue accounts, bank details
Telephone directories	None – these are public records
Register Office records	None – this is public information
Medical records	Personal information relating to medical histories
Search engine information	None – these are public records

4 Answers are:

a False – unless there is inadequate protection

b True.

5 The most effective ways of storing each are:

a Purchase invoice – alphabetically/chronologically. You are most likely to look for them under the name of the supplier and the date of the order.

b National insurance numbers – alpha-numerically because they consist of letters and numbers.

c Vehicle registrations – alpha-numerically because they consist of letters and numbers.

Learning outcome 2
Be able to gather and store information

1 Confidential information must be disposed of in a way that makes it impossible to retrieve. Paper records should be shredded, electronic records must be deleted in a way that cannot be recovered.

2 The answer will depend on the organisation the learner works for.

3 The answer to this question will be personal to the learner.

Learning outcome 3
Be able to retrieve information

1 The answer to this question will be personal to the learner.

2 The answer to this question will be personal to the learner.

CHAPTER 11 UNIT 227 (B&A 39)

Employee rights and responsibilities

Learning outcome 1
Understand the role of organisations and industries

1 The answer to this question will be personal to the learner.

2 The answer to this question will be personal to the learner.

3 Two sources of information on training are the human resources department and the relevant trade union.

4 A code of practice is a set of professional standards or written guidelines agreed on by members of a particular profession, or written guidelines issued by an official body or a professional association to its members to help them comply with its ethical standards.

5 The answer to this question will be personal to the learner.

6 The role of trade unions is to achieve common goals such as protecting the integrity of their trade, achieving higher pay, increasing the number of employees an employer hires and better working conditions.

Learning outcome 2
Understand employers' expectations and employees' rights and obligations

1 Statutory rights that you have in a workplace could be any of:

- A written statement of terms of employment within two months of starting work.
- An itemised payslip.

- To be paid at least the national minimum wage.
- Not to have illegal deductions made from pay.
- Paid holiday – full-time employees are entitled to at least 28 days a year.
- Paid time off to look for work if being made redundant. This applies once you have worked for two years for an employer.
- Time off for study or training for 16-17 year-olds.
- Paid time off for antenatal care.
- Paid maternity leave.
- Paid paternity leave.
- To ask for flexible working to care for children or adult dependants.
- Paid adoption leave.
- Unpaid parental leave for both men and women (if you have worked for the employer for one year) and the right to reasonable time off to look after dependants in an emergency.
- To work a maximum 48-hour working week.
- Weekly and daily rest breaks. There are special rules for night workers.
- Not to be discriminated against.
- To carry on working until you are at least 65.
- Notice of dismissal, provided you have worked for your employer for at least one calendar month.
- Written reasons for dismissal from your employer.
- To claim compensation if unfairly dismissed.
- To claim redundancy pay if made redundant. In most cases you will have to have worked for two years to be able to claim redundancy pay.
- Not to suffer detriment or dismissal for 'blowing the whistle' on a matter of public concern (malpractice) at the workplace.
- The right of a part-time worker to the same contractual rights (pro rata) as a comparable full-time worker.
- The right of a fixed-term employee to the same contractual rights as a comparable permanent employee.

2 The answer to this question will be personal to the learner.

3 Two pieces of legislation that protect the rights of the employee are:

- the Equality Act
- the Working Time Directive.

4 Advice on rights can be obtained from:

- Health and Safety Executive
- Department of Business, Innovation and Skills
- Chartered Institute of Personnel and Development (CIPD)
- Trades Union Congress (TUC)
- Advisory, Conciliation and Arbitration Service (ACAS)
- your trade union
- Citizens Advice Bureau
- the internet
- public library
- government agencies.

GLOSSARY

A

accruals Income or expenditure that was due in an accounting period but was not received or paid by the end of the period

acid test A company's ability to pay its short-term debts

ad hoc 'For the purpose of', as for example when a temporary sub-committee is set up especially to organise a works outing

adjourn To suspend a meeting until a later date

adopt minutes Minutes are 'adopted' when accepted by members and signed by the chairperson

advisory Providing advice or suggestion, not taking action

agenda A schedule of items drawn up for discussion at a meeting

amendment An addition or alteration to a motion

apologies Reasons given in advance for inability to attend a meeting

archive A collection of documents such as documents or computer records, kept for future reference

articles of association Rules required by company law that govern a company's activities

articulate To express thoughts, ideas or feelings coherently

asset Anything owned by the company that has a monetary value

asset turnover A measure of operational efficiency that shows how much revenue is produced per £ of assets available to the business

assumption Presuming something to be the case without knowing for sure

attendance list In some meetings a list is passed round to be signed as a record of attendance

audit An independent assessment of the finances of the organisation by a qualified person

autonomy Functioning independently, without supervision

B

balance sheet A 'snapshot' in time of who owns what in the company, and what assets and debts represent the value of the company. The balance sheet equation is basically: capital + liabilities = assets

bank reconciliation A method of confirming that an organisation's accounting records agree with those of the bank as shown in the bank statement

bed in To give something time to establish itself and fit firmly into place

benchmark To provide a standard against which something can be measured or assessed

bias The distortion of a set of statistical results either by a variable not considered in the calculation or by the variable itself

bottleneck Delays caused when one part of a process or activity is slower than the others and so hinders overall progress

bottom-line effect The effect on the net profit or loss

budget An amount of money that it is planned to be spent on a particular activity or resource, usually over a trading year, although budgets can also apply to shorter and longer periods

buffer storage An element used between two different forms of storage

bureau de change An office, often found in a bank, that allows consumers to exchange one currency for another. The bureau de change charges a commission for the currency exchange service

bylaws Rules regulating an organisation's activities

capital employed The value of all the resources available to the company, typically comprising share capital, retained profits and reserves, long-term loans and deferred taxation

capital gain The amount by which an asset's selling price exceeds its initial purchase price. For most investments sold at a profit, capital gains tax is payable

capitalised An asset that is regarded as a capital asset when determining Income Tax liability

cascade A downward flow of information

cash flow The movement of cash in and out of a business from day-to-day direct trading and other non-trading or indirect effects, such as capital expenditure, tax and dividend payments

cash flow statement Shows the movement and availability of cash through and to the business over a given period

casting vote Some committee chairpersons may use a 'casting vote' to reach a decision if votes are equally divided

chairperson The person running a meeting

chairperson's agenda Based on the meeting agenda but also containing explanatory notes

classify To assign things or people to categories

climatic Of or pertaining to the climate and weather conditions

collaborative Involving people or groups working together to produce something

collective responsibility A convention by which all meeting members agree to accept and support a majority decision, even if they disagreed with it during the discussion

commercially sensitive Information that an organisation would not like to be in the public domain as it may give an advantage to a competitor

committee A group of people, usually elected or appointed, who meet to conduct agreed business and report to a senior body

communism A political theory or system in which all property and wealth is owned in a classless society by all the members of that society

consensus Agreement by general consent, no formal vote being taken

constitution A set of rules governing the activities of an organisation

consulate The office of a government official living in a foreign city to promote the commercial interests of the official's own state and protect its citizens

contingency plan A plan about how to react to an event that might occur in the future, especially a problem that might arise unexpectedly

convene To call a meeting

conventions The customary way in which things are done within a group or organisation

corporate governance Company management techniques and processes in general, or the way a particular company is managed

cost of debt ratio The amount of interest charged on a debt over a given period, expressed as a percentage of the average outstanding debt over the same period, or the cost of interest divided by the average outstanding debt

cost of goods sold (COGS) The directly attributable costs of products or services sold, usually comprised of materials, labour and direct production costs. Sales – COGS = gross profit

cost of sales (COS) Cost of sales is the value, at cost, of the goods or services sold during the period in question, usually the financial year. Uses the formula: opening stock + stock purchased – closing stock

creditor A person to whom money is owed by a debtor; someone to whom an obligation exists

cross-referencing A reference from one part of a file to another part containing related information

current assets Cash and anything that is expected to be converted into cash within 12 months of the balance sheet date

current liabilities Money owed by the business that is generally due for payment within 12 months of the balance sheet date, for instance creditors, bank overdraft and taxes

current ratio The relationship between current assets and current liabilities, indicating the liquidity of a business, ie its ability to meet its short-term obligations. Also referred to as the *liquidity ratio*

D

data controller The person who decides the purpose for which personal data is to be processed

debtor Another person or organisation that owes your organisation money; someone who has the obligation of paying a debt

decision Resolution minutes are sometimes called 'decision minutes'

delegate Give authority to somebody else to act, make decisions or allocate resources on one's behalf

demographics Groups of people characterised by age, income, sex, education, occupation, socio-economic group etc

depreciation The sharing of the cost of a large capital item over an agreed period, based on its life expectancy or when it is expected to be out of date

differentiate To establish a difference between two things or among several things

discretion The power to make decisions sensitively on the basis of one's knowledge and the ability to keep sensitive information secret

dividend A payment made per share by a company to its shareholders, based on the profits of the year (but not necessarily all the profits)

E

eject To remove someone (by force if necessary) from a meeting

empathy The ability to understand how someone feels because you can imagine what it is like to be them

empowerment To give somebody a greater sense of confidence or self-esteem

engagement The feeling of being involved in a particular activity

equity The remaining value or interest of investors in assets after all liabilities are paid

ergonomics The scientific study of people at work. The goal of ergonomics is to reduce stress and eliminate injuries and disorders associated with the overuse of muscles, bad posture, and repeated tasks

ethical Consistent with agreed principles of correct moral conduct

ethics A system of moral principles governing the appropriate conduct of a person or group

evolve To develop gradually, often into something more complex or advanced

executive having the power to act upon taken decisions

exemplary So good or admirable that others would do well to copy it

exemption Permission or entitlement not to do something that others are obliged to do

ex officio Given powers or rights by reason of office

experiential Relating to experience as opposed to other methods of acquiring knowledge

extrapolate To say what is likely to happen or be true by using information that you already have

F

fixed assets Assets held for use by the business rather than for sale or conversion into cash, for instance fixtures and fittings, equipment and buildings

fixed cost A cost that does not vary with changing sales or production volumes, for instance building lease costs, permanent staff wages, rates and depreciation of capital assets

fluctuate To change often from high to low levels or from one thing to another

fiduciary Adjective describing a legal or ethical relationship of trust between two or more parties

G

gearing The ratio of debt to equity, usually the relationship between long-term borrowings and shareholders' funds

goodwill any extra money paid when acquiring a company that exceeds that company's net tangible assets value

governance The process of governing a country or organisation

Gross profit or loss sales less cost of goods or services sold

guillotine To cut short a debate usually in parliament

H

honorary post A duty performed without payment, eg honorary secretary

house style A set of rules concerning spellings, typography etc to be applied within a company

hybrid Something made up of a mixture of different aspects or components

hypothesis A statement that is assumed to be true for the sake of argument

I

implicit Not specifically stated but understood in what is expressed

income The monetary payment received for goods or services, or from other sources such as rents or investments

inflection The way a speaker's voice rises and falls when they speak

intangible Something non-physical that cannot be seen or touched

intelligence services An organisation that gathers information about the secret plans or activities of an adversary or potential adversary

interim An interval of time between one event, process or period and another

inter-related In a relationship in which each depends on or is affected by the other or others

intra vires From Latin, within the power of the committee or meeting to discuss, to carry out

itinerary A plan for a journey listing different places in the order in which they are to be visited

J

jargon Language that is used within a group or profession that might not be understood or used by other people

L

liabilities General term for what the business owes. Liabilities are long-term loans of the type used to finance the business and short-term debts or money owing as a result of trading activities

lie on the table To leave an item to be considered instead at the next meeting

liquidity ratio Indicates the company's ability to pay its short-term debts by measuring the relationship between current assets against the short-term debt value. Uses the formula: current assets ÷ current liabilities

lobbying A practice of seeking members' support before a meeting

longevity Duration

M

margin Net income divided by revenue, or net profit divided by sales

methodologies The methods and principles used for doing a particular kind of work

missive A formal letter or other written communication, often a legal communication

motion A proposal put forward for discussion at a meeting

motivate To make somebody feel enthusiastic, interested and committed to something

mover Someone who speaks on behalf of a motion

multinational A large company that operates or has investments in several different countries

musculoskeletal disorders Musculoskeletal pain is pain that affects the muscles, ligaments and tendons, and bones

N

National Insurance Compulsory state-run social security scheme based on contributions from employees and employers. It provides medical and financial assistance, including pensions, to people who are ill, retired or unemployed

nem con From Latin, literally, 'no one speaking against'

net assets Also called *total net assets*, total assets, fixed and current, minus current liabilities and long-term liabilities that have not been capitalised, for instance short-term loans

net current assets Current assets minus current liabilities

net profit or loss Profit or loss after deducting all operating expenses

network To build up or maintain informal relationships, especially with people whose friendship could bring advantages such as job or business opportunities

niche A specialised part of a market

O

objective Based on facts rather than thoughts or opinions; free of any bias or prejudice caused by personal feelings

operating expense Any expense incurred in running a business, such as in sales and administration, as opposed to an expense incurred in production

opposer One who speaks against a motion

optimise To make something such as a method or process as good or as effective as possible

optimum The best or most suitable within a range of possibilities

other business Either items left over from a previous meeting or items discussed after the main business of a meeting

overhead An expense that cannot be attributed to any one single part of the company's activities

P

parameters Limits

patents A set of exclusive rights granted to an inventor for a limit period of time

penultimate Second to last in a series or sequence

peripheral Externally related or connected, for example a device linked to a computer to provide communication (as input and output) or auxiliary functions (such as additional storage)

phasing Any distinct or characteristic period or stage within a sequence of events

philosophical Concerned with or given to thinking about the larger issues and deeper meanings in life and events

phishing To trick somebody into providing bank or credit card information by sending a fraudulent email pretending to be from a bank or similar institution

placebo Something prescribed for a patient that contains no medicine but is given for the positive psychological effect it may have because the patient believes that he or she is receiving treatment

point of information The drawing of attention in a meeting to a relevant item of fact

point of order Proceedings may be interrupted on a 'point of order' to draw attention to a breach of rules or procedures

pre-existing Something that already existed

prescriptive Establishing or adhering to rules and regulations

procurement The process of buying supplies or equipment for a government department or company

profit and loss account (P&L) A trading account for a period, usually a year, which shows profit performance

proposal The name given to an item submitted for discussion (usually in writing) before a meeting takes place

pros and cons The arguments for and against something

proxy Literally 'on behalf of another person', a proxy vote

psychological Relating to the mind or mental processes

punitive Causing great difficulty or hardship

Q

qualified buyer An individual or company who is in the market and displays some evidence of being financially able to buy

quorum The number of people needed to be in attendance for a meeting to be legitimate and so commence

R

rationale The reasoning or principle that underlies or explains something, or a statement setting out this reasoning or principle
read-only tag A computer setting that means users are unable to change the content of a file
recompense Compensation for an injury or loss
refer back To pass an item back for further consideration
remuneration The paying or rewarding of somebody for their work or input
reserves The accumulated and retained difference between profits and losses year on year since the company's formation
resolution A firm decision to do something
return on capital employed (ROCE) A percentage figure representing profit before interest against the money that is invested in the business. Calculated as: profit before interest and tax ÷ divided by capital employed × 100
revenue The income generated from the sale of goods or services, or any other use of capital or assets, associated with the main operations of an organisation before any costs or expenses are deducted

S

seconder One who supports the 'proposer' of a motion or proposal by 'seconding' it
secretary Committee official responsible for the internal and external administration of the committee
secret ballot A system of voting in secret
sector A component of an integrated system such as an economy or a society
share capital The balance sheet's nominal value paid into the company by shareholders at the time the shares were issued
shareholders' funds A measure of the shareholders' total interest in the company represented by the total share capital + reserves
shelve To drop a motion that has no support
sine die From Latin, literally 'without a day', that is to say indefinitely, eg 'Adjourned sine die'
SMART A target that is specific, measurable, achievable, realistic and time-bound
spam An unsolicited, often commercial, message transmitted through the internet as a mass mailing to a large number of recipients
stagnation Failure to develop, progress or make necessary changes
stakeholder A person or group with a direct interest, involvement or investment in something
standard operating procedure A process that is followed when carrying out an operation or dealing with a situation
standing committee A committee that has an indefinite term of office
standing orders Rules of procedure governing public sector meetings
statutory Covered by a permanent established rule or law, especially one involved in the running of a company or other organisation, and subject to the penalty laid down by that statute
sterling The currency in pounds and pence used in the United Kingdom
subjective Based on somebody's opinions or feelings rather than on facts or evidence

T

table To introduce a paper or schedule for noting at a meeting
taken as read To save time, it is assumed that meeting members have already read the minutes
teething problems Problems that you experience in the early stages of an activity
telecommuting Working from home on a computer linked to the workplace via modem
tenet A principle, belief or doctrine that is generally held to be true
terms and conditions Arrangements laid down formally in an agreement or contract, or proposed by one side when negotiating an agreement
transact To conduct or carry out something such as business
transcribe To make a written copy of something
treasurer Committee official responsible for its financial records and transactions

U

ultra vires From Latin, beyond the authority of the meeting to consider
unanimous Everyone being in favour

V

value added tax (VAT) A consumption tax that is applied at each stage of production based on the value added to the product at that stage
variable cost A cost that varies with sales or operational volumes, for instance materials, fuel and commission payments
variance A difference between two or more things
verbatim Word for word

viability The long-term survival of an organisation and its ability to have sustainable profits over a period of time

viable Able to be done or worth doing

visa An official endorsement in a passport authorising the bearer to enter or leave, and travel in or through, a specific country or region

working capital Current assets less current liabilities, representing the required investment continually circulating to finance stock, debtors and work in progress

INDEX